Postcard History Series

Manassas

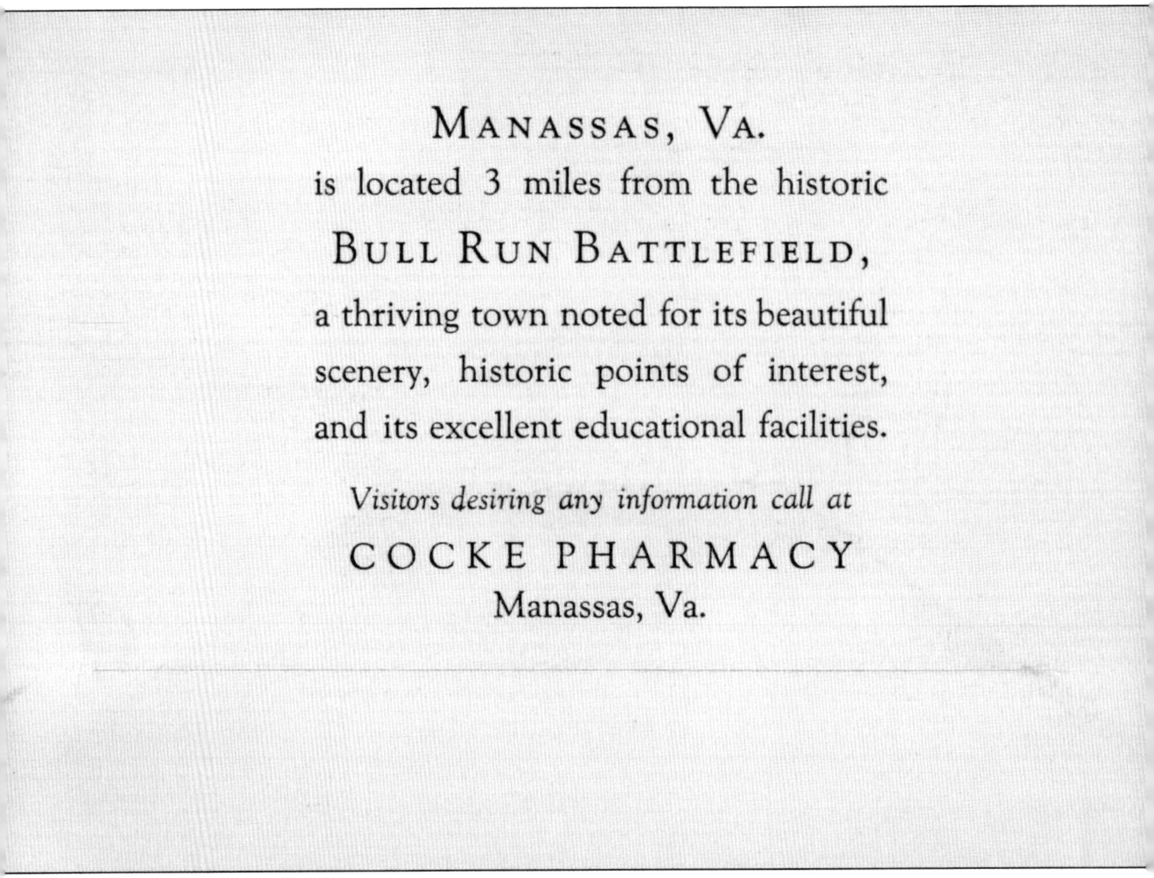

MANASSAS, VA.
is located 3 miles from the historic
BULL RUN BATTLEFIELD,
a thriving town noted for its beautiful scenery, historic points of interest, and its excellent educational facilities.

Visitors desiring any information call at
COCKE PHARMACY
Manassas, Va.

Cocke's Pharmacy, Prince William Pharmacy, and Wenrich's Jewelry Store were among the businesses that sold many postcards like this souvenir foldout booklet of Manassas images. Locals could take pride in sending postcards with images of a prosperous town, and tourists could take home a souvenir of their time visiting the battlefield and other sites. (Nancy Mitchell.)

ON THE COVER: Center Street, shown here in about 1915, was a bustling commercial hub and major road through town, much as it is today. Nash Hardware and the Conner Opera House, at left, are still occupied by restaurant and retail space. The post office no longer occupies the building bearing its name on the corner of Battle Street, at right, but commercial space does. (Author's collection.)

POSTCARD HISTORY SERIES

Manassas

Lisa Sievel-Otten

ARCADIA PUBLISHING

ISBN 978-1-4671-1619-0

Published by Arcadia Publishing
Charleston, South Carolina

Printed in the United States of America

Library of Congress Control Number: 2015956864

For all general information contact Arcadia Publishing at:
Telephone 843-853-2070
Fax 843-853-0044
E-mail sales@arcadiapublishing.com
For customer service and orders:
Toll-Free 1-888-313-2665

Visit us on the Internet at www.arcadiapublishing.com

To Bob, Lindsay, and Alex, for cowriting the most important history of all: our family story

Contents

ACKNOWLEDGMENTS

All of us who appreciate local history owe a debt of gratitude to those who find it hard to part with photographs, mementos, letters, and postcards of another era. Those dusty boxes we stack in attics have become the basis of many a museum. The Manassas Museum began in much the same way, thanks to the generosity of the Rohrs, Conners, Ratcliffes, Bushongs, and many others too numerous to mention, who wanted simply to mark the centennial of the town. The museum they built is a testament to their love of this city, and it offers all of us a glimpse of another time that would otherwise be forgotten.

Thank you, to family, friends, and colleagues at the City of Manassas who have provided encouragement for this project and most especially to those who have reviewed the manuscript. Thank you, to Barbara Breeden, Chip and Nancy Rohr, and Don Wilson, Virginiana librarian of the Prince William Public Library System, for sharing their knowledge of Manassas. Thank you, to Jim Burgess, Manassas National Battlefield Park Museum specialist, for reviewing the facts and offering invaluable suggestions.

Thank you, to all those who saved those dusty boxes and researched and documented this little southern town. You have enabled all of us to imagine life in a different time but in the same place.

And finally, thanks go to my husband, Bob, daughter, Lindsay, and son, Alex, for indulging in and sharing my enthusiasm for historic sites and for offering advice on this project and to my brother Tom, who has always inspired me to notice the markers, visit the sites, and read the local history.

Unless otherwise noted, all images appear courtesy of the Manassas Museum.

Introduction

Not long after the echoes of artillery fire finally receded from memory, survivors of the war, along with their newcomer neighbors, must have ached to build a new community free of conflict. Despite—or perhaps because of—its proximity to Civil War battlefields and graveyards, Manassas became a refuge for those looking to start fresh. Seated side by side on the town council, in Center Street businesses, and in church pews were veterans, both Confederate and Union.

By the late 1800s and early 1900s, life revolved around concerts at Conner's Hall, plays at the Baldwin School, summer horse shows for both whites and African Americans, the Piedmont Dairy Festival, autumn agricultural fairs, rides on the merry-go-round, and Christmas church services. Citizens—often spurred by the encouragement of George Carr Round, the town's leading cheerleader—mostly supported the rapid development that transformed dusty Center Street into an electrified commercial and social hub and the proposals that built schools, utilities, and magnificent homes. A few naysayers rejected the first attempts to establish electric service or to build the landmark town hall and expanded depot, but the town passed bond issues that made possible a historic downtown that survives today.

African Americans, restricted to their own schools and neighborhoods south of the railroad tracks by local ordinances, nonetheless found healing grace in the halls of the Manassas Industrial School, in the American Legion, and among congregations like the historic First Baptist Church. In the early days of the new 20th century, when the stillness of summer twilight would settle over the town, men who lived in the Liberty Street neighborhood would sing outside their homes to an appreciative audience. Like their neighbors north of the tracks, it was school concerts, church suppers, football games, and homecomings at Manassas Regional High School that bound their community.

We can only imagine how proud residents must have been to purchase a postcard at Wenrich's Jewelry Store, send it to a far-flung relative, and hear his or her response about the splendid new buildings in Manassas. Civic pride was palpable in the way that residents hung bunting and opened their doors to veterans attending the National Jubilee of Peace or in the way that newspapers could call on citizens to have a cleanup day to improve the appearance of downtown. Townspeople were such avid readers of local news that two daily newspapers stayed in business for years. Debates were lively among well-informed citizens when town councilmen or the mayor suggested spending tax dollars on some new initiative.

Tourists came through town purchasing postcards that would be reminders of their visits to the battlefield. In a town where Confederate and Union veterans learned to join hands and work together, postcards catered to both Northern and Southern sympathizers. Tributes to Gen. Thomas "Stonewall" Jackson abounded, but so did postcards picturing memorials to fallen Union heroes on what northerners called the Bull Run battlefield. Those with surviving messages on the back speak mostly of the weather, a travel schedule, or the health of a family member. Postcards were, first and foremost, an inexpensive and speedy way to communicate.

The postcard images of the Southern Railway Depot, the post office, the Conner Building, the old town hall, the Old Manassas Courthouse, Trinity Church, Manassas Presbyterian Church, Hibbs and Giddings, and Hynson's that were captured 100 years ago do not look all that different from the scenes we see today. We walk the same sidewalks, shop in the same stores, conduct business in the same offices, and worship in the same churches. Our local government still wrestles with road and utility maintenance, improving schools, and keeping taxes in check.

Some of the places we see in those images, like the Manassas Industrial School or Milford Mills, no longer exist. Other places, like Robert Portner's Annaburg or Liberia Plantation when it was a dairy farm, appear substantially altered. Some battlefield vistas remain pristine, but others now include the snaking lines of cars navigating nearby commuter routes. These humble postcards are often the only visual record we have of so many of these places, but their blue-sky optimism does not tell the whole story of life in Manassas.

Those who settled here may not have moved across the country to a windswept plain, but they were pioneers nonetheless. This land—and all who lived here—was scarred by the war. They were incorporating a town, worrying about digging another well, and trying to purchase enough buckets and ladders to fight the next fire. They were navigating dusty dirt roads on a hot August afternoon or when those roads turned to knee-deep mud after a cold October rain. They shared the road with cattle, goats, and pigs. They hauled the family's water from a town well. They watched fire repeatedly consume homes and businesses. They tended those frequently injured on the railroad tracks. They wept when the Spanish flu epidemic claimed family, neighbors, and even the town doctor. Still, they kept opening businesses, paving roads, building schools, and most importantly, building community.

This book does not present a complete history of Manassas—there are many fine books that do—but follows instead the ebb and flow of the places and people pictured in this postcard collection. The resilience of those first citizens who restored fields destroyed by warring armies, built consensus in an emerging local government, or passed water-filled buckets in nightclothes while fighting a great fire on a cold December night should remain an inspiration to a new generation helping to reinvent a diverse city.

One

A Railroad Town

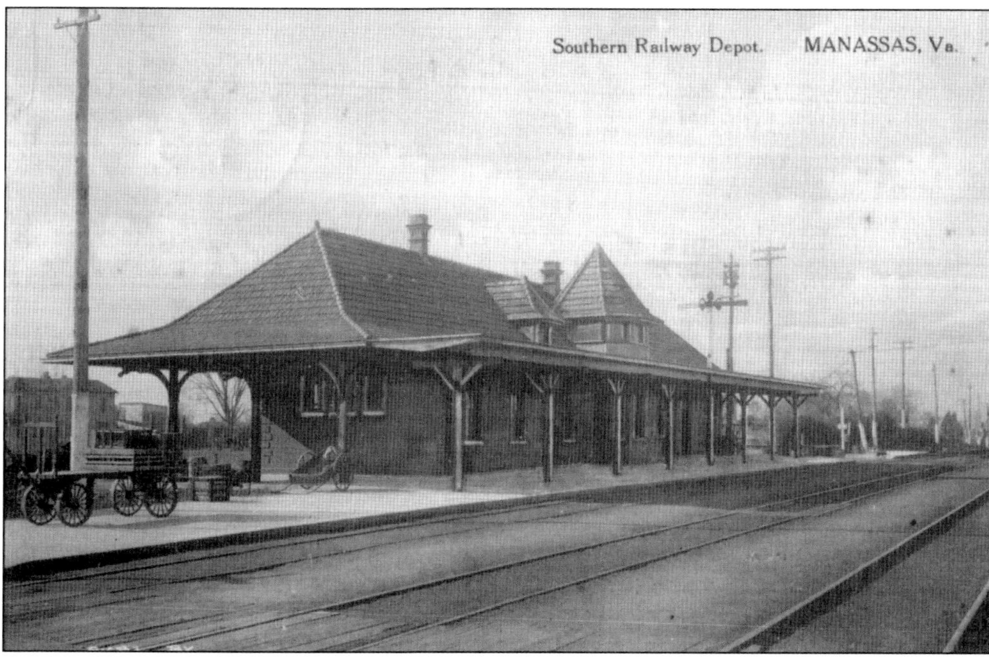

The fortunes of Manassas—and its establishment as a town—were inextricably tied to the railroad. When the Orange & Alexandria Railroad reached what was then called Tudor Hall in 1851, its Alexandria-to-Gordonsville route created an opportunity for farmers to move their grain to market. The Manassas Gap Railroad, which extended to Strasburg, connected to the Orange & Alexandria here, creating the famous Civil War–time moniker "Manassas Junction."

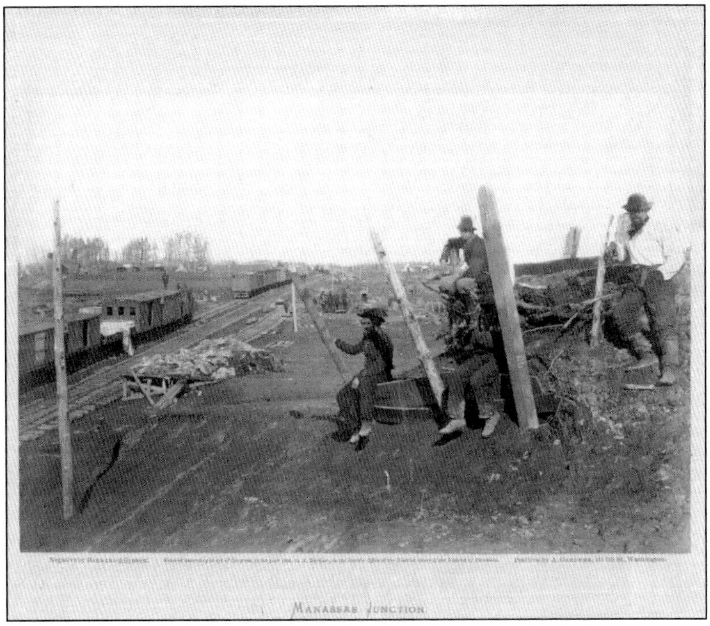

Confederate soldiers descended on Manassas Junction in the spring of 1861 to build a series of earthworks defending the railroad. Both Northern and Southern troops realized the strategic importance of controlling a rail line that stretched from Washington to the Shenandoah Valley, but through most of the war, Union troops controlled the junction. This 1862 image shows soldiers beside damaged rail lines after Confederates evacuated. (Library of Congress.)

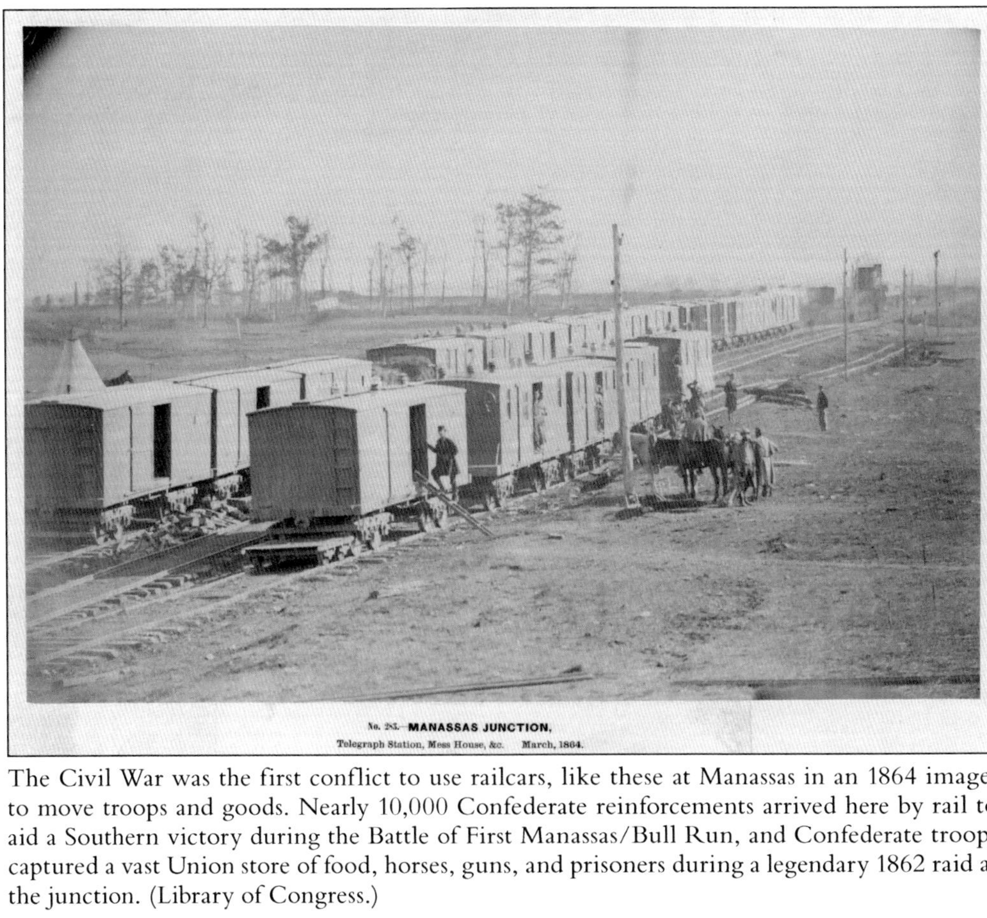

The Civil War was the first conflict to use railcars, like these at Manassas in an 1864 image, to move troops and goods. Nearly 10,000 Confederate reinforcements arrived here by rail to aid a Southern victory during the Battle of First Manassas/Bull Run, and Confederate troops captured a vast Union store of food, horses, guns, and prisoners during a legendary 1862 raid at the junction. (Library of Congress.)

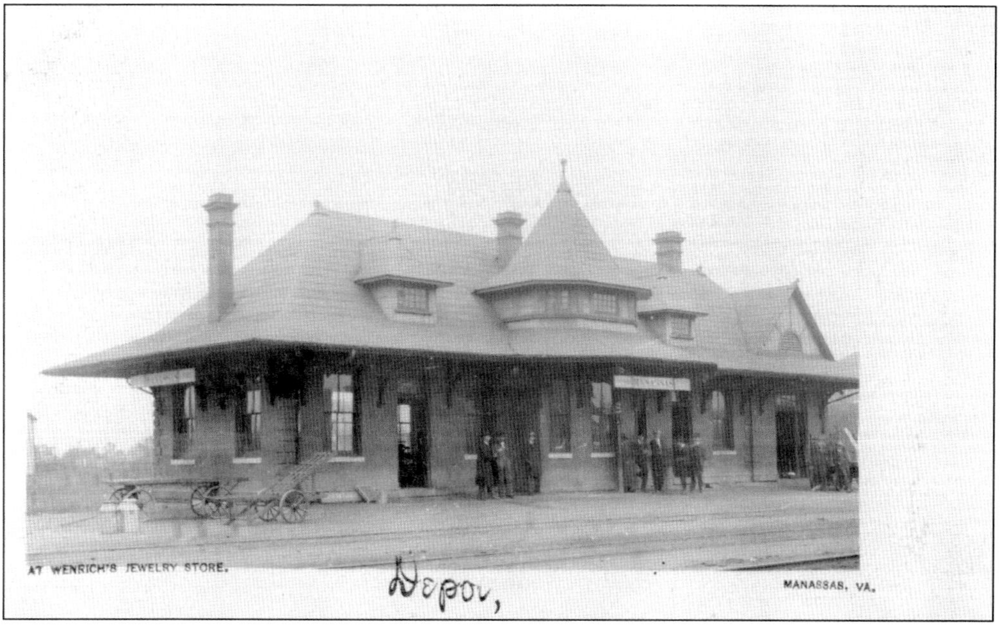

The first Manassas railroad depot was a small log building located east of the present site between Battle and West Streets. The first depot built on the present site was a simple wooden structure, which was dismantled and replaced by this brick depot in 1904. In June 1914, a fire broke out in the baggage room, and the depot burned, leaving only the foundation and walls.

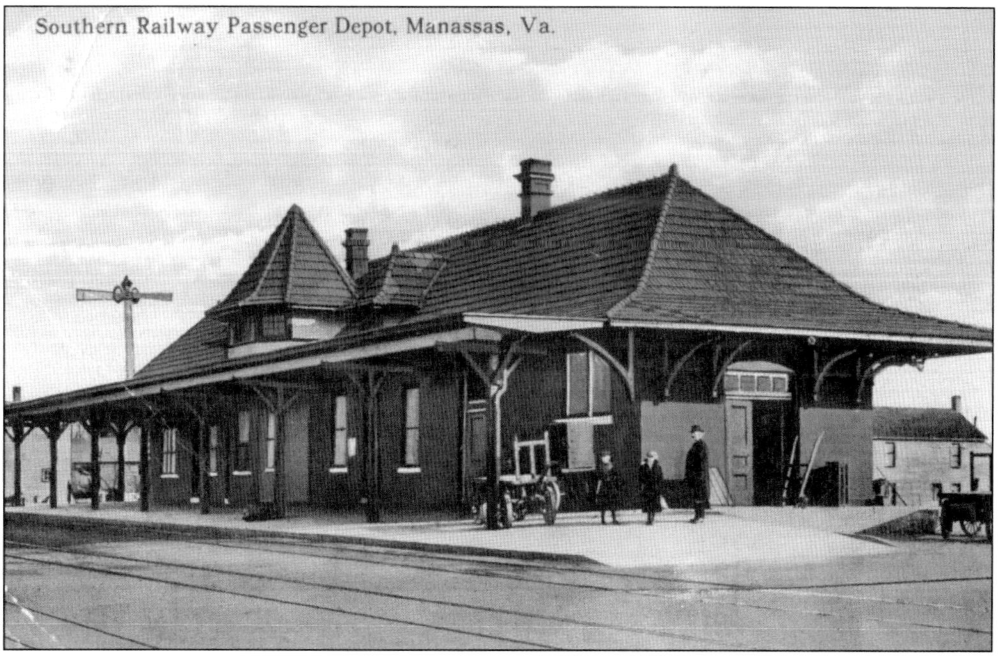

This new larger depot opened just four months later, partially incorporating the walls of the burned depot. Its new features included an office; waiting rooms for ladies, men, and "colored" passengers; a ladies' restroom; running water; a larger baggage room; and sidewalks. This view of the newly constructed depot shows a new umbrella shed on two sides, new electric lights, and a clay tile roof.

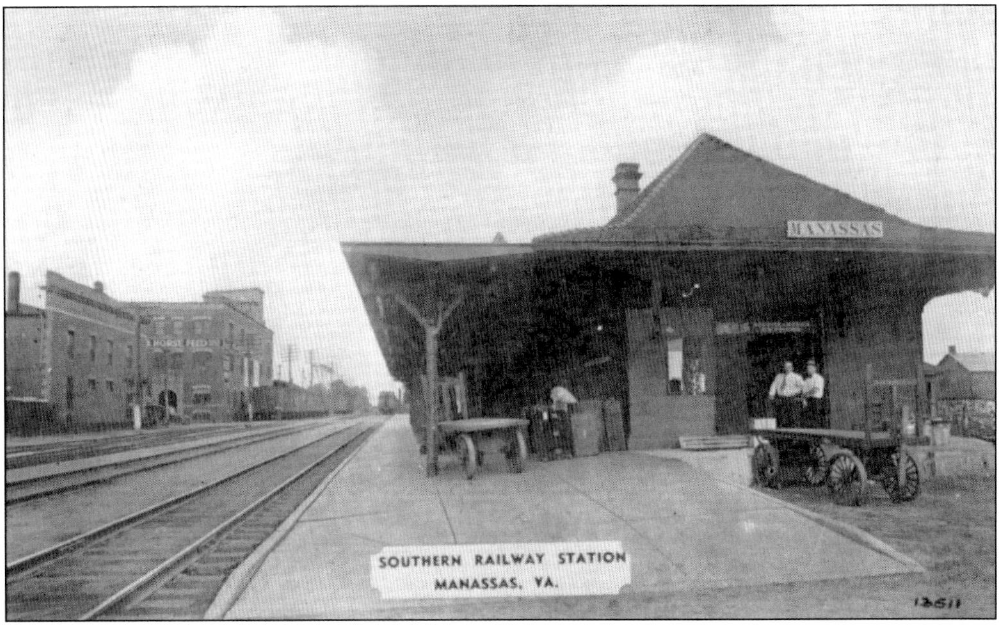

Those who stayed or settled here after the Civil War quickly realized the importance of restoring routes, rebuilding bridges, and resuming commercial and passenger rail service. By the early 1900s, passengers could board the train in Manassas and travel for work or pleasure to Washington and beyond. Railroad workers built grand homes along Prescott Avenue and helped spur the local economy and population growth.

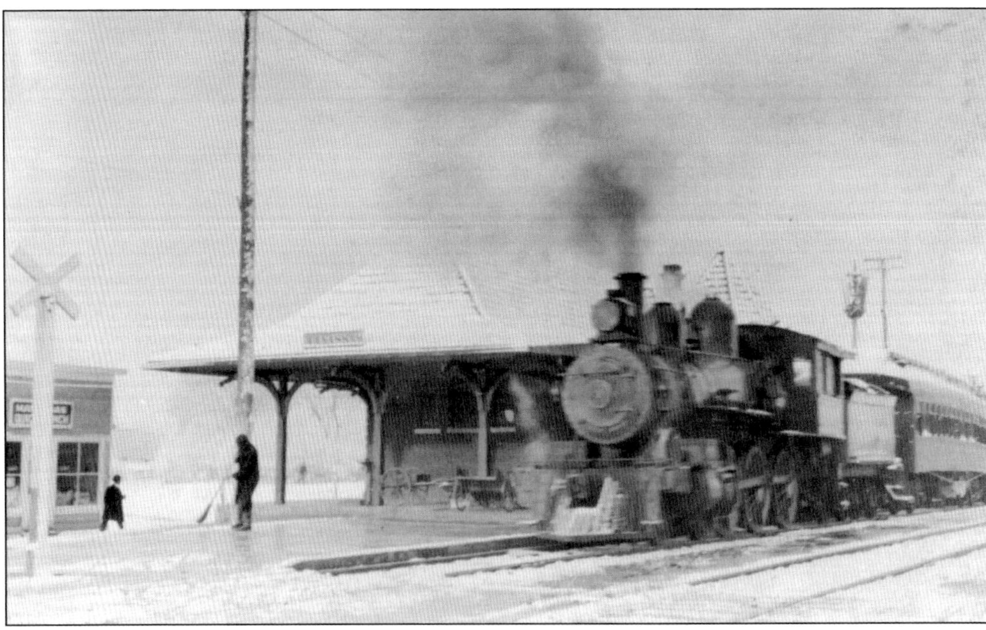

Manassas dairy farmers sent milk and eggs on the train to Washington markets, while Model Ts and Sears, Roebuck and Co. kit houses arrived here on the train from distant points. Townspeople gathered at the depot waiting for the mail clerk to pick up and sort the mailbag dropped by a passing train or for telegrams passed from conductors.

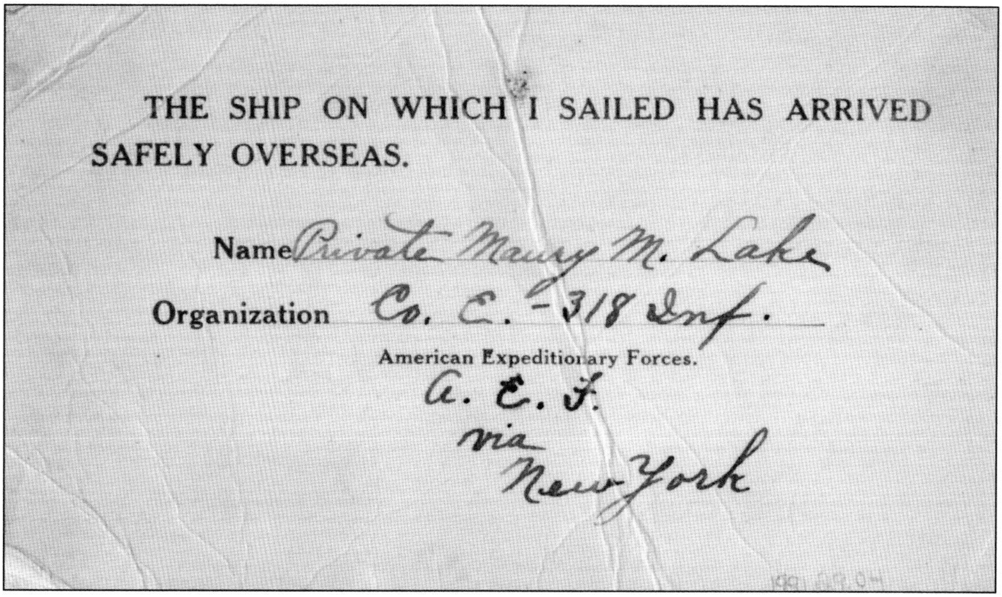

Area families anxiously waited for the train to deliver postcards from their World War I soldiers and to know they arrived safely overseas. Before embarking for Europe from New York, soldiers signed and addressed the cards with the help of YMCA volunteers. When the military post office received cablegrams that a ship arrived safely, the postcards were mailed from New York. Pfc. Maury Montgomery Lake, a Fauquier County native, was appointed postmaster of the Wellington Post Office in 1917, shortly before he left for the war. His family lived in Culpeper County, so Mrs. O. Wells must have been a friend in Wellington, a small community outside Manassas. Sadly, Private 1st Class Lake never made it home. He was killed in action on October 4, 1918, and is buried in Meuse-Argonne American Cemetery in Romagne-sous-Montfaucon, France.

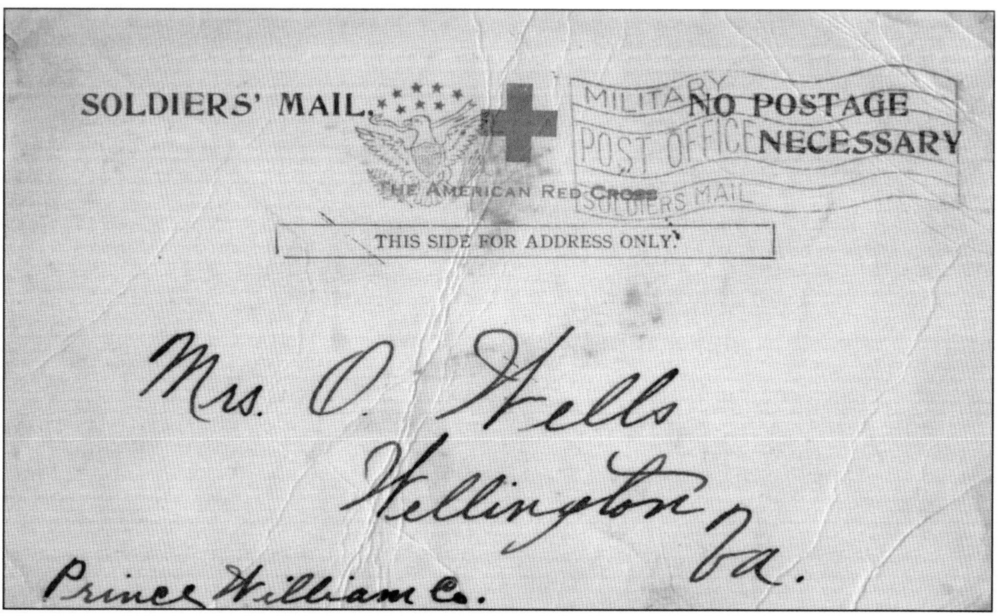

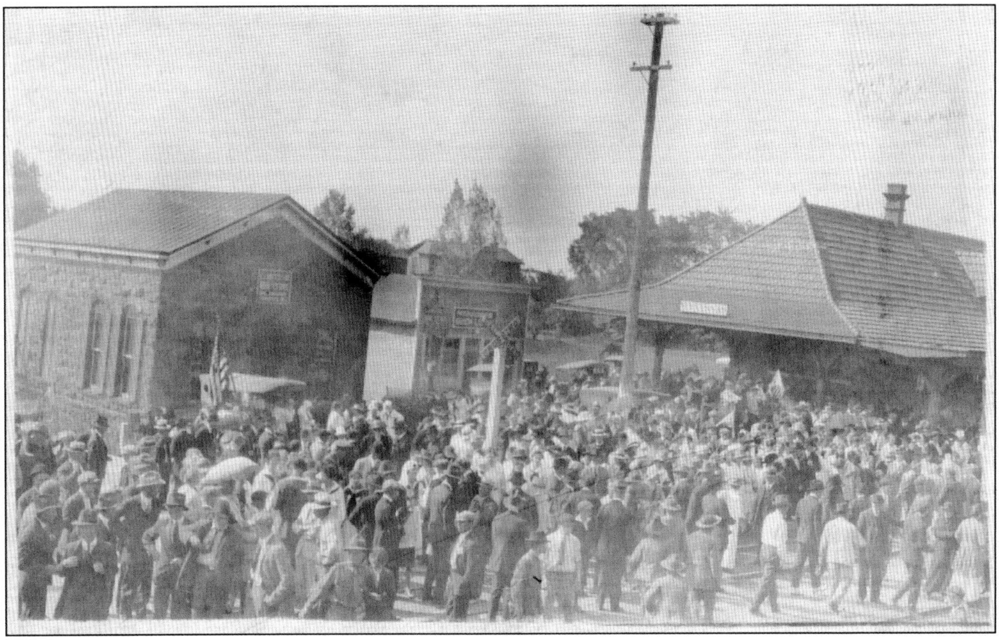

Townspeople gathered at the Southern Depot for many momentous events, like this one in about 1920, including send-offs and welcomes for soldiers in both world wars; the arrival of trains for horse shows; Piedmont Dairy Festivals; church dedications; the 1911 Peace Jubilee; or the passing of funeral trains. The Metz family ran the real estate business, at rear left, and the Manassas Quick Lunch, at rear right.

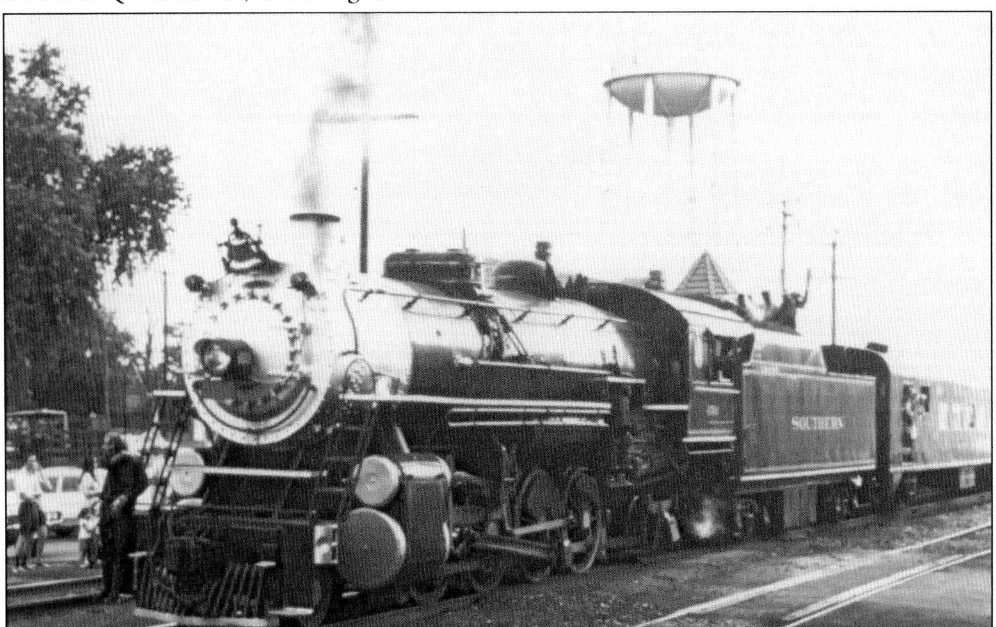

Manassas still honors its railway heritage with the annual Manassas Heritage Railway Festival and hosts occasional steam excursion trains, like this 1911 steam locomotive that came to town in 1973. The earliest commuters traveled to Washington on trains like this, affectionately called "milk trains" for the cargo they carried from area dairy farms.

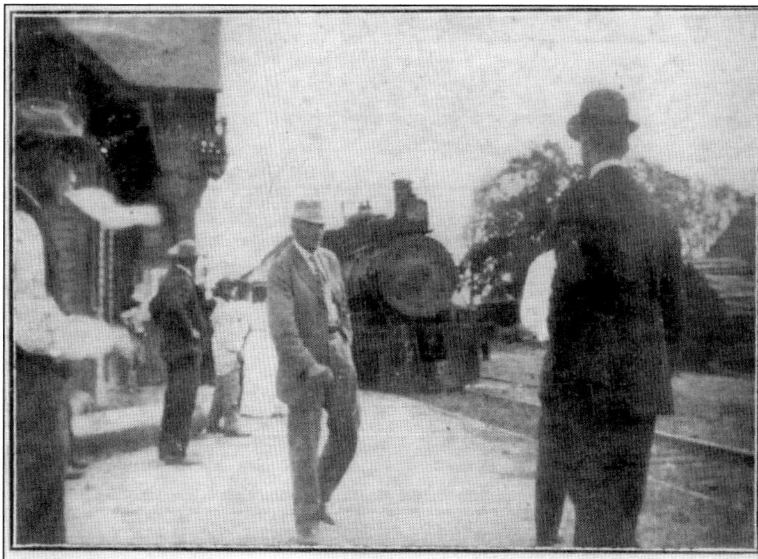

322 D. Station, Gainesville, Va. M. Cave, Publisher.

The nearby Gainesville station opened when the Manassas Gap Railroad was finished in 1852. It became an important stop for tourists headed to the Sudley Springs Hotel in the late 1800s, a resort where those on vacation could sample the waters of the local spring. Wagons transported visitors the five miles from the station to the hotel, which burned down in the early 1900s.

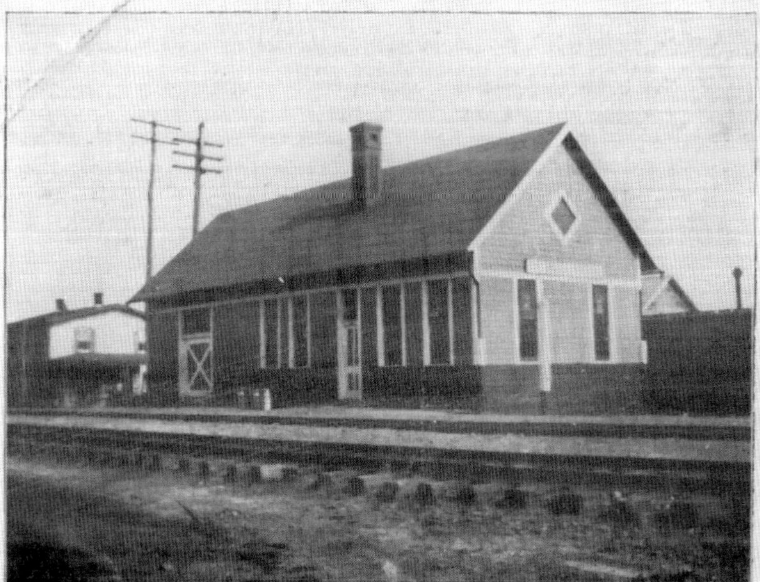

RAILROAD DEPOT, BRISTOW, VA.

Although this depot no longer exists, Bristow is still a popular stop for commuters. Like Manassas, Bristoe Station (the spelling at the time) was attacked during the Civil War when Confederate forces heading to the Battle of Second Manassas derailed and burned two Union railcars, captured Federal soldiers, and destroyed tracks to prevent their use by Union troops.

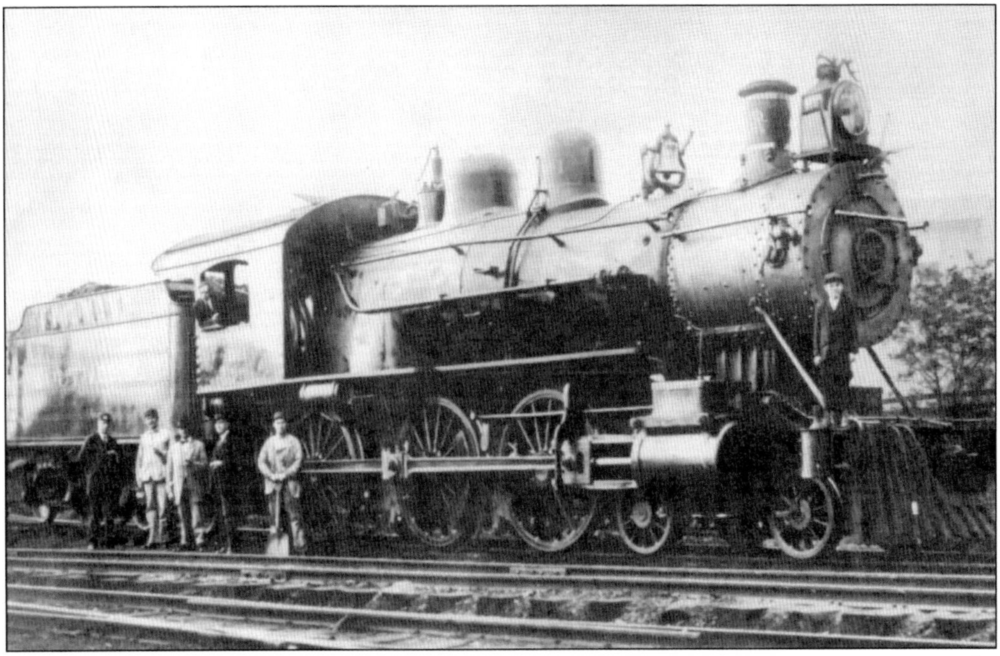

This 1973 souvenir postcard commemorates the steam excursion train visit to Manassas. The image shows a Southern Railway locomotive used on the Harrisonburg Branch in 1911. Union veteran George C. Round was said to like what he saw when he disembarked from a similar train in Manassas. He soon met his bride and stayed to help build the community where he earned the nickname "town father."

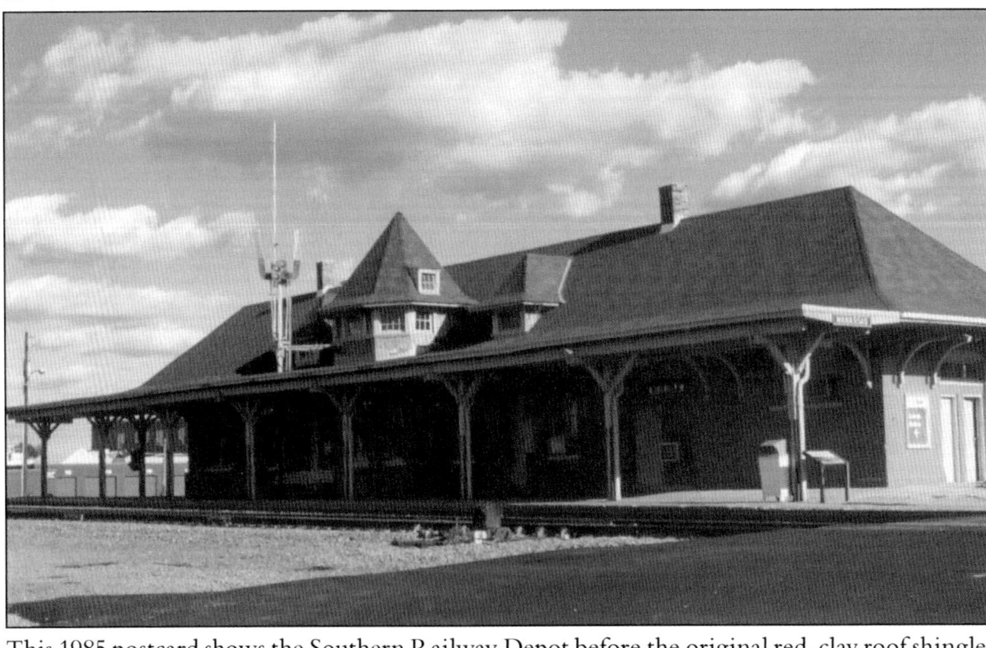

This 1985 postcard shows the Southern Railway Depot before the original red-clay roof shingles were restored in a 1997 renovation. The depot had fallen into disrepair until James and Marion Payne led a campaign to revitalize it. In 1914, the Manassas Business Men's League led a similar effort to persuade officials to build an improved depot after it was destroyed by fire.

Two

First in Education

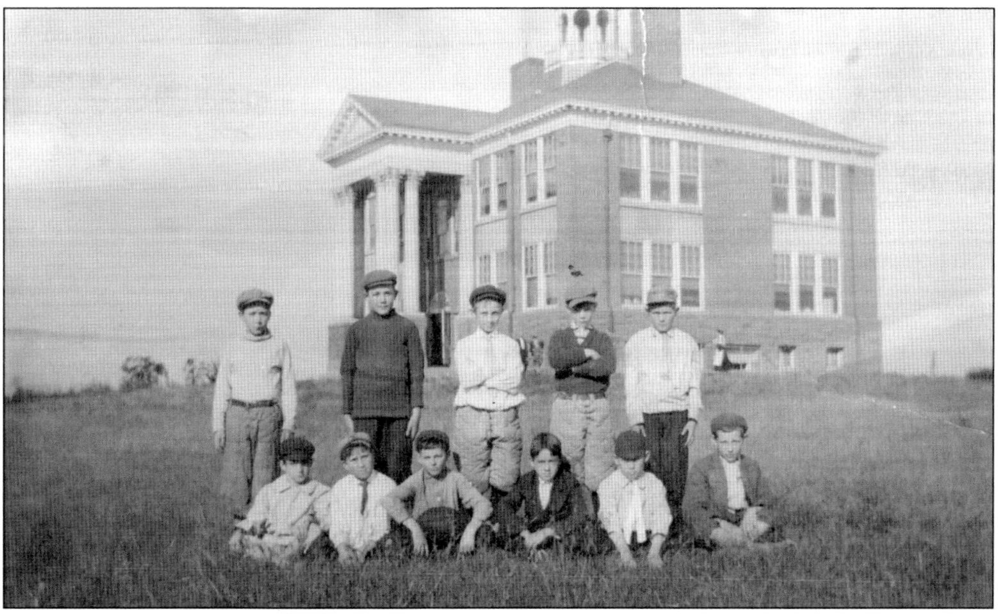

Union veteran George C. Round had ambitious plans for his adopted hometown. He and fellow citizens helped establish the first public schools in Virginia for both whites and African Americans. Although the schools were at the center of the small town's life and helped smooth relations between Northerners and Southerners, they remained segregated until 1966. Students pose here before the new Bennett School, built in 1909.

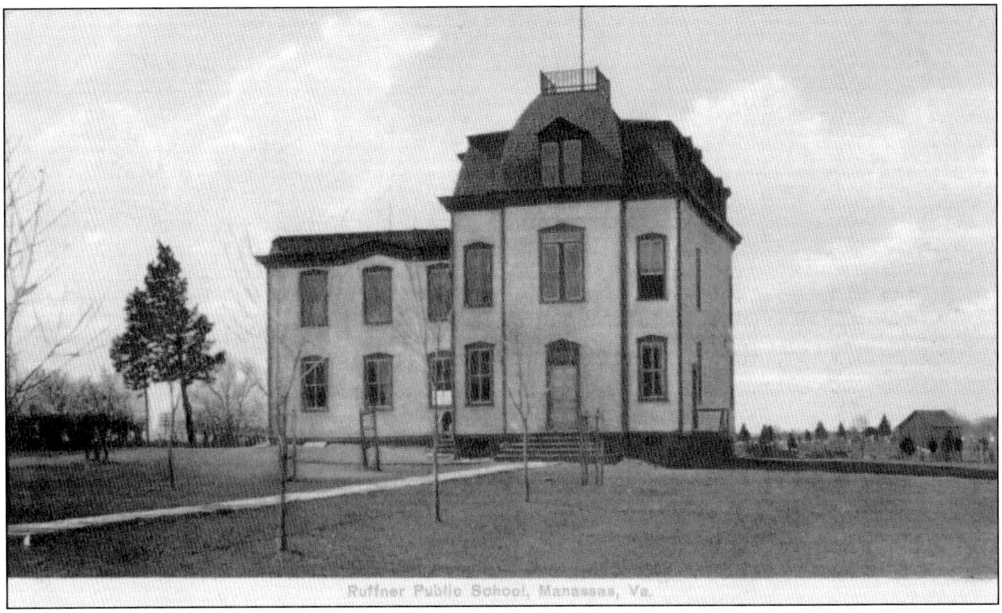

The first public school for white children in Virginia opened in 1872 at Peabody and Center Streets. Ruffner School No. 1, named for the commonwealth's first superintendent of schools, began meeting in a church in 1869, even before the state mandated public schools. Ruffner educated both elementary and secondary students until 1927.

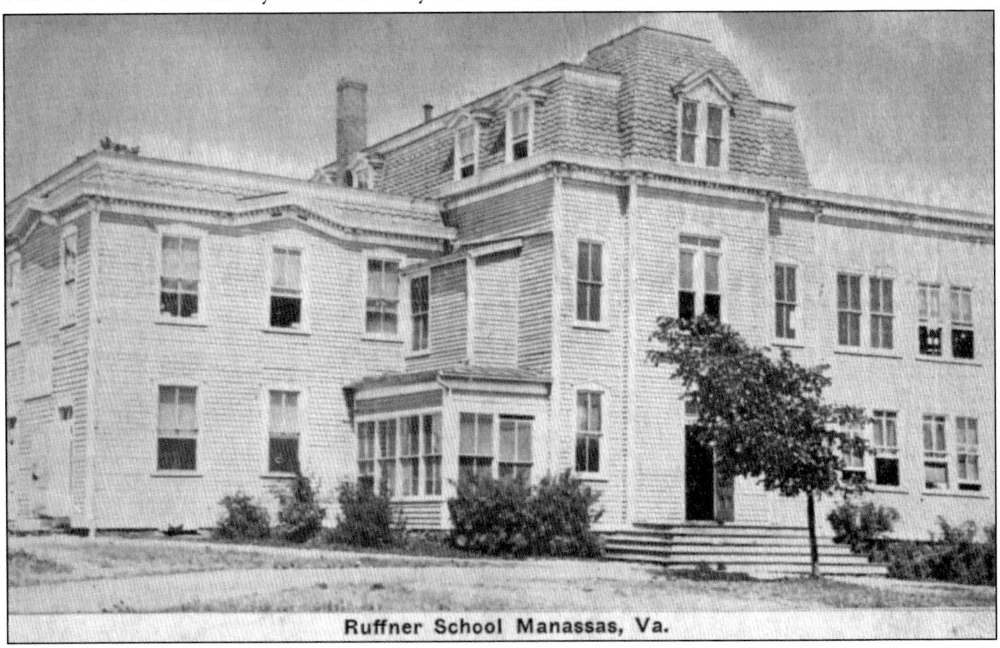

Ruffner was originally built as a two-room schoolhouse, and Andrew Carnegie donated funds in 1899 for a third-story addition, which housed the county's first library. Although initially designed as a grade school, Ruffner later educated secondary students. By 1908, the school expanded to accommodate a growing high school population, but by 1925, it risked losing its accreditation due to overcrowding. The building was razed in 1930 after students began attending classes in the new high school.

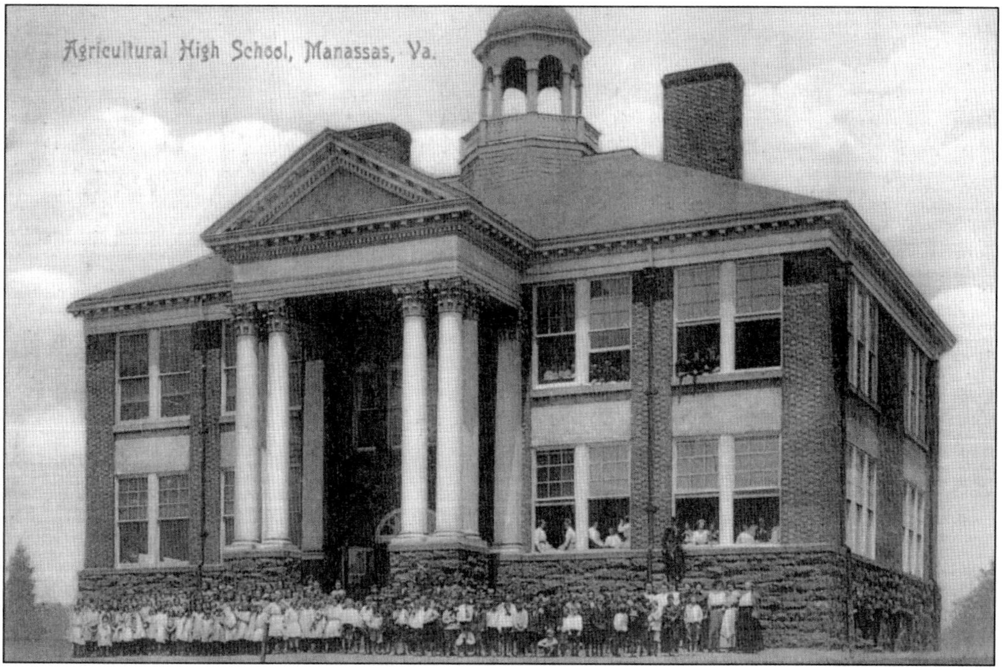

Although the Bennett School on Lee Avenue was commissioned as Virginia's first agricultural high school, and sometimes mistakenly called a college, only elementary students ever attended there. The growing population of younger students used the building from 1909 until 1953, and teachers later trained there. Here, students celebrate the 1909 opening of the building.

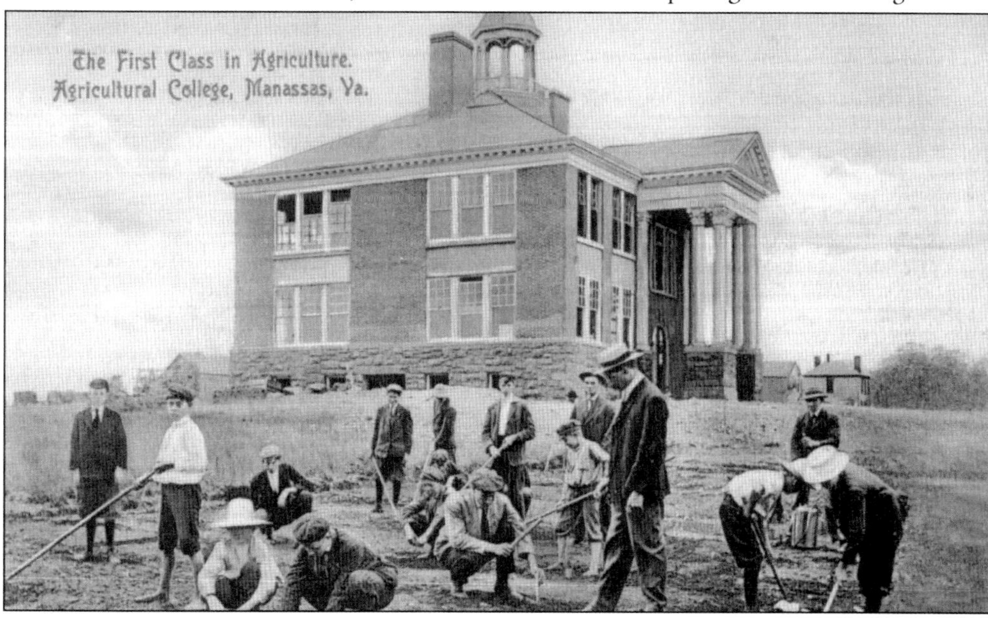

High school students remained in the nearby Ruffner School building, now renamed the Agricultural High School, where a new wing was constructed to house them. Boys used the school's experimental plot to determine fertilizing needs and the best methods of soil cultivation and crop rotation, while girls learned cooking and sewing. Bennett, still standing on Lee Avenue near the Prince William General District Court, is now a county property.

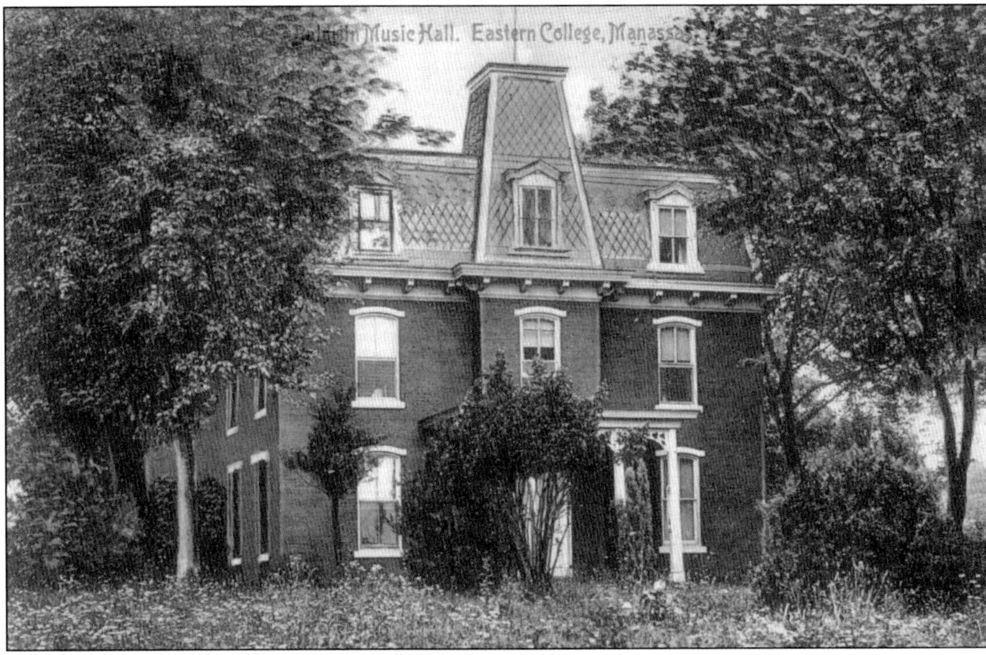

The Manassas Institute, pictured above, was founded by sisters Fannie and Eugenia Osbourn in 1890 and opened in what was then called the Baldwin House, built by Isaac Baldwin in the 1880s and located on the present grounds of the Manassas Museum. After the institute moved to larger quarters on Grant Avenue, as seen below, in 1896, the Baldwin House became part of Eastern College and the Swavely School. The Temple School—founded by Margaret Temple Hopkins, the daughter of the Hopkins Candy Company founder—then began educating young men and women in the musical arts in 1924 at that location. Their recitals at the Conner Opera House were the talk of the town. "Miss Hopkins and her two very able associates have accomplished much in music among the younger generation of Manassas," reads a front-page story in the *Manassas Democrat*.

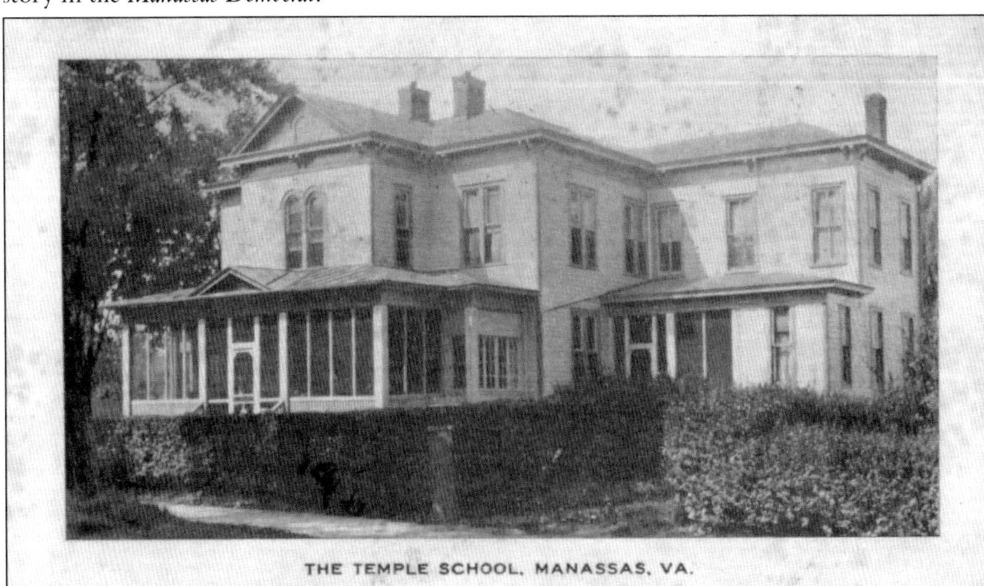

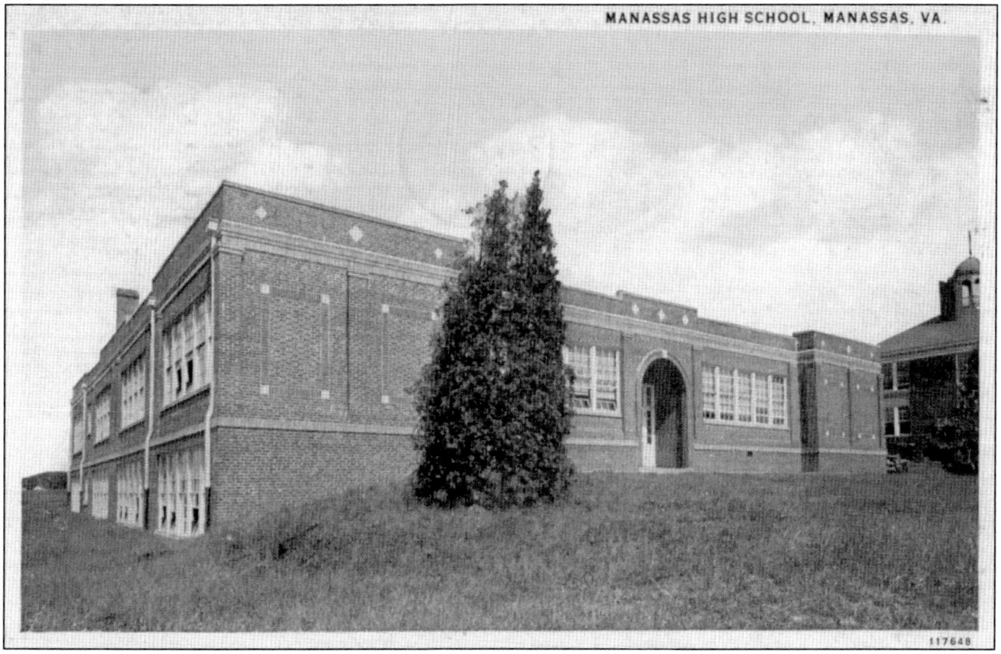

Eugenia Osbourn and her sister Fannie Osbourn Metz were pioneers in private and public education in Manassas. Fannie, a private teacher in the 1870s, opened the Manassas Institute with her sister for students in grades first through twelfth in 1890. By 1906, the institute merged with the public Manassas High School, where Fannie served as principal until her death in 1912. Eugenia then stepped in as principal, a job she held until her retirement in 1935. Even after retirement, she stayed on as the school's librarian until 1943. To ease overcrowding, this new high school building (shown here in about 1940) was erected in 1928 next to the Bennett School.

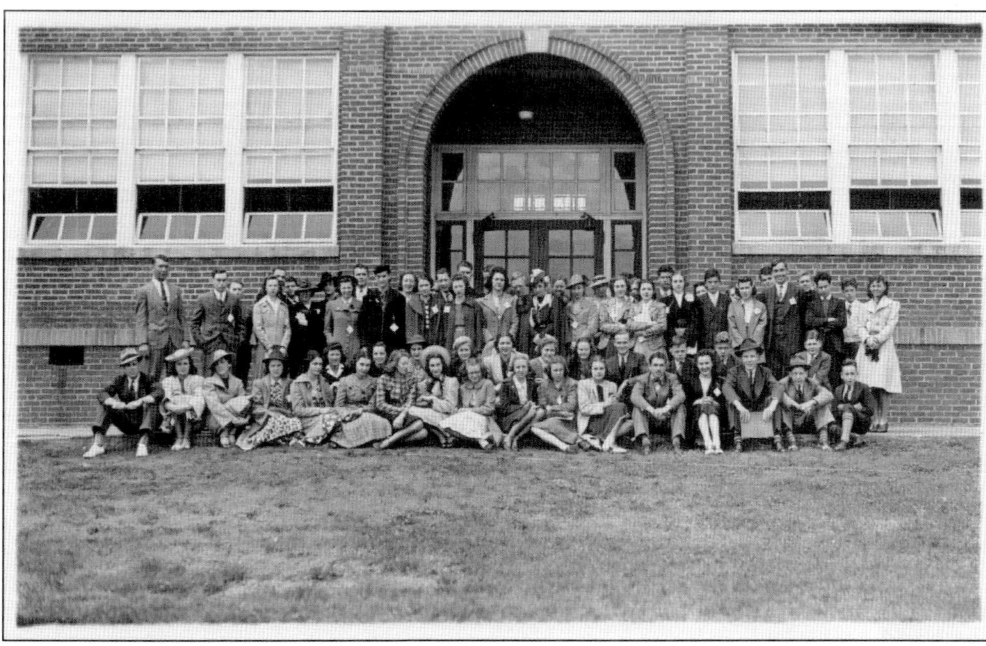

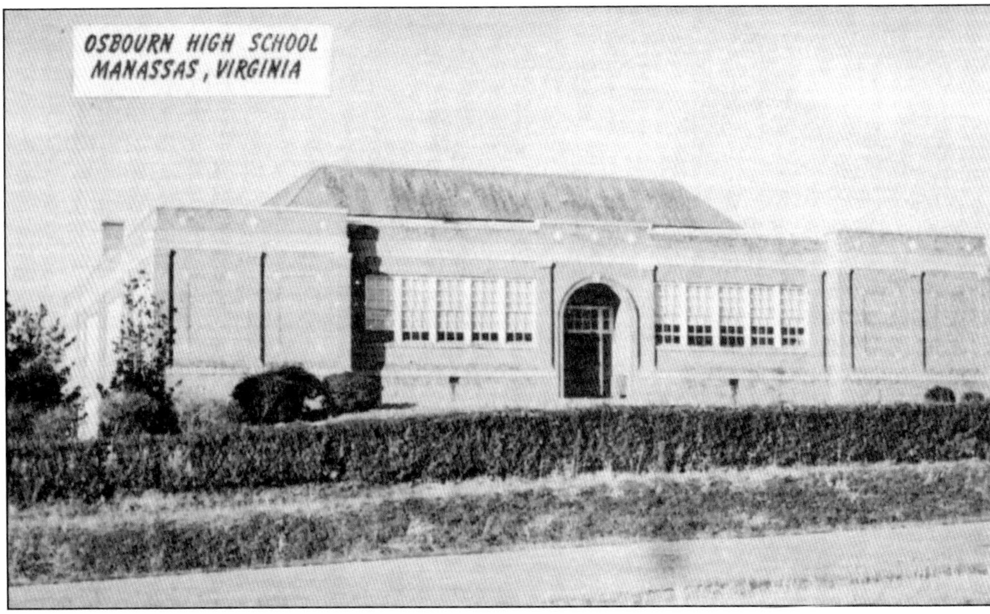

In the 1930s, the old Manassas High School on Lee Avenue was renamed Osbourn in honor of the Osbourn sisters. At the dedication, school officials cited the "excellent standards attained by the schools that were in a very large measure due to the life time of loyalty and dedication to public education in this community by Miss Eugenia H. Osbourn and her sister Mrs. Fannie Osbourn Metz."

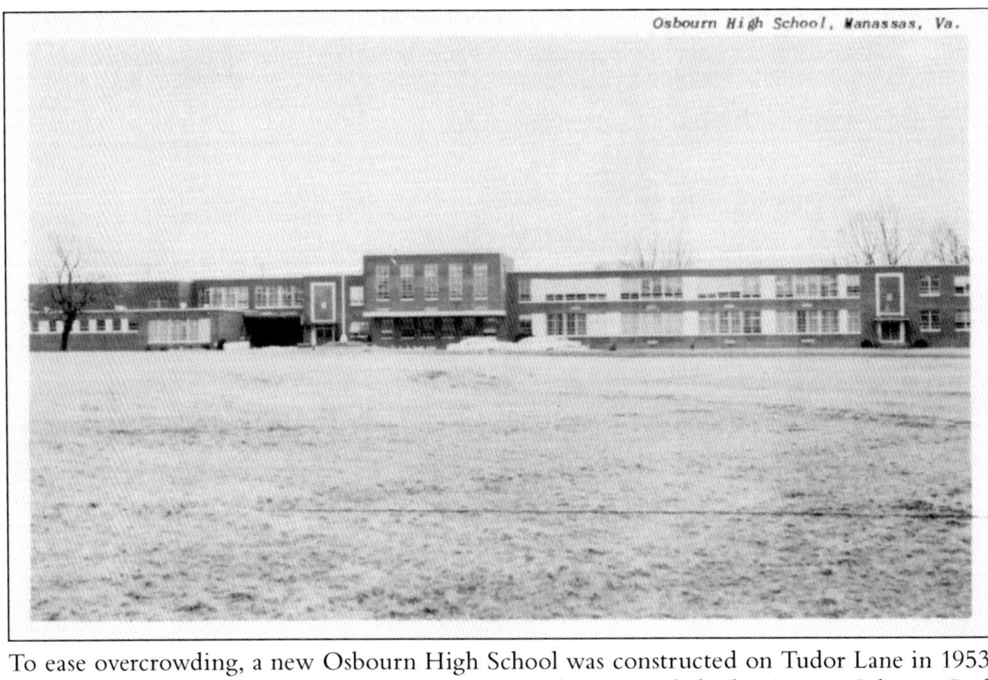

To ease overcrowding, a new Osbourn High School was constructed on Tudor Lane in 1953, but by 1975, the population outgrew that space. Students attended what is now Osbourn Park High School on Euclid Avenue until the city created its own school system and built the present school in 1977. Older portions of the building were razed when the newest wing was completed in 1999.

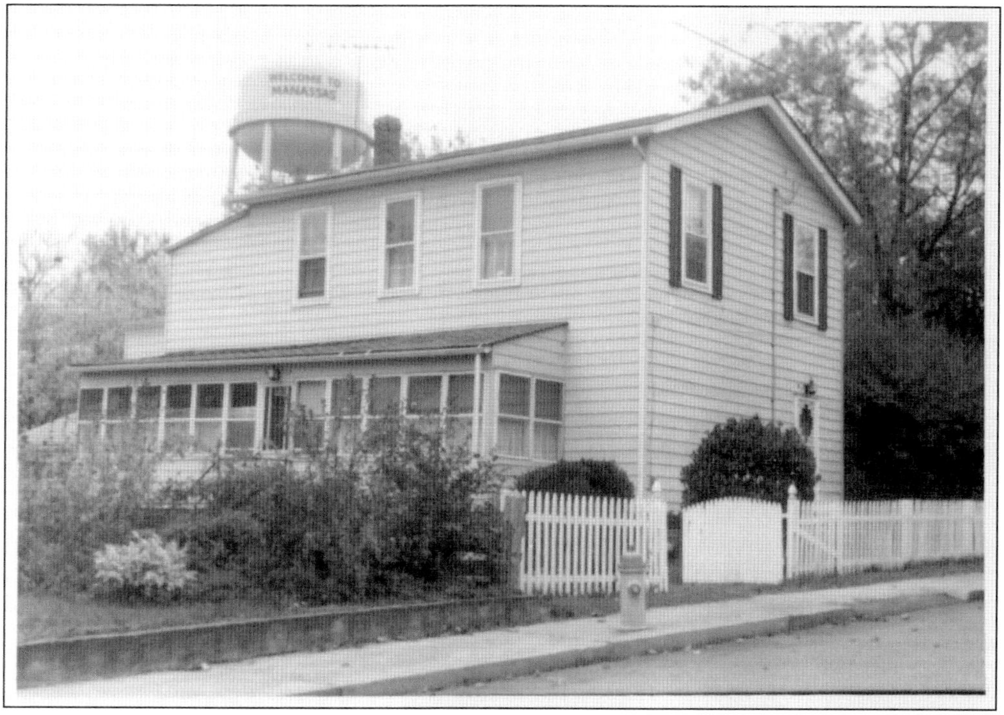

In the years after the Civil War, African Americans established schools with little help from the newly formed public school system. The Manassas Village Colored School (above) became the second public school in Manassas in 1870, evolving from a private school funded by both white and African American donors. Located on Liberty Street, it was renamed the Brown School a year later for a benefactor of the Philadelphia Friends Society, a group that had for years been sending funds for the education of young African Americans. The original school—and a larger school built in 1926 with the sweat equity of supporters—was the educational and social center of the African American community for 83 years. Prominent physician and Brown alumnus Dr. John Williams (pictured at right) bought and installed radiators and laid a water line to the new school during the heat of summer.

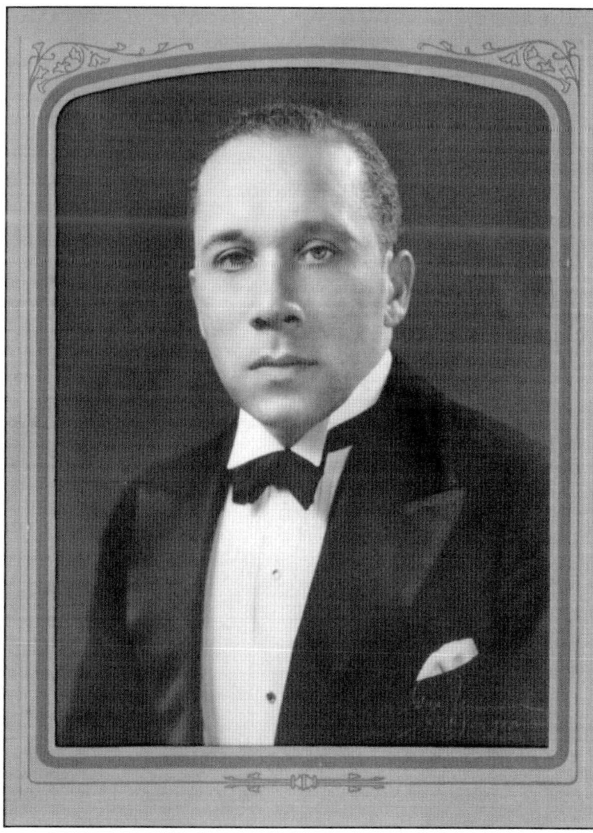

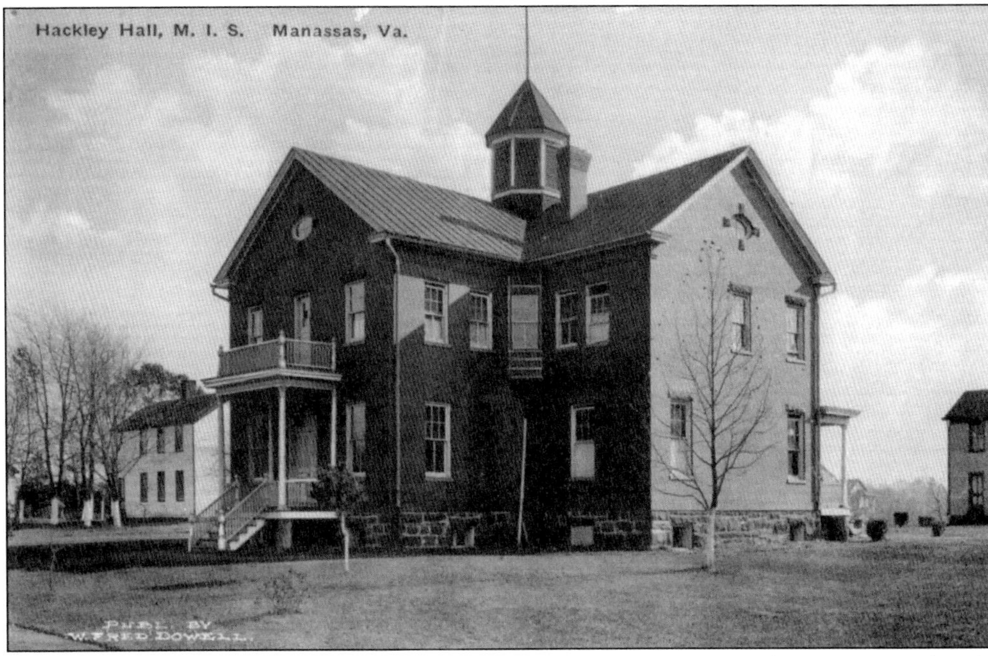

After almost a decade of fundraising by its visionary founder, Jennie Dean, the Manassas Industrial School for Colored Youth opened in 1894. The school was designed as a private residential institution for secondary students, and provided both academic and vocational training within a Christian setting. Although local citizens contributed to the school, Andrew Carnegie and other East Coast philanthropists largely financed construction of the campus. Hackley Hall served as the boys' dormitory.

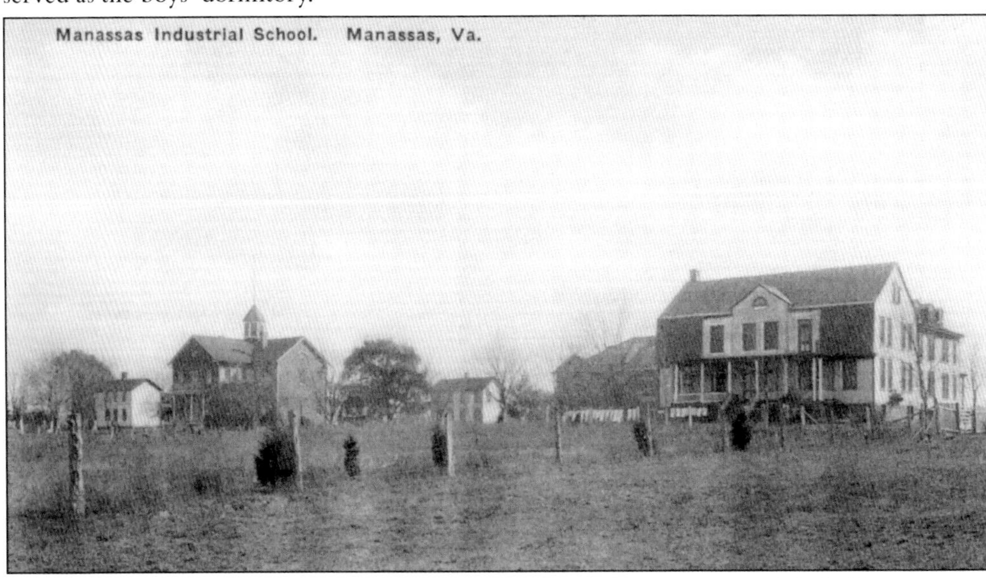

By 1900, over 150 students studied academic subjects, music, and vocational skills like carpentry, blacksmithing, shoemaking, sewing, cooking, domestic arts, and laundry methods. Students earned their tuition and board by selling products they harvested and made. The school produced 100 barrels of corn, 435 bushels of potatoes, 300 bushels of sweet potatoes, numerous vegetables, and hay in 1915.

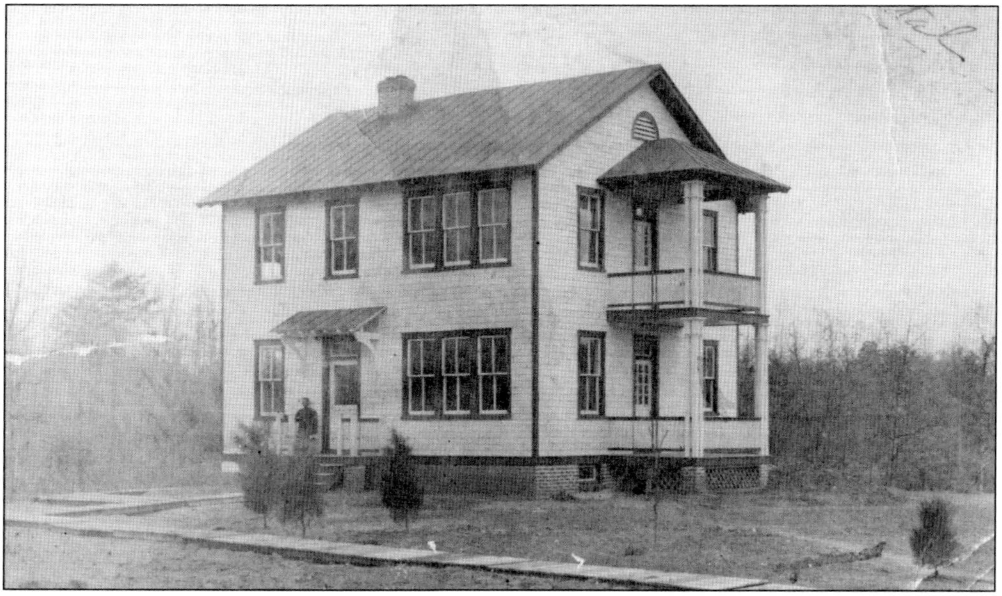

The 1915–1916 Manassas Industrial School catalogue notes the aim of the school: "to teach Negro youth the need and importance in a democratic society of all kinds of useful labor intelligently done, and as far as possible to send them back to their homes efficient teachers and leaders in industry and civic welfare." This home was the industrial school's hospital.

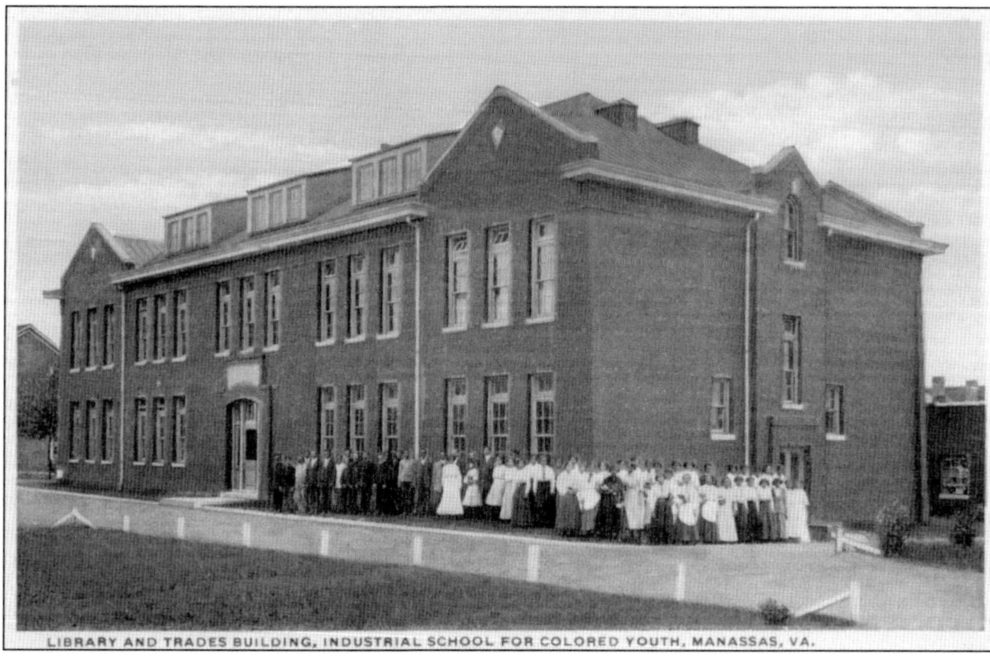

"The upkeep and care of the school's 200 acre farm, the farm implements, the stock, the dormitories and cottages—and all this is done by the students themselves—most helpfully supplement the work of the classroom and the shop," the Manassas Industrial School catalogue explains. "Particular stress is laid upon the study and practice of agriculture and upon the adequate training and preparation of teachers for the colored elementary rural schools." The Carnegie Building, shown here, housed classroom, office, and library space.

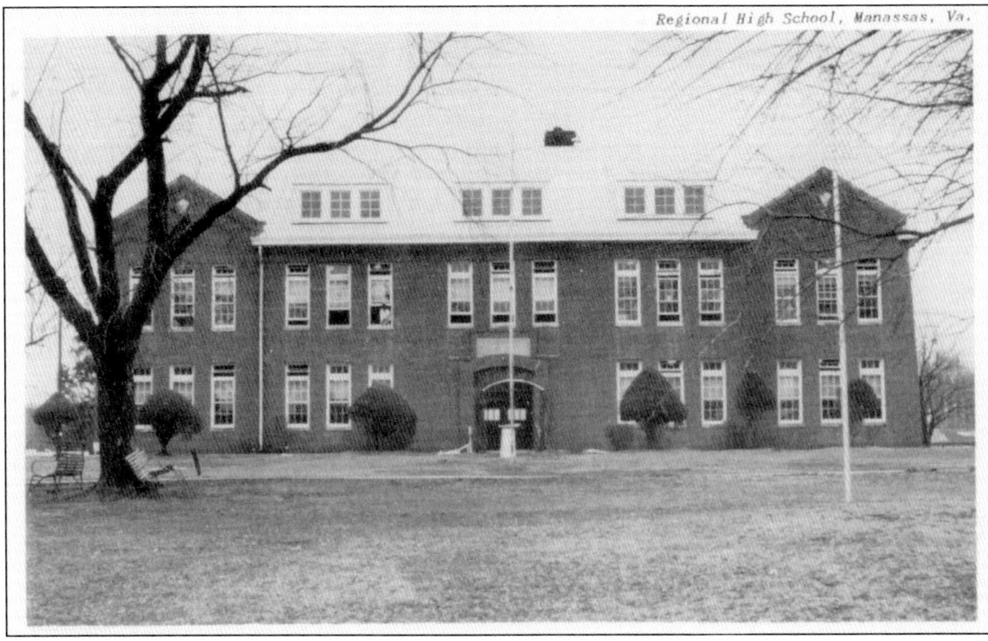

After the Manassas Industrial School closed in 1938, the segregated high school for African Americans—operated by Prince William, Fairfax, Fauquier, Warren, Rappahannock and Shenandoah Counties—opened on the campus. Both day and resident students traveled great distances to study courses in college preparatory, home economics, agriculture, carpentry, and other trades at the Manassas Regional High School. Students repaired and improved the facilities, and cooked and cleaned in the dormitories.

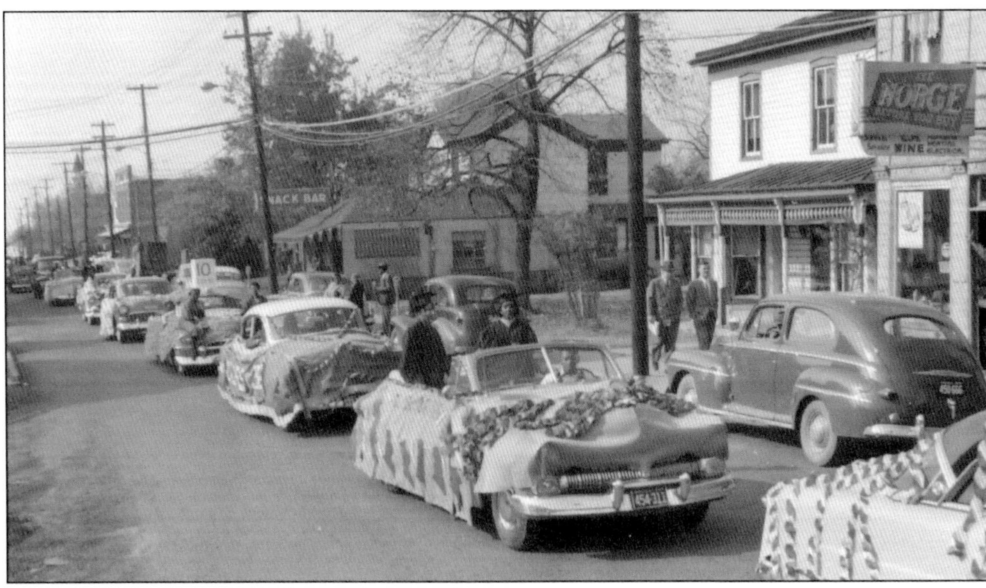

Homecoming celebrations at the Manassas Regional High School, like this one in 1953, featured elaborate parades through town, football games, and dances. The school was also known as the Manassas Industrial School until 1960, when a new Jennie Dean High School, accommodating grades first through twelfth, was built on the site. After schools desegregated in 1966, the school became Jennie Dean Junior High School and then Jennie Dean Elementary.

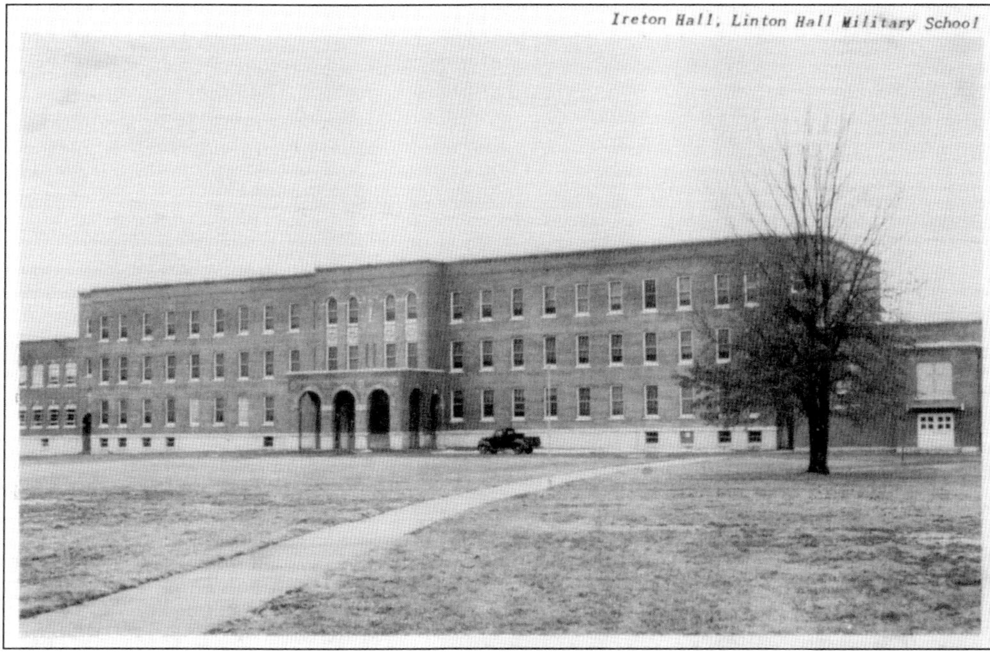

Benedictine monks and sisters first opened St. Joseph's Industrial School for boys and St. Edith's Academy for girls at what is now Linton Hall School in Bristow in 1894. By 1922, the girls' school moved to Richmond while the residential school for boys remained, becoming Linton Hall Military Academy in the late 1930s. By employing a disciplined regimen, the school promised to instill leadership, character, and integrity in boys ages six through high school. It became a coeducational day school in 1989.

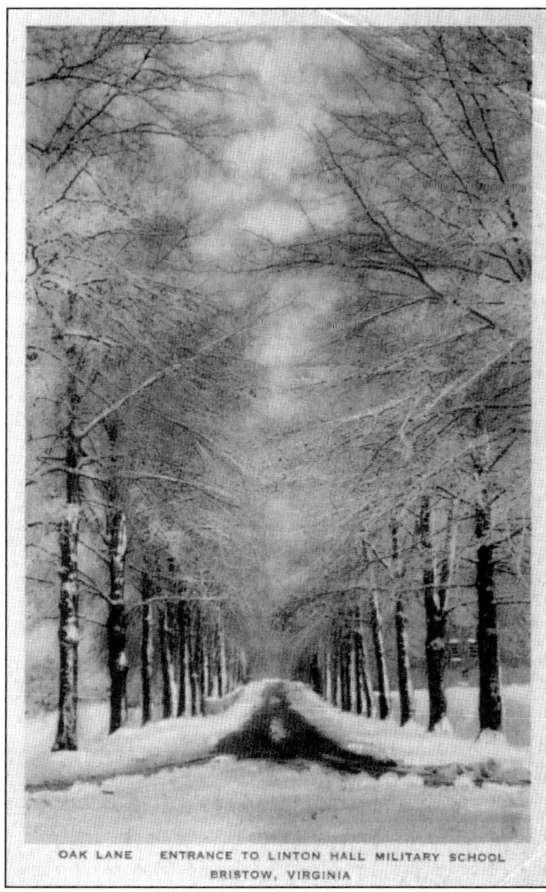

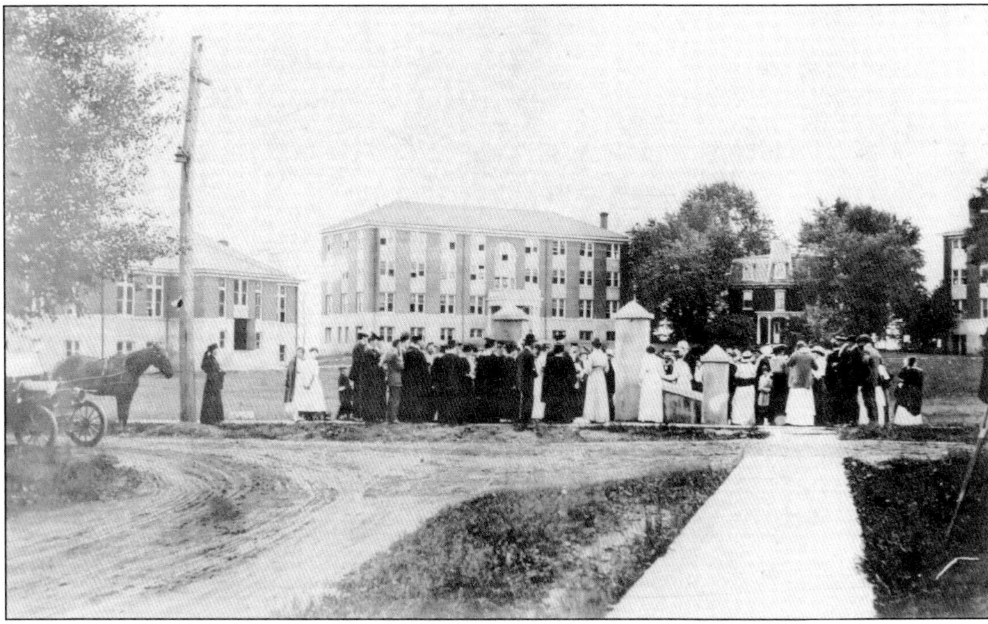

Eastern College, established in Front Royal in 1902, moved to Manassas in 1909 after the Business Men's League presented a petition to the town council asking for a levy to pay for land where the college could be built. In addition to building boys' and girls' dormitories, the school borrowed funds to construct two additional buildings on Battle Street for classrooms, offices, and dormitories. Alumni and the town provided funding for a new gymnasium, erected in 1910. The campus was built on Isaac Baldwin's property, where the Manassas Museum stands today. The original Baldwin House (seen at center in the above photograph) that formerly housed the Manassas Institute was used as a music hall. The school closed its doors in 1920 amid mounting debt and leased the buildings to Eastern College-Conservatory for Women, a brief venture that was open for only two years.

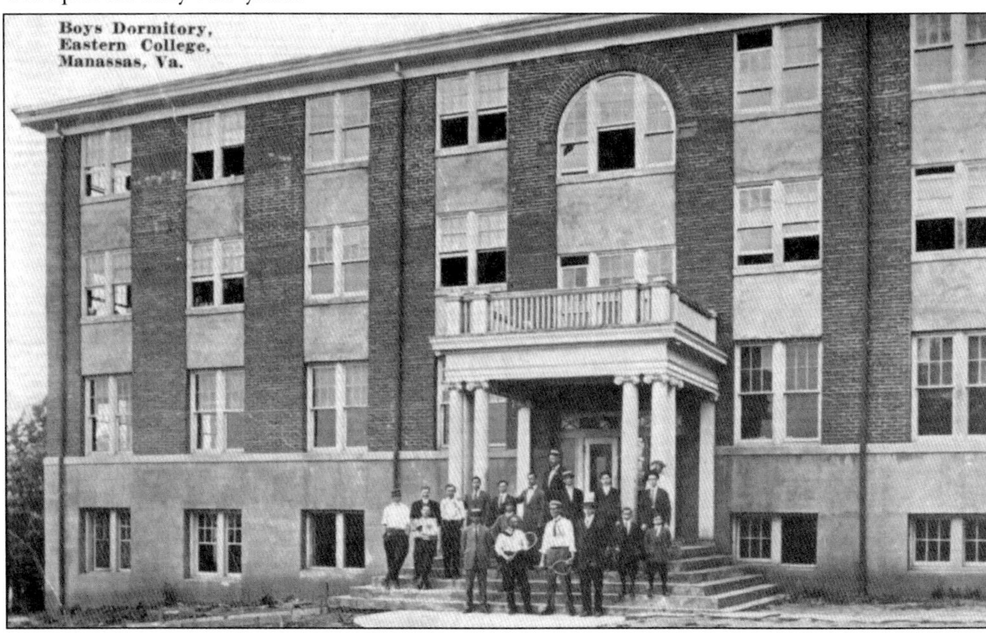

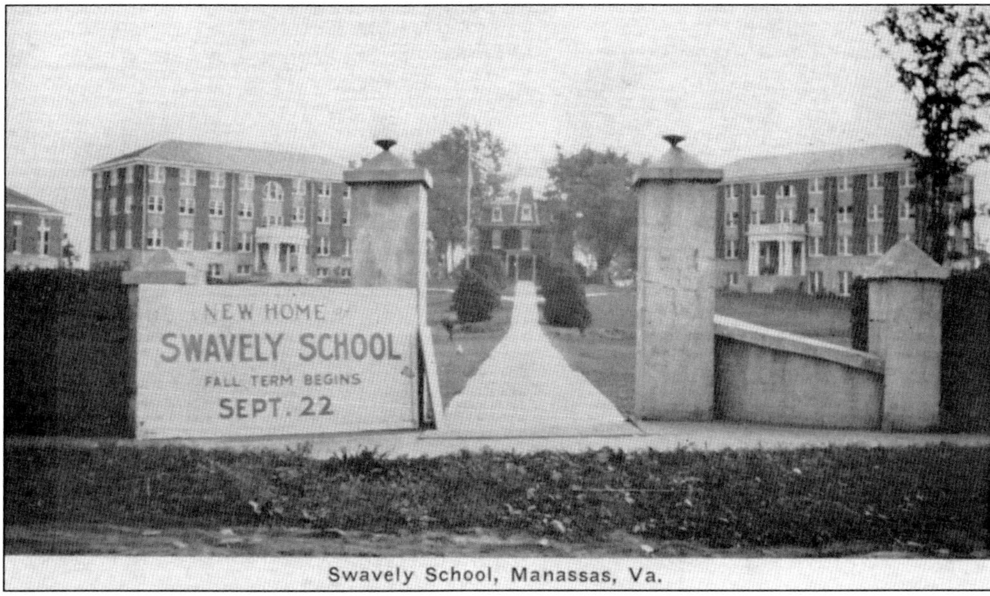

Swavely School, a prep school specializing in preparing young men for the military academies and Ivy League schools, took over the Eastern College campus in 1924. The Swavely catalogue extolls the virtues of its location, proclaiming, "The Virginia countryside which surrounds it provides beautiful vistas on every hand. The locality is high, a plateau of about 400 feet elevation, and the air is always clear and bracing."

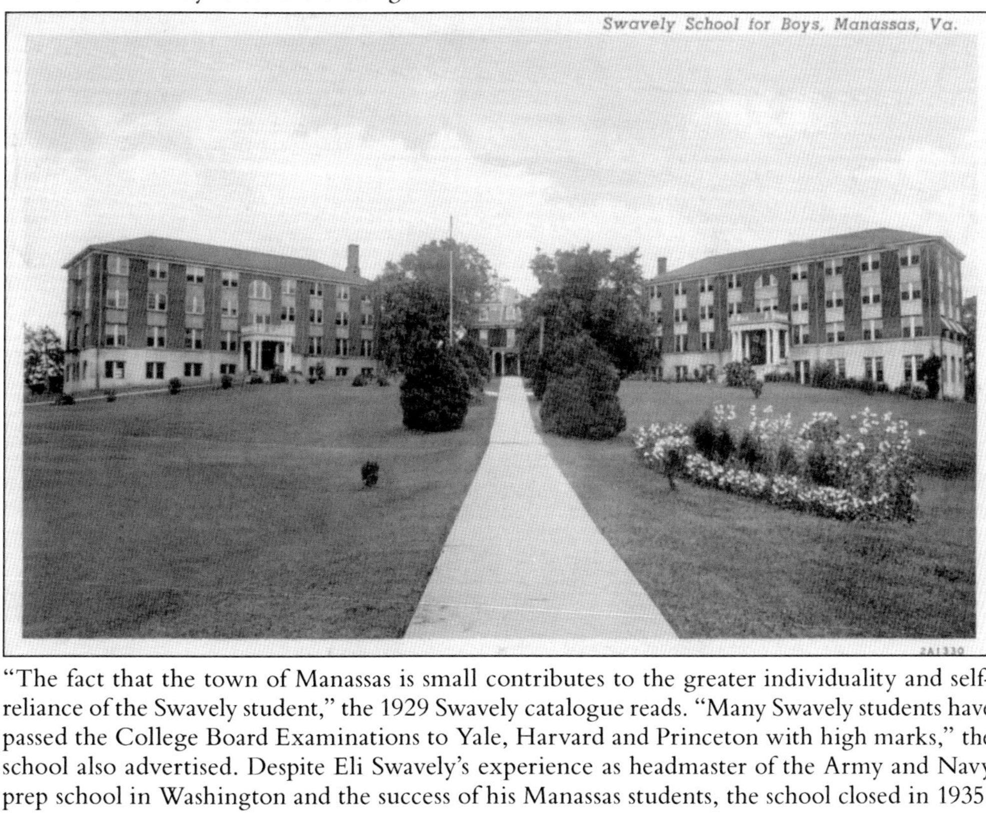

"The fact that the town of Manassas is small contributes to the greater individuality and self-reliance of the Swavely student," the 1929 Swavely catalogue reads. "Many Swavely students have passed the College Board Examinations to Yale, Harvard and Princeton with high marks," the school also advertised. Despite Eli Swavely's experience as headmaster of the Army and Navy prep school in Washington and the success of his Manassas students, the school closed in 1935.

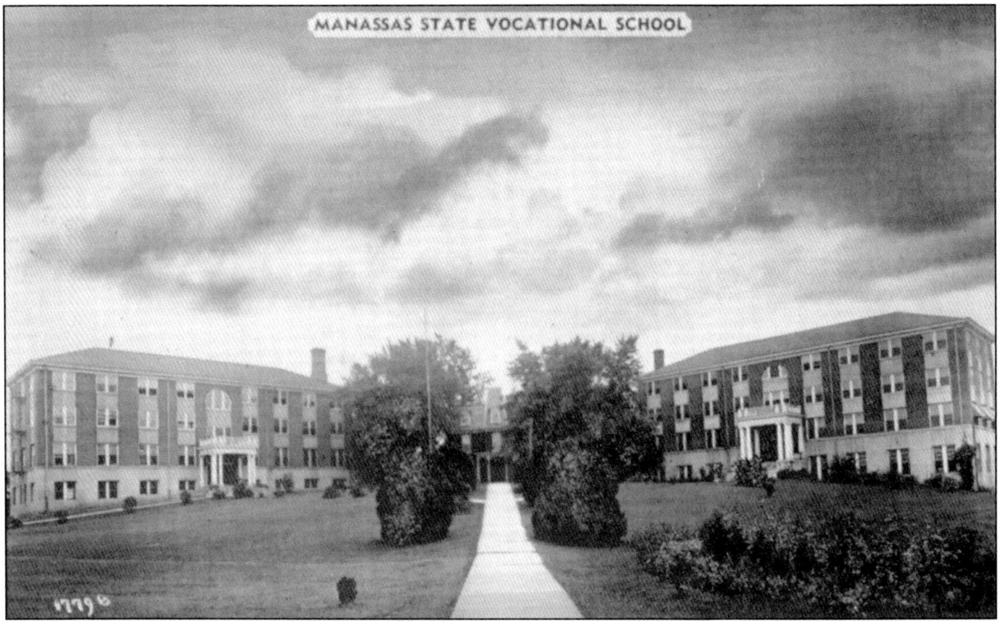

For several years at the start of World War II, the commonwealth and the National Youth Administration transformed the former Swavely School into Manassas State Vocational High School for 300 boys. Where Eastern College and Swavely students had once read classics, students now learned plumbing, carpentry, auto mechanics, welding, electric skills, and many more trades in the year-long program. Students practiced their skills on the long-neglected campus buildings and grounds.

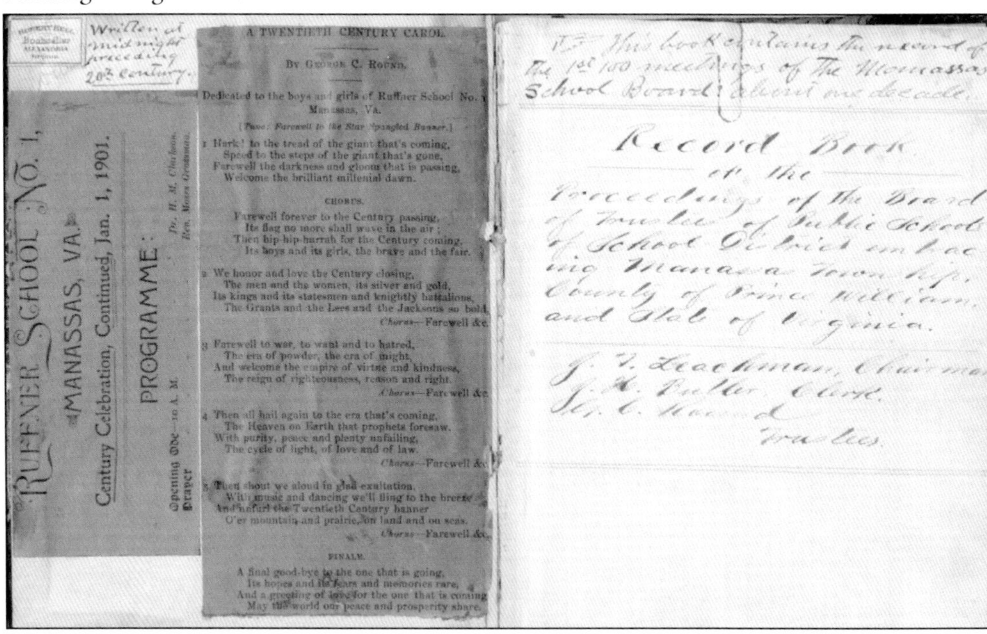

The record book containing the "proceedings of the Board of Trustees of the Public Schools of the School District embracing Manassas Township" details meeting minutes. The cover also contains portions of a program commemorating the turn of the 20th century and a carol written by George C. Round with the notation "written at midnight preceding the 20th century."

Three

Worshipping Together

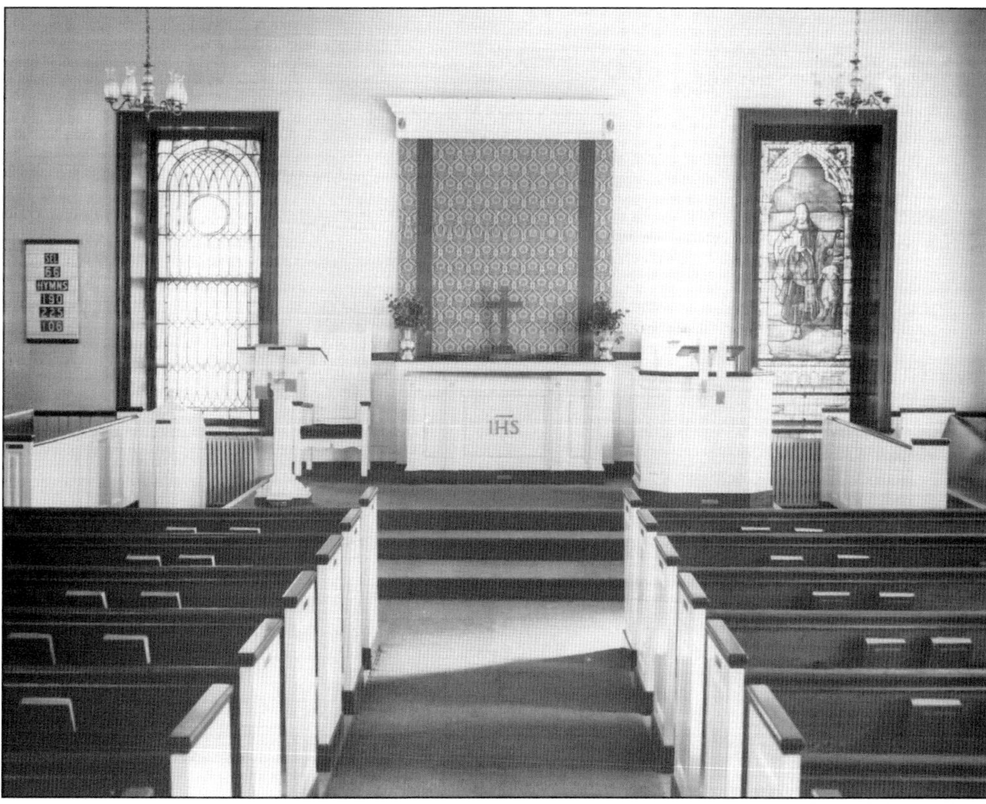

As Manassas began to recover from the destruction of the Civil War and the town grew alongside the railroad tracks, newcomers, immigrants of several nationalities, and former slaves established churches and religious traditions that would help to define life for the new residents. The Methodists first met in a Main Street home in 1867, and the Presbyterians were the first to build a church (shown here) in 1875.

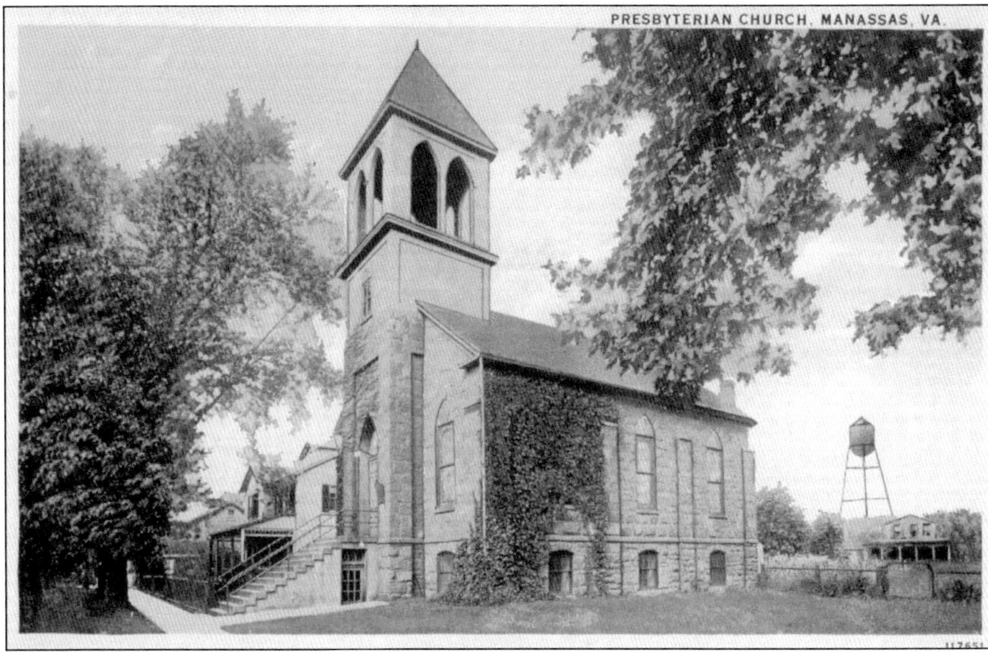

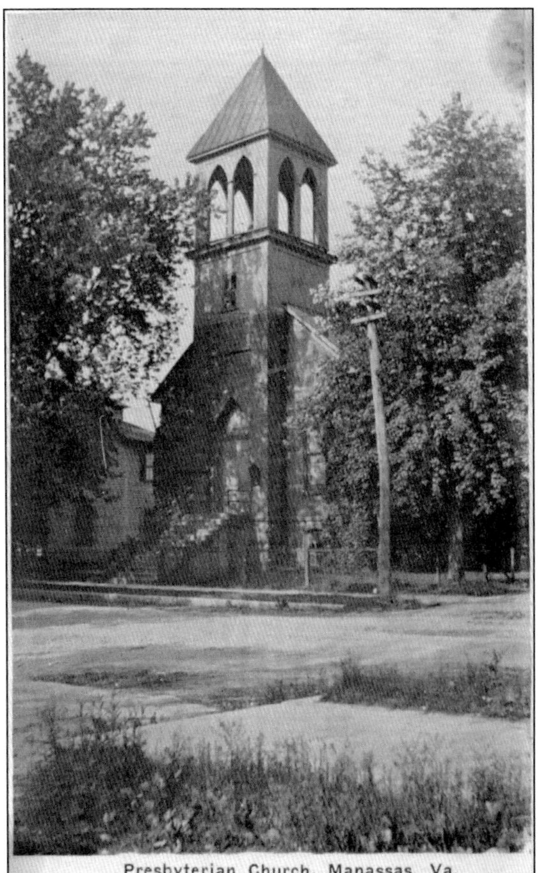

The Manassas Presbyterian Church, located on Main and Church Streets, grew from a congregation established in 1850 near Nokesville. Although the congregation scattered during the Civil War, members purchased a lot for $250 and secured a discarded government structure to use as a church in 1867. The Presbyterians allowed Methodists and Episcopalians to use the building before they were able to construct their own churches. In 1875, the congregation realized its dream of building a more permanent native brownstone church, complete with sanctuary windows made of Tiffany glass. The original belfry was torn down in 1957 after hurricane damage. The congregation moved to an expanded location on Ashton Avenue in 1977, and the brownstone has been occupied by several restaurants.

When Rev. Marshall Downing Williams (pictured) found some African Americans pitching horseshoes rather than attending church on Sundays, he established prayer services under a tree by the Brown School in 1872. In 1879, his followers founded the First Baptist Church, built on donated land. In 1905, the growing congregation purchased land for $800 and built the present-day church on Center Street.

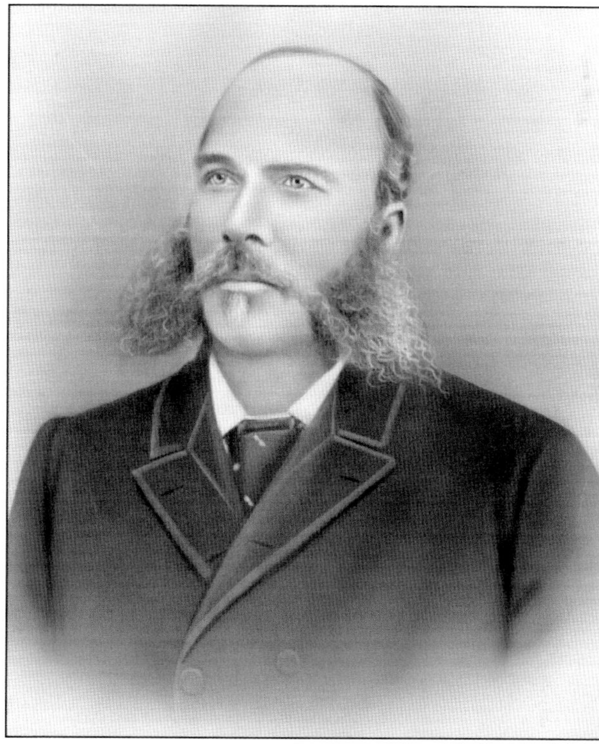

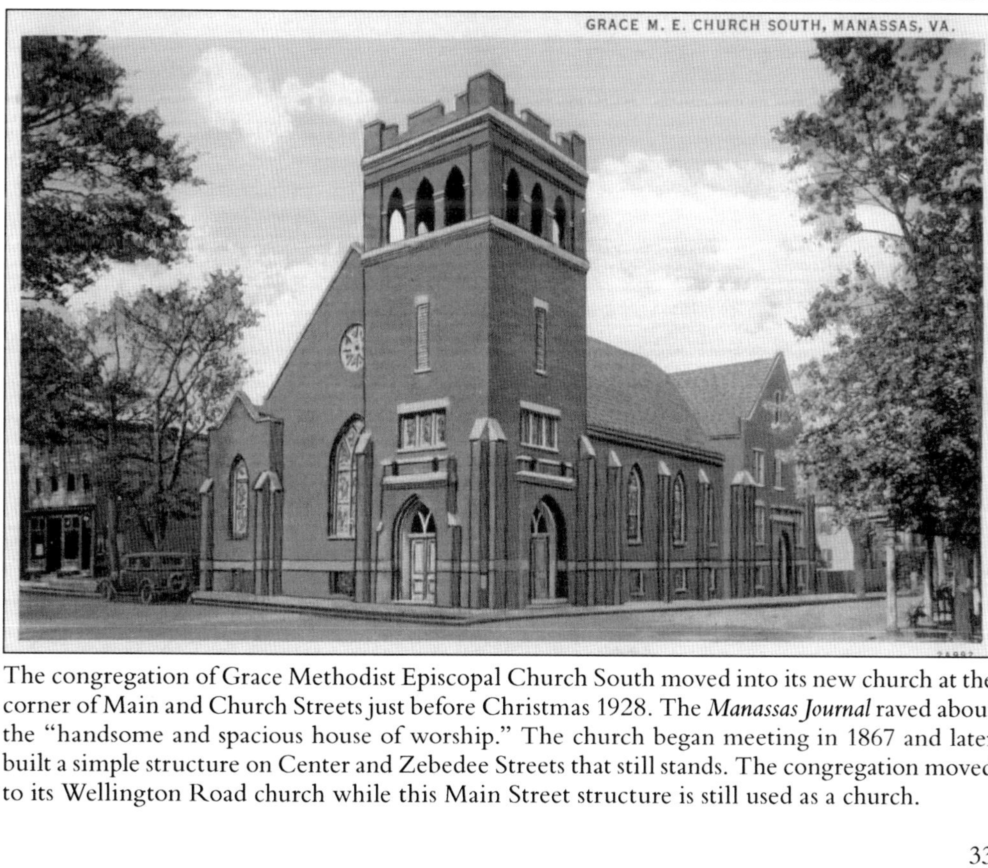

The congregation of Grace Methodist Episcopal Church South moved into its new church at the corner of Main and Church Streets just before Christmas 1928. The *Manassas Journal* raved about the "handsome and spacious house of worship." The church began meeting in 1867 and later built a simple structure on Center and Zebedee Streets that still stands. The congregation moved to its Wellington Road church while this Main Street structure is still used as a church.

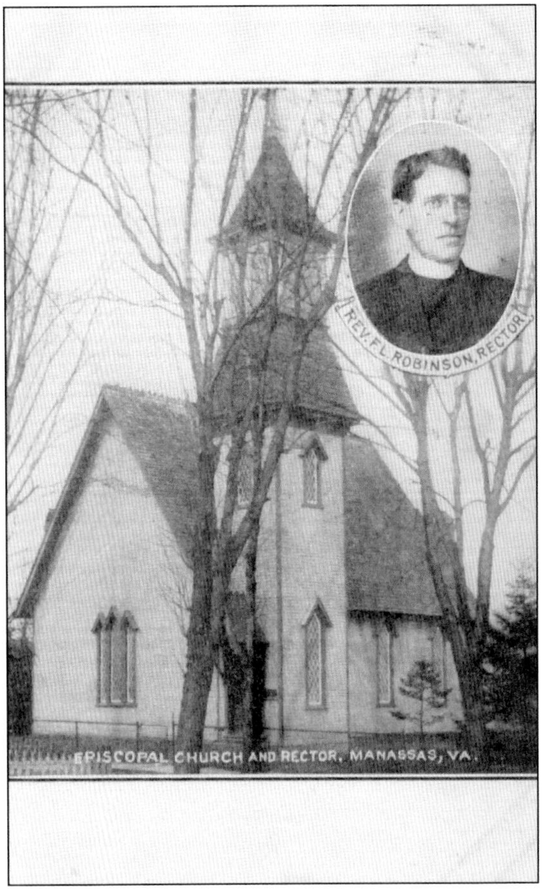

Trinity Episcopal Church grew out of the Dettingen Parish established in 1744 in Dumfries and began as a mission church in 1872. When the Reverend Arthur Gray, the first rector, arrived at the mission church, he found "23 communicants, a debt of $60.00 on the organ, no tower, a mere shell of a building, no chancel, no pews, no furniture." The small congregation banded together to build the new church on West Street in 1879. The Reverend F. Leslie Robinson (pictured in the inset at left) served as Trinity's sixth rector, from 1907 till 1910. As the church grew, a new sanctuary was constructed in 1922, and further additions have since been built.

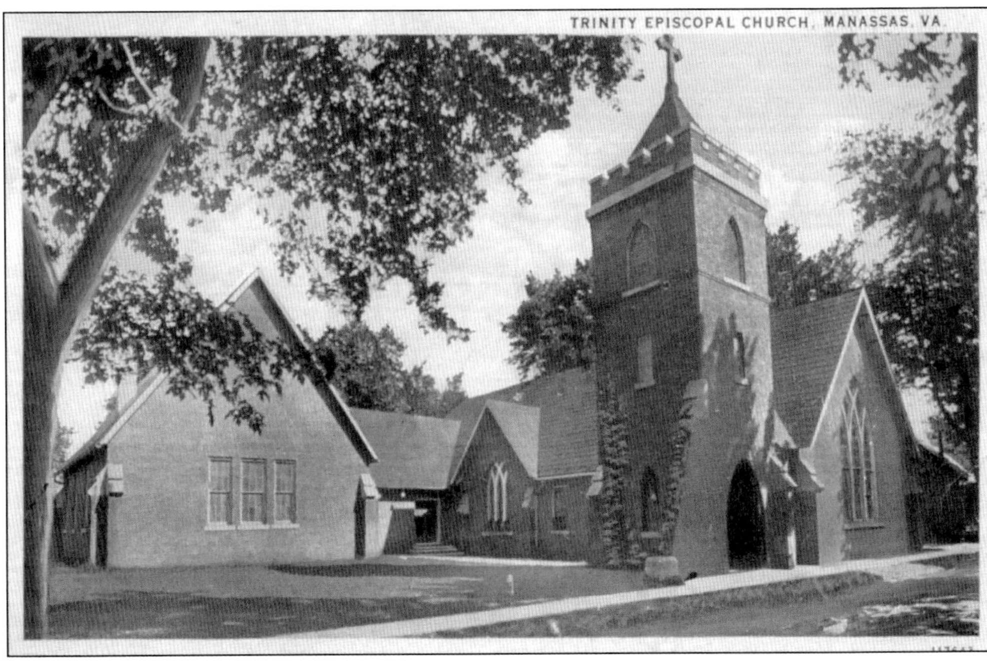

Three trains carried worshippers from Washington to the All Saints Catholic Church (pictured at right) dedication in 1879, and an estimated 5,000 processed to the little church at the corner of Center Street and Fairview Avenue. "The living crowded to see the gaily-adorned procession marching under banners consecrated to a different mission than that of war," the *Washington Post* reported. Its 75-foot steeple became a landmark for Catholics from the Potomac to the Bull Run Mountains until All Saints moved to a new campus a mile west in 1974. The church has since been home to the Reformed Presbyterian congregation. The Church of God (pictured below) was built in 1899 on Fairview Avenue and established a popular nationally known summer meeting camp on Rixlew Drive in the 1940s. The camp still meets near its new church, and the Fairview Avenue structure has been home to other congregations.

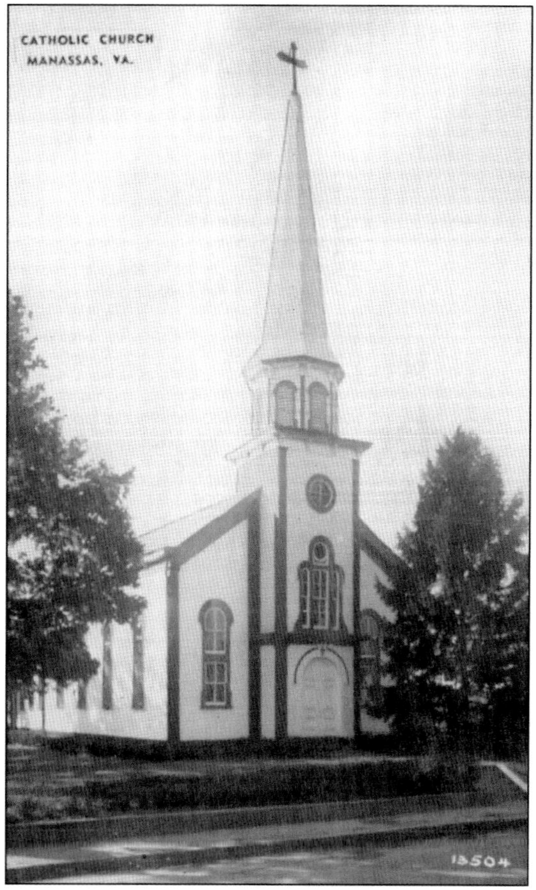

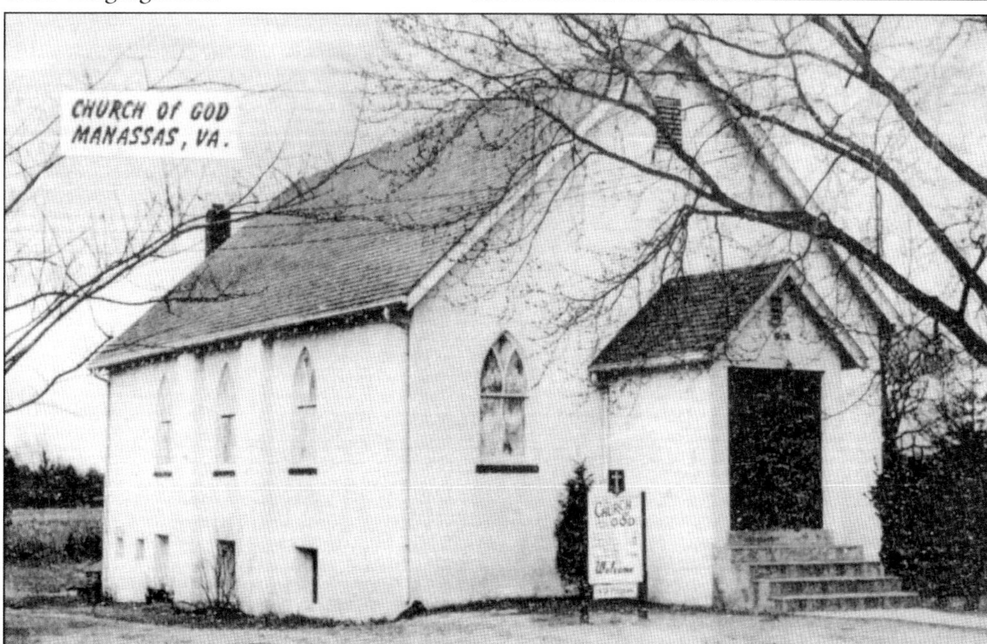

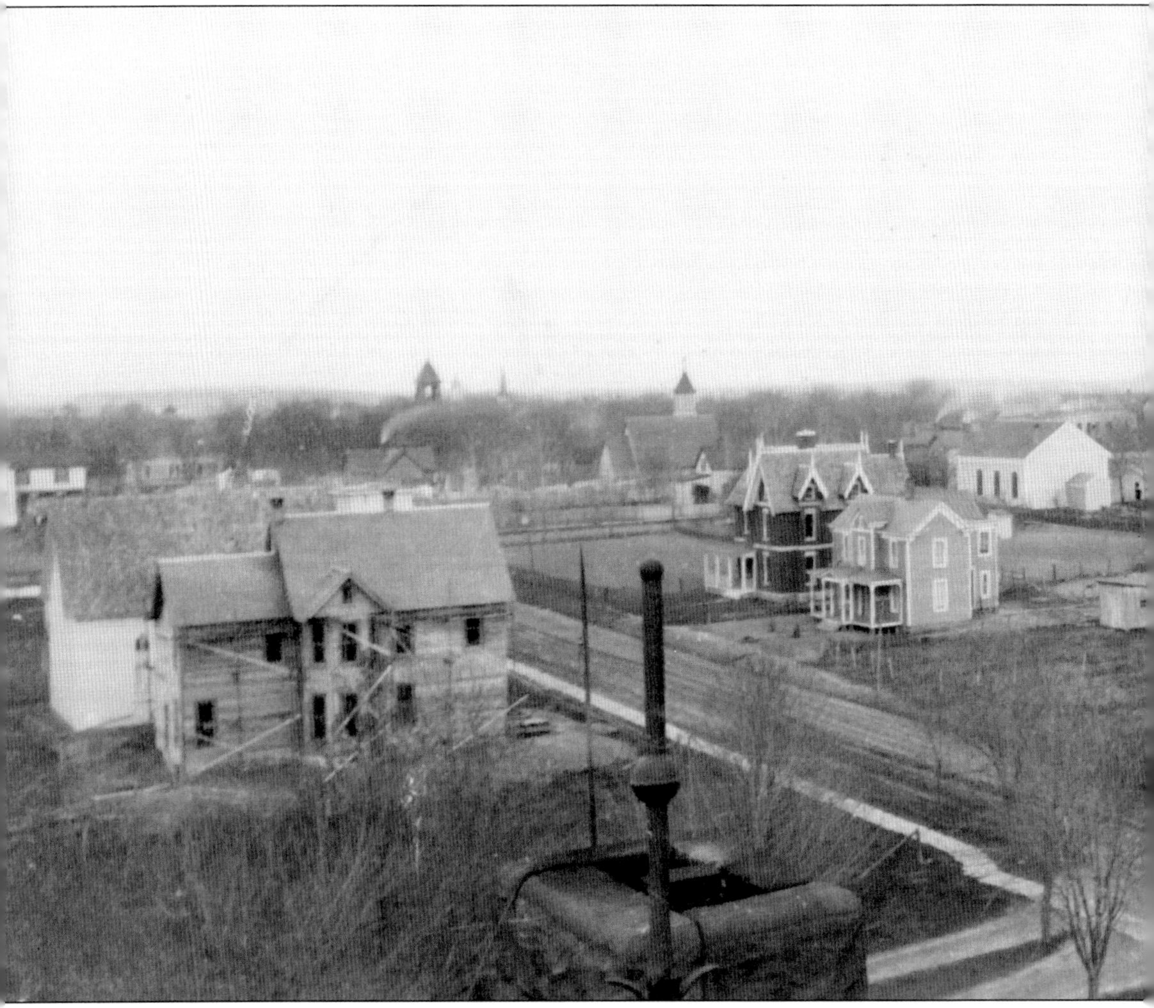

Newcomers from Pennsylvania and Maryland established Bethel Lutheran Church in 1889 in a borrowed space on Center Street. When the congregation bought land on Lee Avenue and began constructing a new church, a windstorm moved the building eight inches from its foundation. As the first services were held there in 1897, plastering and painting were not finished. Bethel later moved to a roomier site on Plantation Lane. Bethel is the white building pictured at far left in 1900 while its parsonage was under construction next door. The image, which also shows the

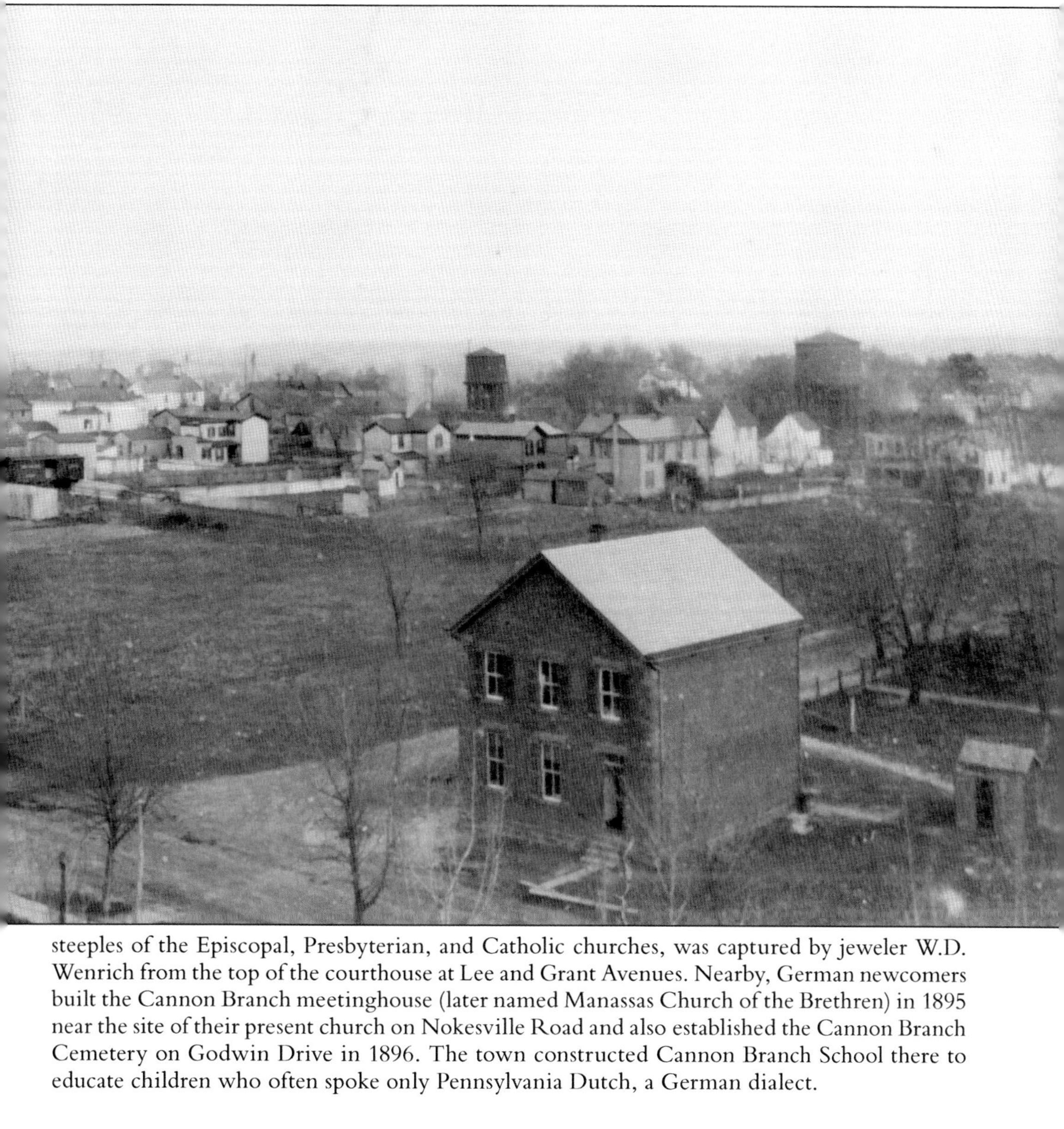

steeples of the Episcopal, Presbyterian, and Catholic churches, was captured by jeweler W.D. Wenrich from the top of the courthouse at Lee and Grant Avenues. Nearby, German newcomers built the Cannon Branch meetinghouse (later named Manassas Church of the Brethren) in 1895 near the site of their present church on Nokesville Road and also established the Cannon Branch Cemetery on Godwin Drive in 1896. The town constructed Cannon Branch School there to educate children who often spoke only Pennsylvania Dutch, a German dialect.

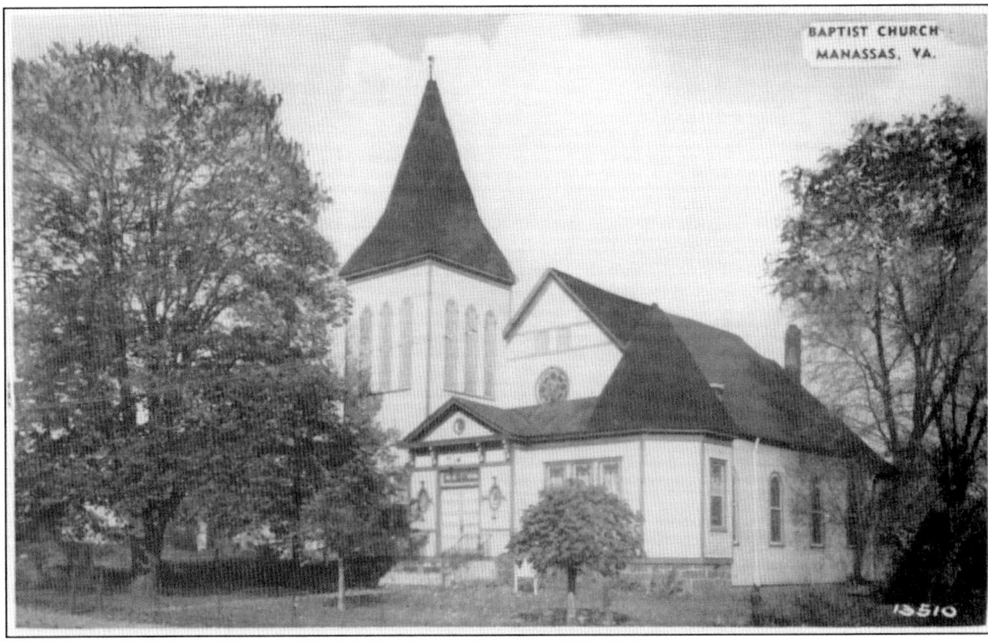

The Manassas Baptist Church formally began in 1884 with eight members who met in the home of an elder on Main Street, soon after the Potomac Baptist Association observed that the county was "suffering" for religious work and that there was "appalling destitution such as we have hardly dreamed of." As membership grew, the Baptists built a Center Street church in 1889 with the help of members' donated labor. A new Albert Speiden–designed church (above) was built in 1906, and his daughter Virginia played the town's first pipe organ there. After a fire damaged this wood-frame building in 1935, members built a new brick structure in the late 1930s (below), adding an educational wing in 1947. Manassas Baptist moved to a new campus on Sudley Road in 1967, and its former church has served other congregations and commercial uses.

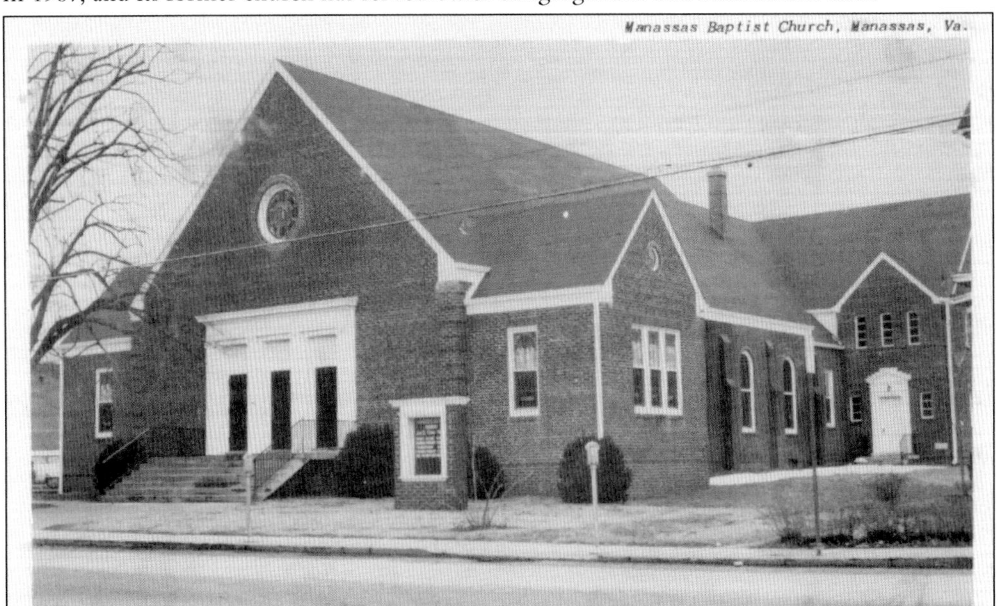

Four

Building a Town

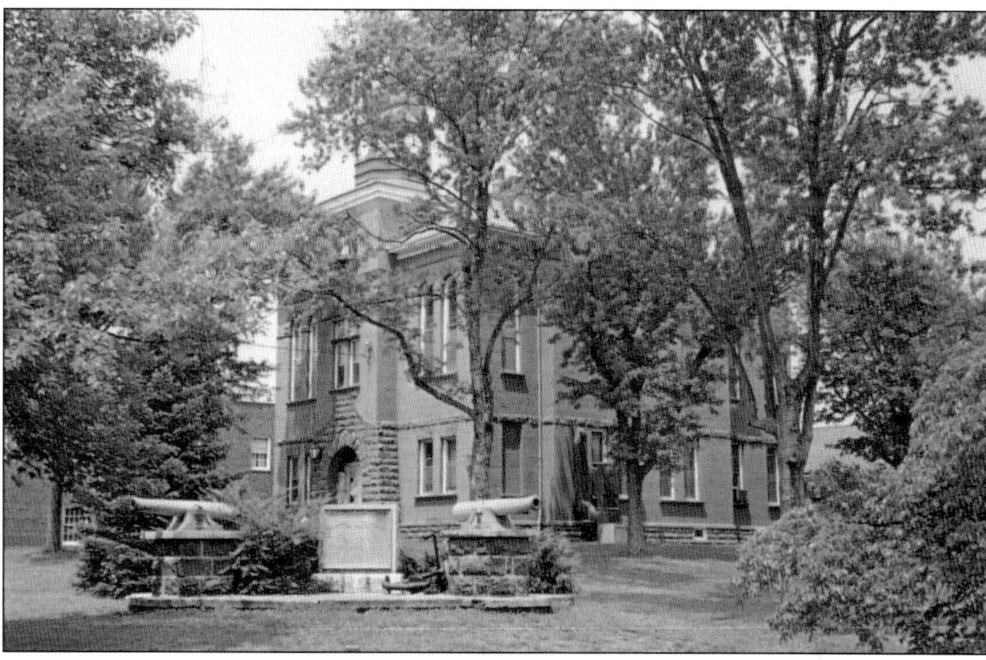

It was the construction of the county courthouse that spurred a building and population boom in Manassas. As the town grew, leaders and citizens faced issues that are still important today: building and maintaining roads and sidewalks, establishing and maintaining fire and utility services, investing in public buildings and an air landing strip, writing ordinances, and balancing budgets. Like today, lively debate accompanied any decision on town spending or taxation.

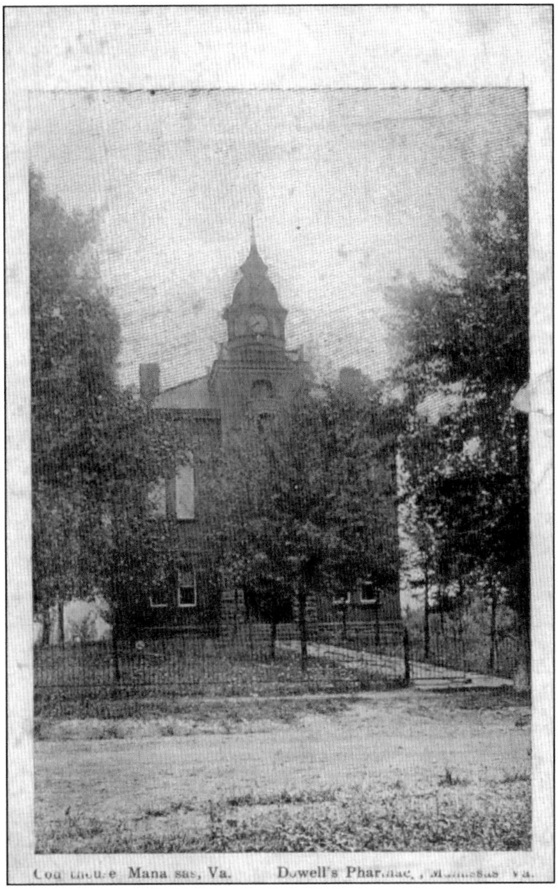

It was not until the third try in 1892 that voters passed a referendum to move the county seat from Brentsville to Manassas, after an intensive lobbying campaign led by George C. Round argued that the move would bring prosperity to the town. The protests of Brentsville lawyers and tavern keepers could not overcome the fact that the old 1820 courthouse was inconvenient to the railroad.

A full Masonic ceremony with music from the town band marked the laying of the cornerstone in 1893. The courthouse and adjacent jail, built of native brownstone and brick, opened on New Year's Day in 1894. A special real estate tax of 15¢ per $100—in addition to the regular 40¢ per $100 tax—was levied on town residents to pay off the $3,000 building bonds.

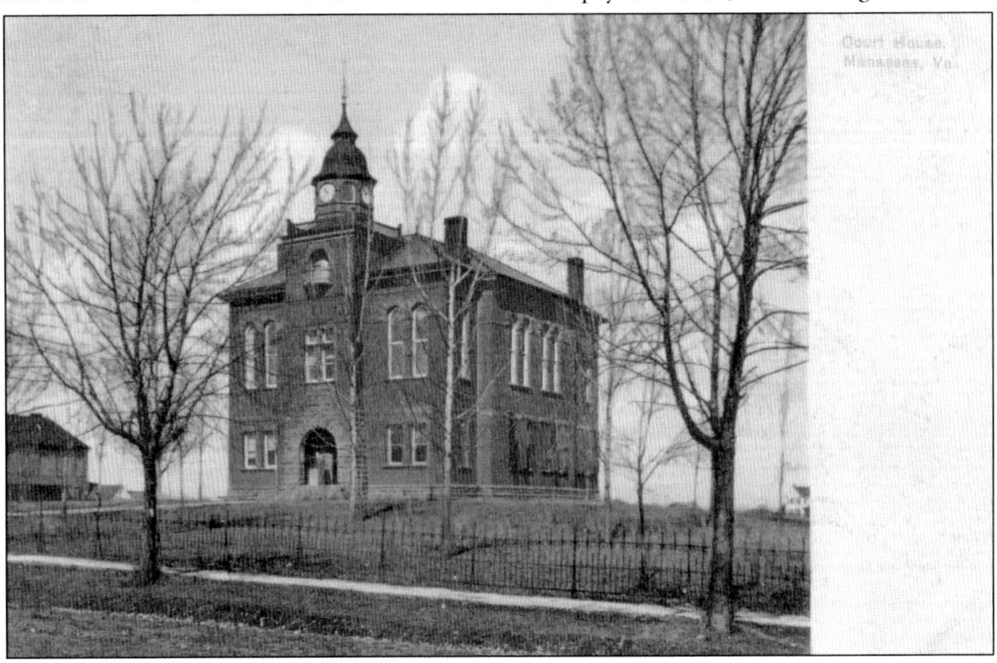

The 1911 National Jubilee of Peace began on the Manassas battlefield, where veterans who had fought against each other 50 years earlier clasped hands. Thousands attended ceremonies on the courthouse lawn later that day, where the appearance of Pres. William Howard Taft caused a sensation in the small town. George C. Round, who organized the event, quickly enlisted the support of all citizens. The ladies of Manassas cooked and prepared for weeks to feed and lodge hundreds of veterans, while their daughters played the part of peace maidens, who dressed in white and donned sashes representing each state. Others shuttled visitors from the railway depot to the battlefield, built a speaking platform, or played in the band. The *Manassas Democrat* called on all citizens to decorate homes and businesses for the occasion or risk "a glaring evidence of lack of civic pride."

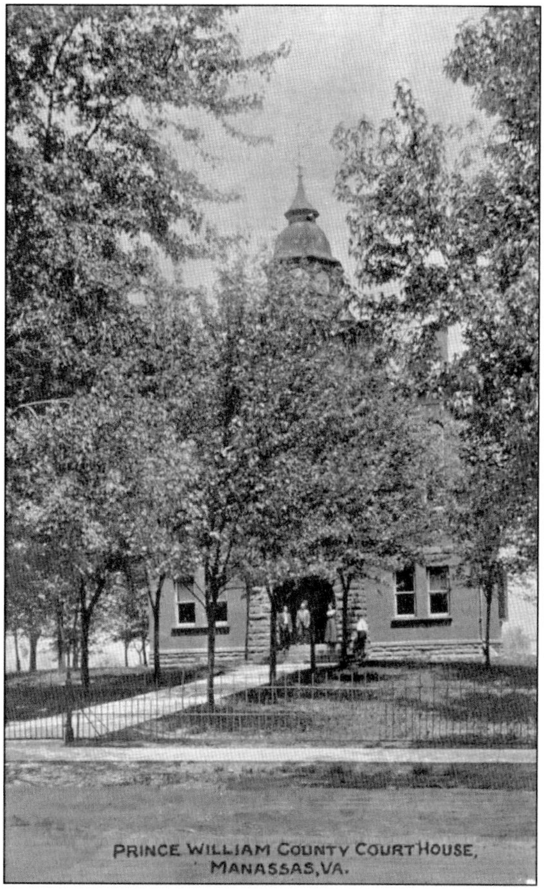

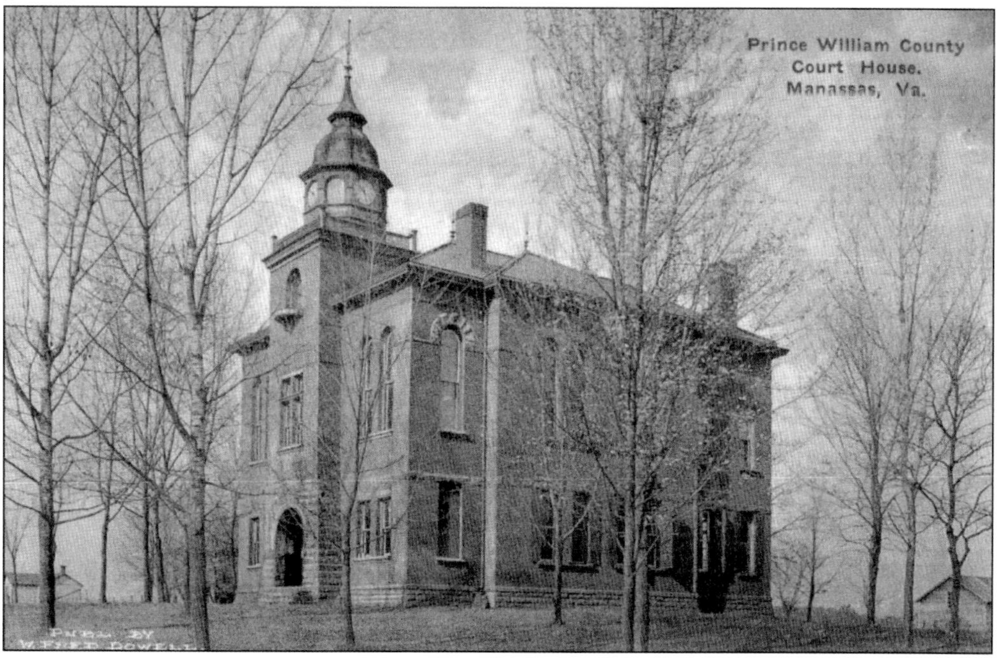

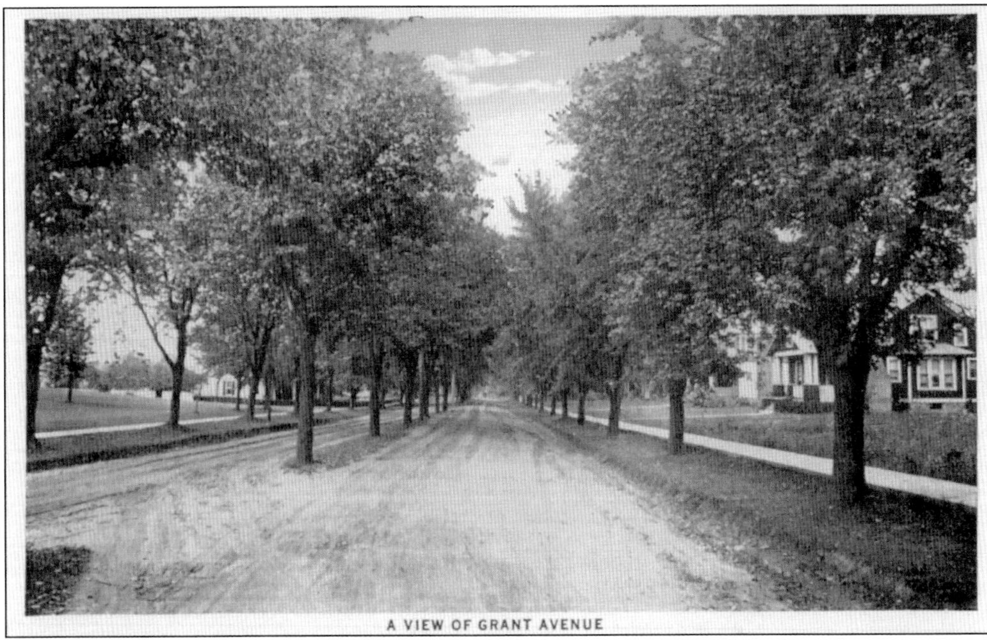

Once the county courthouse moved to Manassas in 1894 and ushered in a period of prosperity and expansion, grand residences sprang up along the wide, tree-lined Grant Avenue. The road was not yet paved, and sidewalks were all wooden until 1878, when the town incurred a $1,000 debt to start building sidewalks and crosswalks made of native stone.

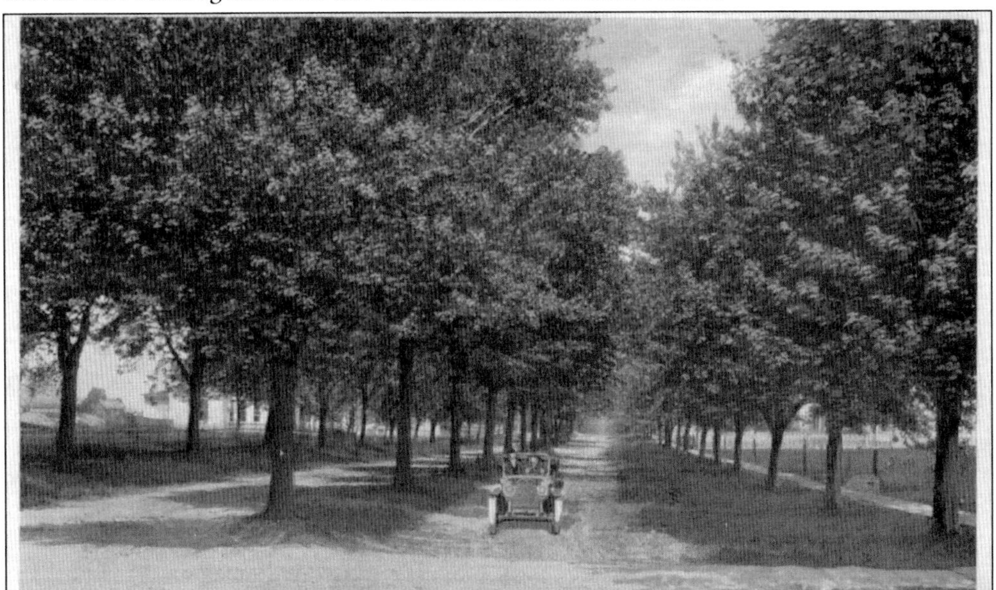

In 1876, the town council planted 500 maple trees along the town's main streets in an effort to create a "wholesome and peaceful atmosphere." Trees were so valued that ordinances were passed prohibiting anyone from marring or breaking trees or shrubbery or tying horses to trees. Taxpayers who planted shade trees in front of properties bordering town streets could claim a 50¢ tax deduction.

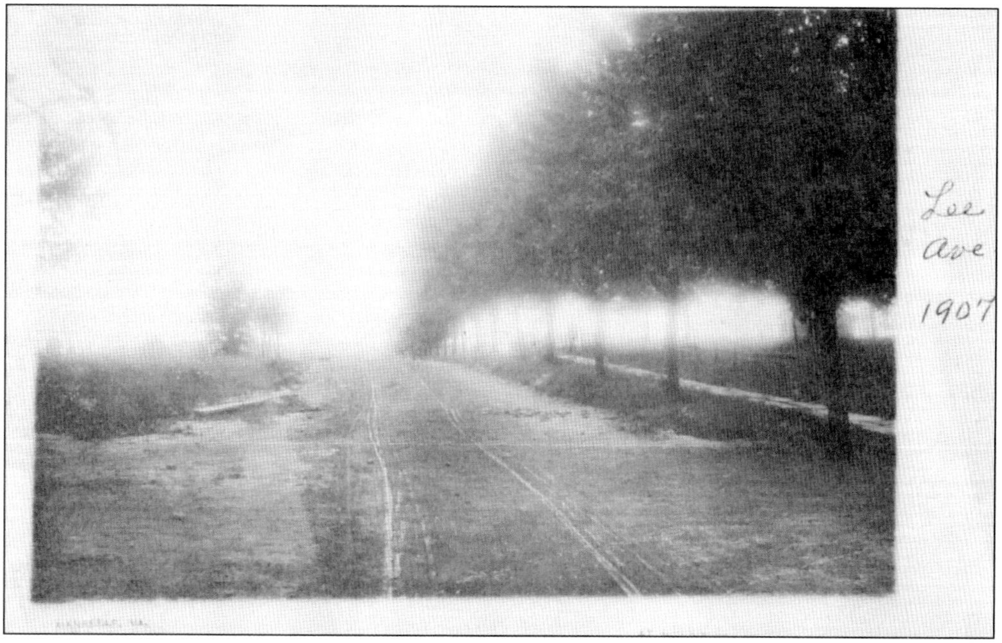

Although those strolling or driving down Lee Avenue enjoyed the shade of trees for years, citizens decided to plant more trees along the street for every resident of Manassas or Prince William County who gave his life in World War I. Town council minutes from 1925 note that the tree planting held on Armistice Day in 1925 honored soldiers and helped beautify the town.

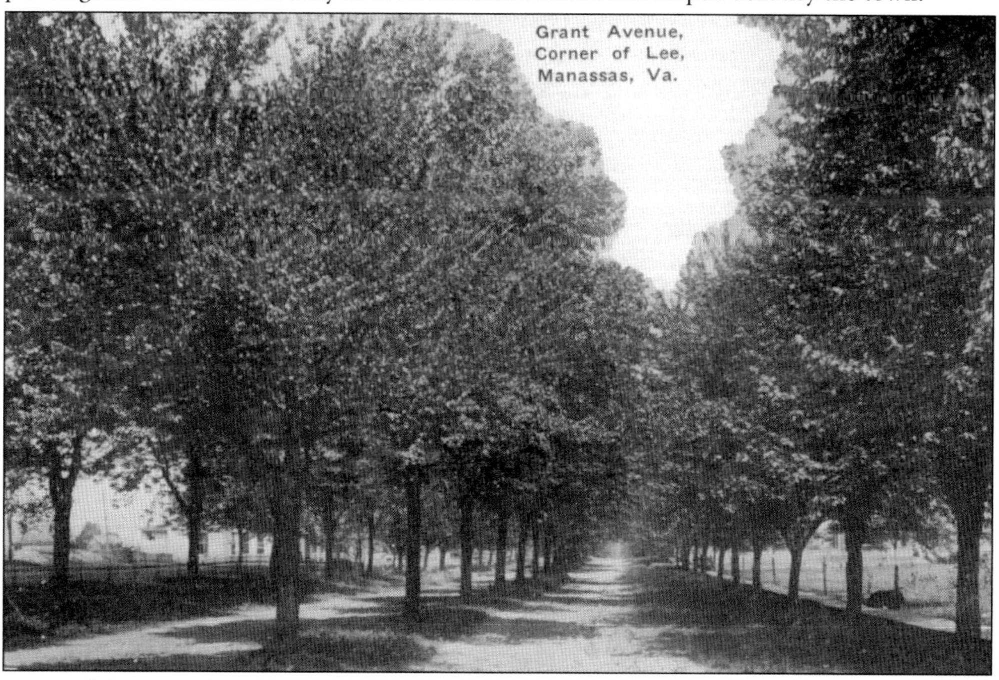

Many of the trees that still grace Grant Avenue were said to be planted by George C. Round after he had surveyed and named Lee and Grant Avenues, the newest and widest streets in town. Round thought it fitting for the new county courthouse that moved here in 1894 to be located on streets named after the Civil War's most prominent opposing generals.

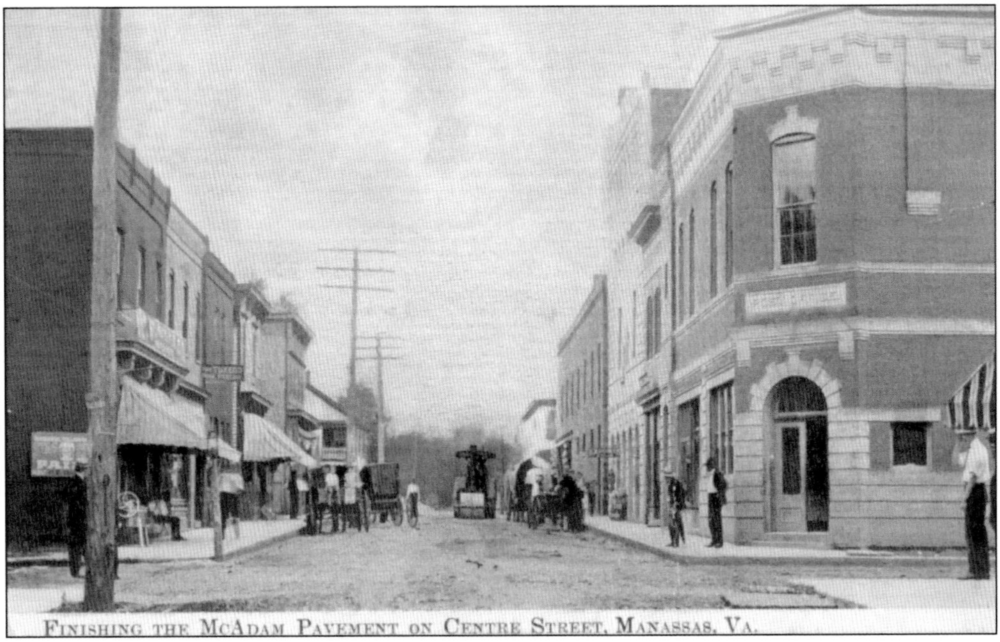

Landowner William S. Fewell laid out and sold the new town's blocks shortly after the Civil War ended. George C. Round described the town as it appeared then: "In those days the town, as laid out by Mr. Fewell after the war, was simply an adjacent cornfield and cow pasture." These 1906 images capture Center Street busy with new construction after the Great Fire of 1905. The Conner Opera House would soon be built on the left, just past Nash's Hardware and the Tuxedo Pool Parlor. From the ladies who stepped out in white dresses only to return home brown with dust or the merchants who toiled to keep dirt from their shops, it seemed everyone in Manassas clamored for street improvements. The town's macadam paving used packed crushed stones to create a cleaner, smoother surface.

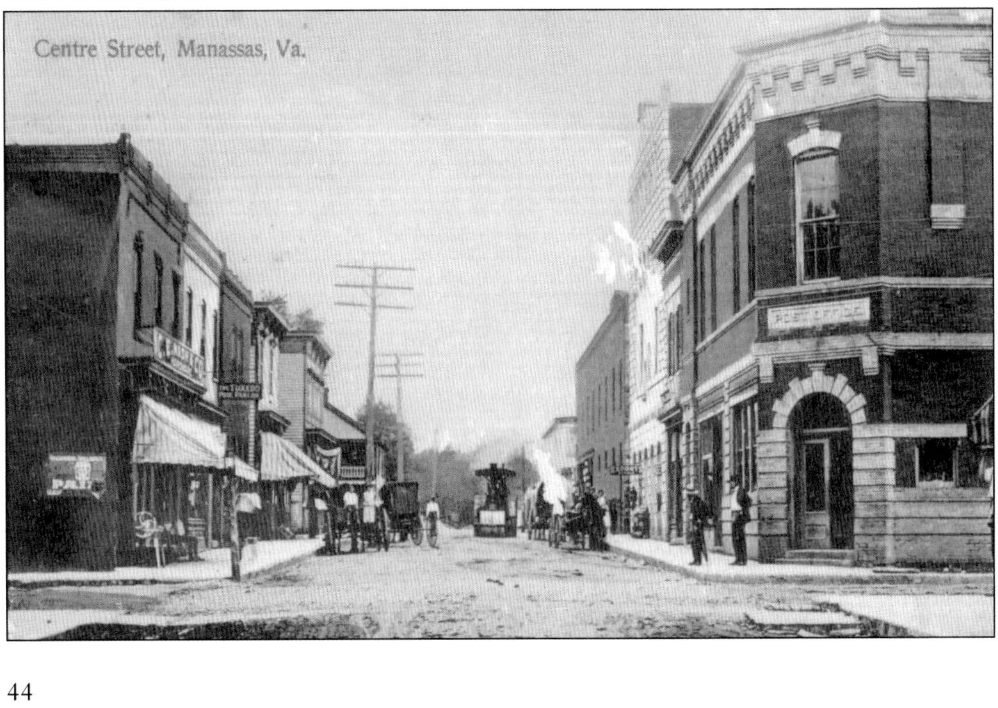

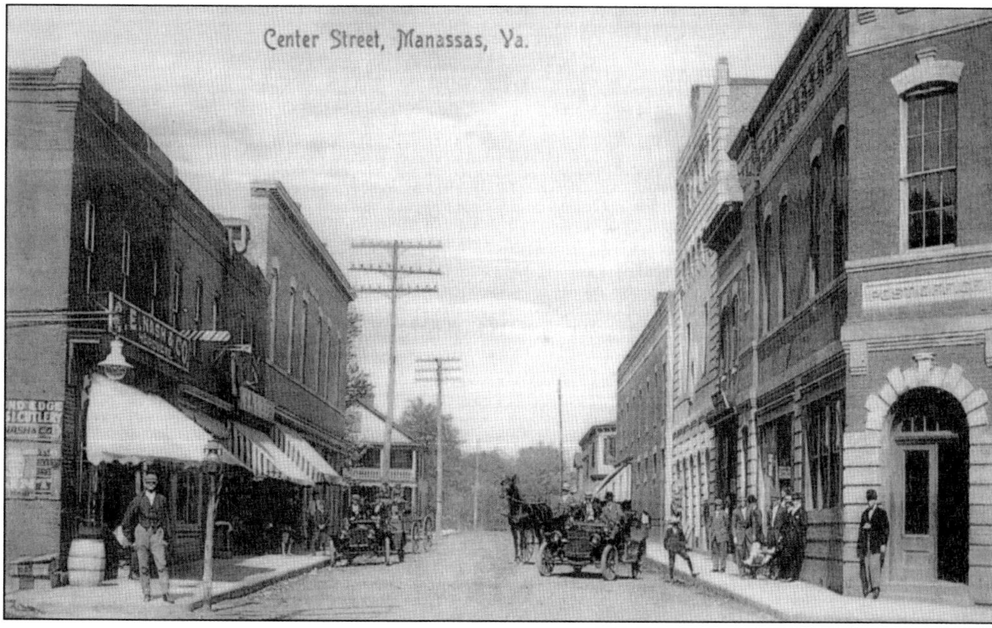

In the town's early years, the council's street committee could call out 20 men to work on the streets whenever necessary. Citizens were required to work, provide a substitute, or pay in cash for street maintenance, which included extending, grading, draining, and graveling the roads. In an effort to beautify the streets, the town spent $1,200 on plank sidewalks and streetlamps in the 1880s.

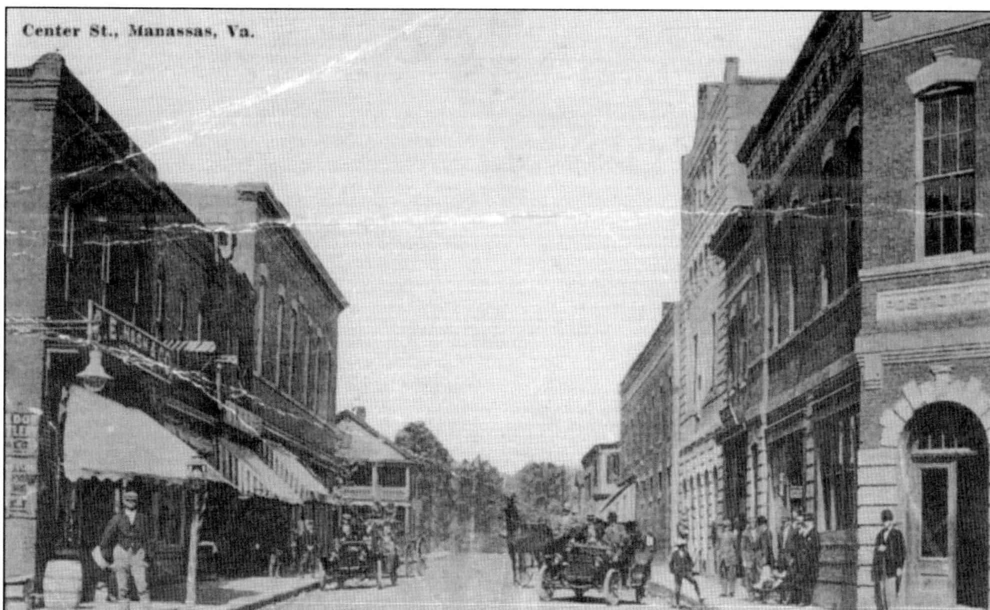

Although the two c. 1910 images on this page originate from the same photograph, this postcard shows a view with all telephone poles and lines removed—a common practice at the time. Photographs would be sent to a postcard company where artists could remove telephone poles, power lines, signs, and other distractions, or improve unpaved or potholed streets. The images were also often colorized and set against blue skies.

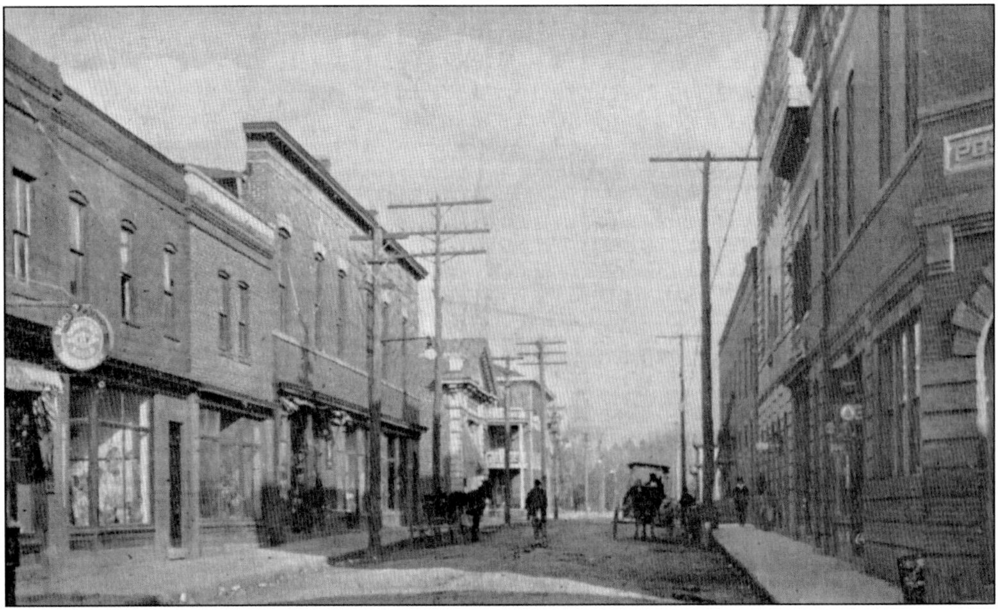

Shown here shortly after the Conner Opera House was built, Center Street became a cleaner commercial center. In the 1890s, no swine, goats, horses, mules, or geese could run free in the streets, and no cattle or sheep were allowed to run free after 9:00 p.m., but residents defeated several ballot measures to restrict cattle from grazing in the streets. It was not until 1900 that animals were prohibited from streets.

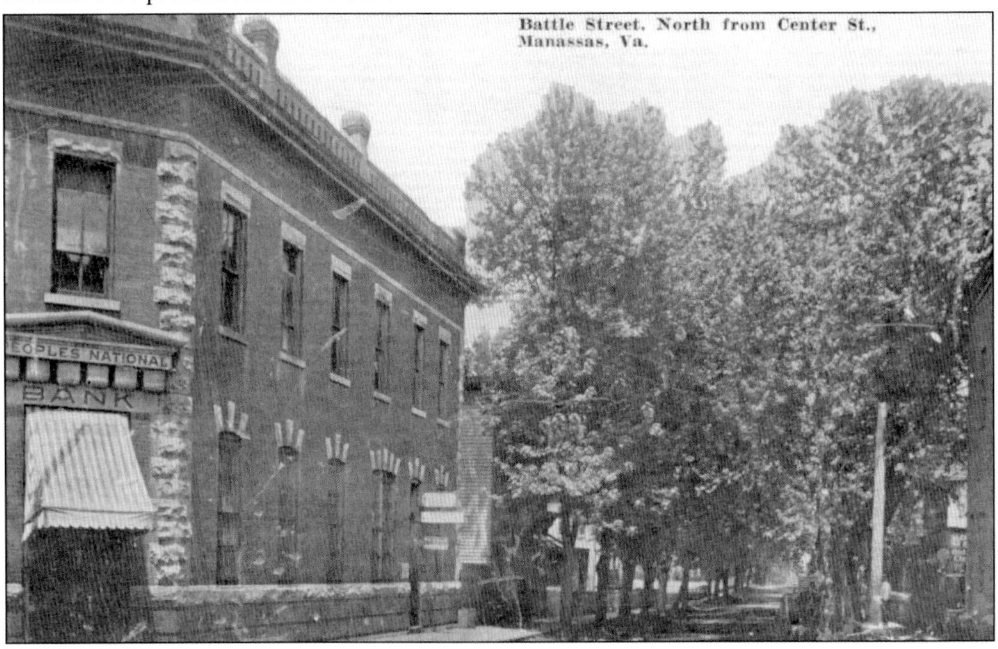

Keeping streets clean was a constant concern. "Many of our vacant lots, even in the business centers, have the appearance of a dumping ground for the town's rubbish. And one lot in particular is a menace to both health and morals and even life, with its disused, dilapidated old stable and ice house, overshadowing the sidewalk," the *Manassas Democrat* said in 1914 while advocating for a town cleanup day.

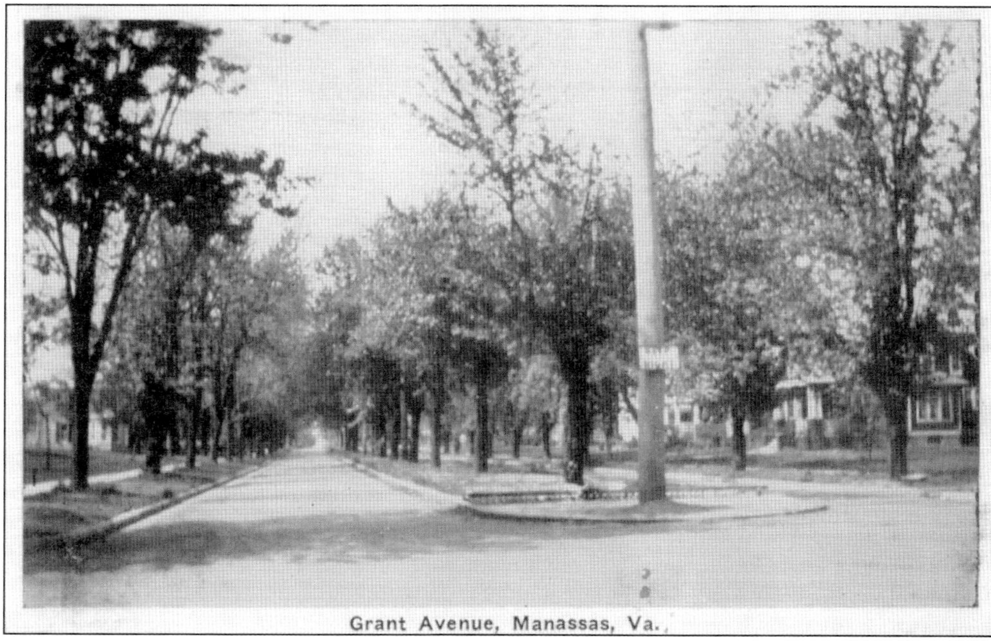

The appearance of wooden poles throughout the town signaled the start of telephone service in 1895, and the following year West Street and Grant Avenue were extended northward. Both Grant Avenue and Church Street were expanded even further by 1904, when the town's limits were one square mile and the total population was 1,109 residents.

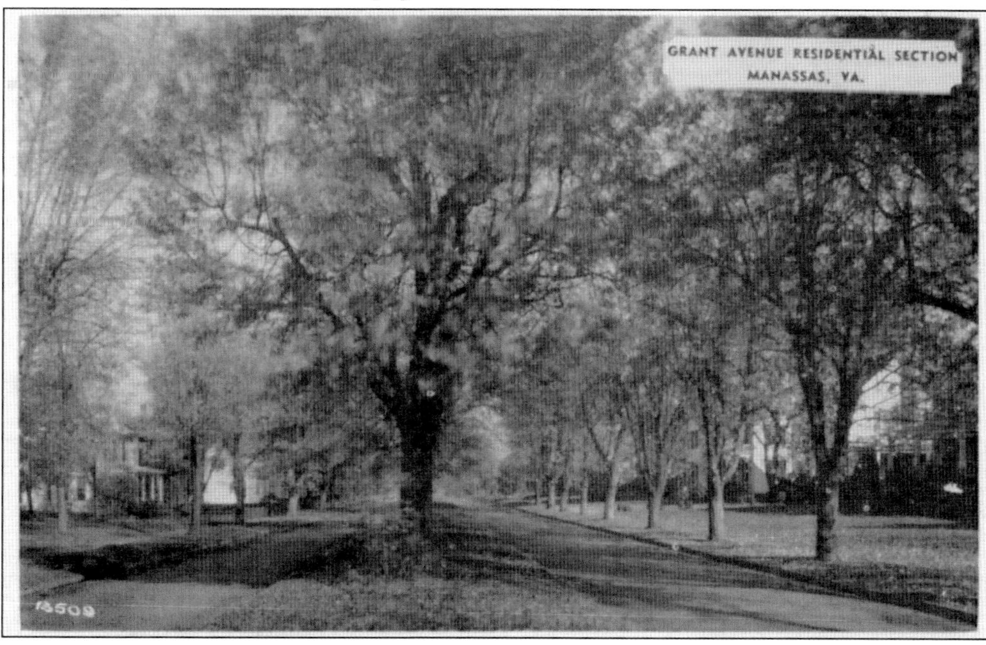

By the 1930s, the gracious Grant Avenue homes of railroad executives, lawyers, and businessmen stood sentry while the town suffered through the Great Depression. An infusion of federal and state funds for building the new Church Street post office, construction work here on Grant Avenue and other streets, sewer expansion, town mapping, and town hall repairs enabled Manassas to weather the storm better than most towns.

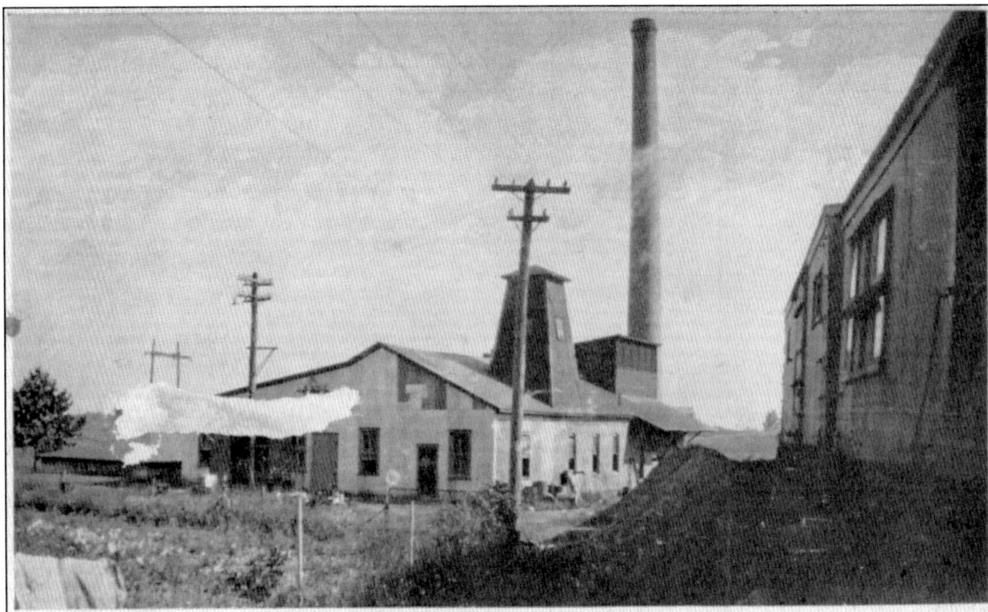

Town Light and Water Plant, Manassas, Va.

Despite repeated attempts to gain votes, both council members and townspeople were reluctant to raise taxes and assume debt for utility services. In 1902, only one vote supported electric power, while a majority favored improving streets instead. By 1914, attitudes had changed, as the *Manassas Democrat*'s headline read "Manassas, the little city of beauty and progressiveness, is soon to be equipped with the modern utilities of water, lights and sewerage."

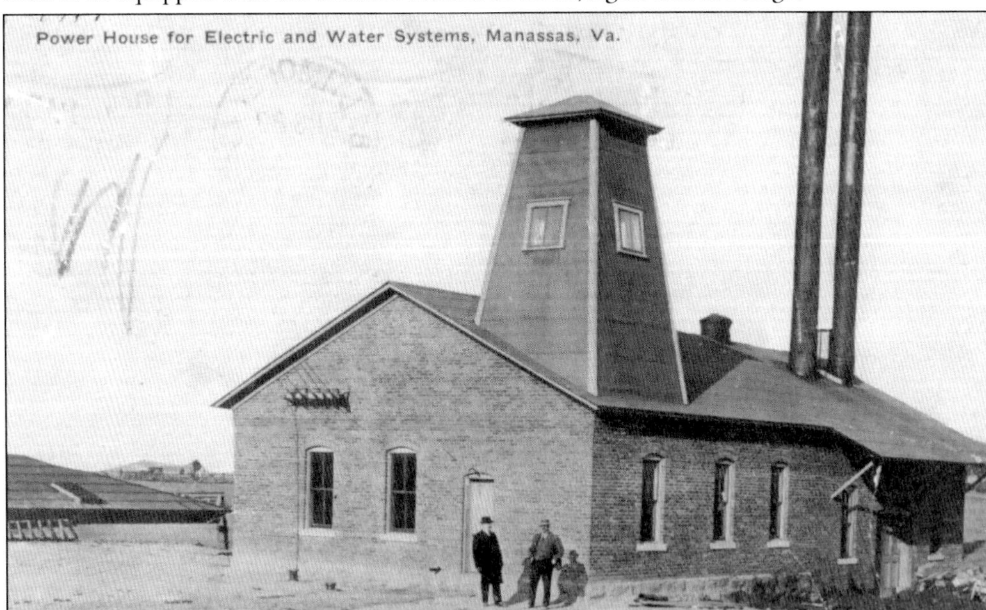

Power House for Electric and Water Systems, Manassas, Va.

A $75,000 bond for town electric and water service as well as street construction was finally passed in 1913, after 15 years of effort. The first powerhouse, originally powered by a steam boiler heated with coal, was constructed on East Church Street, and water lines were laid down Center Street. In 1916, another $20,000 bond for town sewer construction passed.

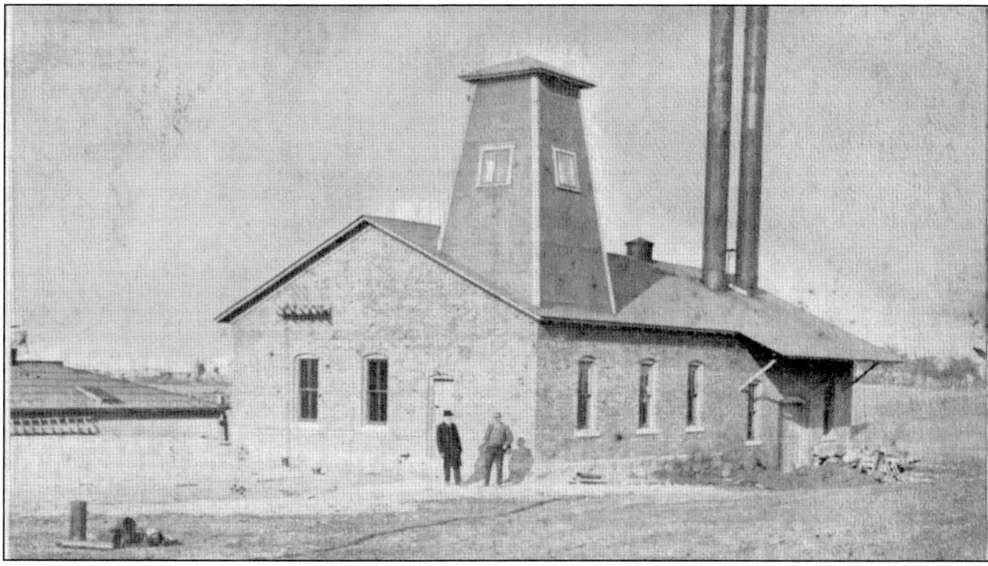

"Last Monday evening at 7:30 o'clock," the *Manassas Democrat* reported in October 1914, "Mr. Herl A. Petersen, president of the Washington Suburban Electric Co., said 'Let us have light,' and the residence of Mr. G. Raymond Ratcliffe was flooded with the best imitation of natural light known to man." Ratcliffe's home was the first illuminated by the new electric plant, but the Conner Building was already using a generator for its lights.

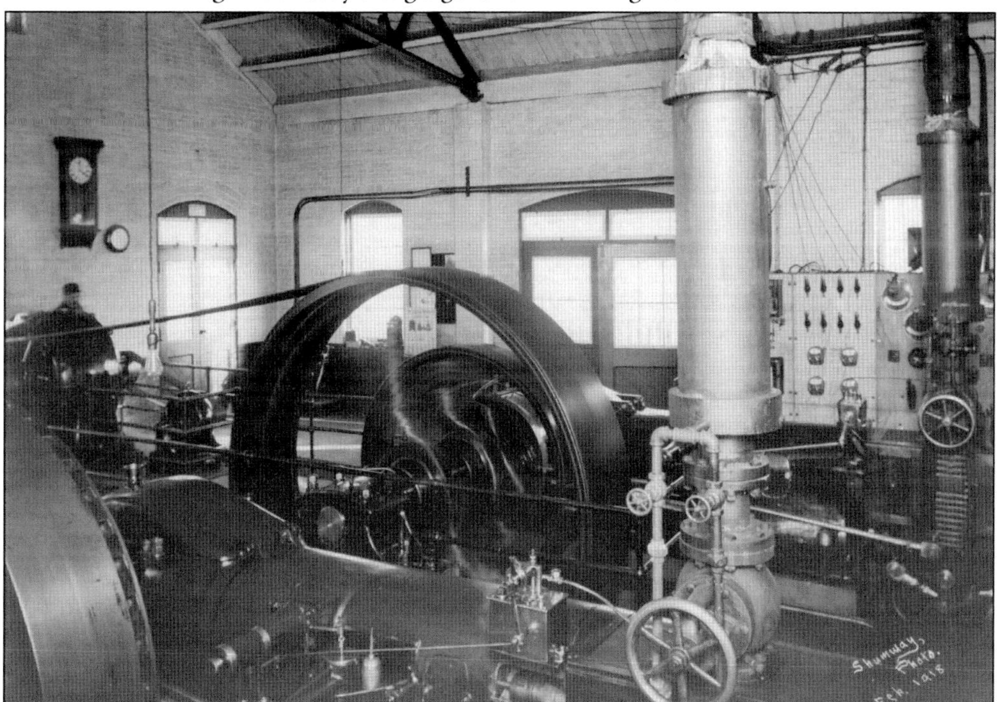

The interior of the power plant, pictured in 1918, was overseen by the new superintendent of public works, and the coal for the power plant was manually carted from the railroad siding to the plant by town workers. The power plant only operated at night until 1915, when it began operating 24 hours a day.

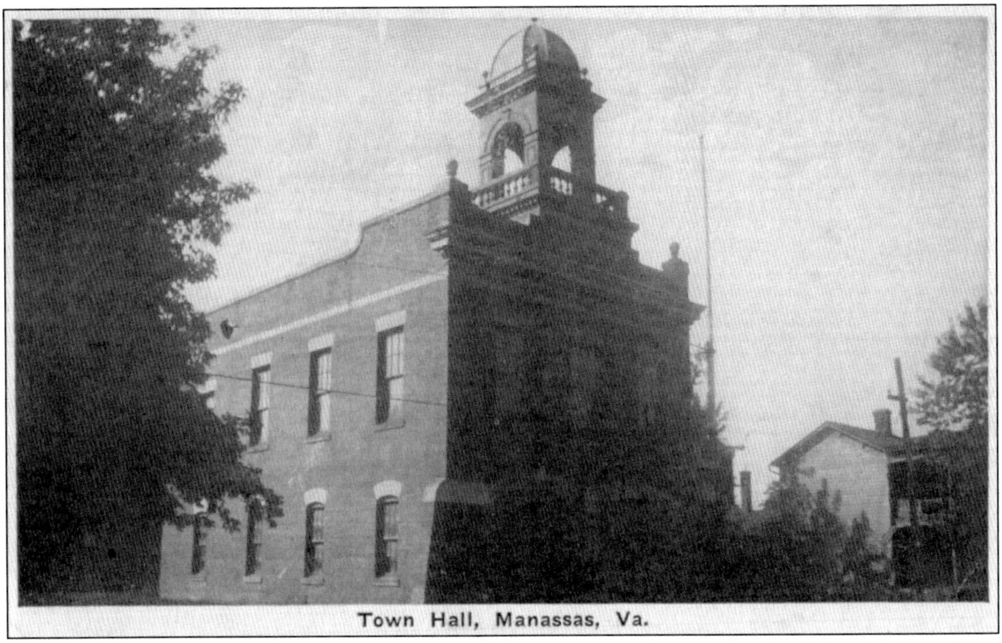

Like initiatives to establish utilities, construction of a new town hall met with opposition from residents who feared the town was assuming too much debt. A taxpayer writing to the *Manassas Democrat* said, "At the present juncture do we not need $5,500 more for other purposes than for a new Town Hall? Let the Council, if necessary, submit the question to those who will have to pay the bills."

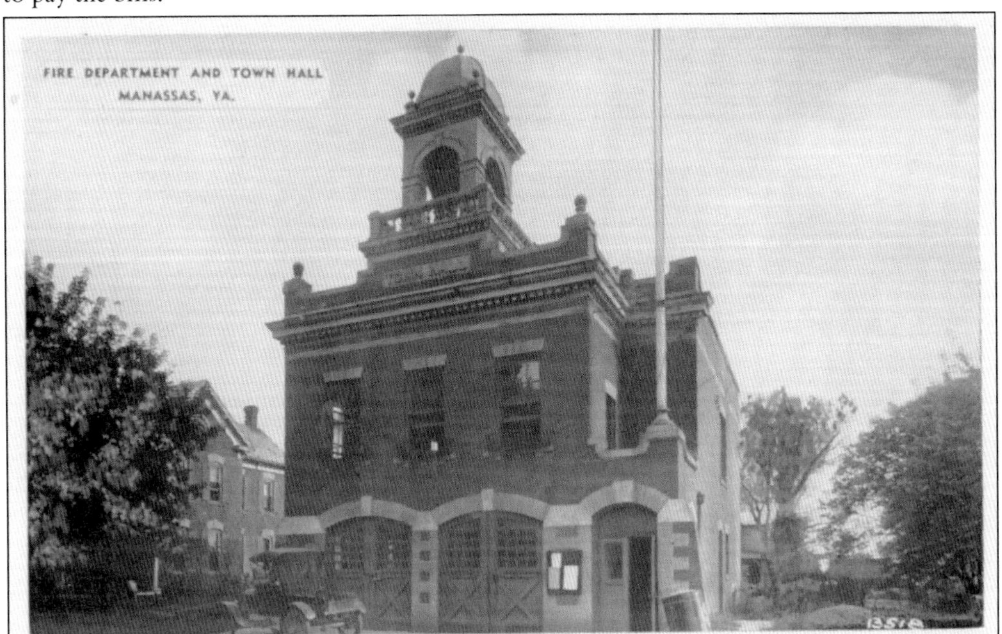

Prominent local architect Albert Speiden designed the new town hall as a multipurpose building. The volunteer fire company was housed on the first floor, and the town council chamber was on the second floor. An office was set up in town hall to be open to the public at specified hours. Until a treasurer's position was added in 1915, the town sergeant handled all monies.

As the town grew, the volunteer fire department gained a prominent sign on town hall, but the fire company quickly outgrew the building and moved to its Centerville Road location in 1956. The move freed the first floor for the town treasurer and other offices, a welcome change for citizens who no longer had to climb steep stairs to conduct business.

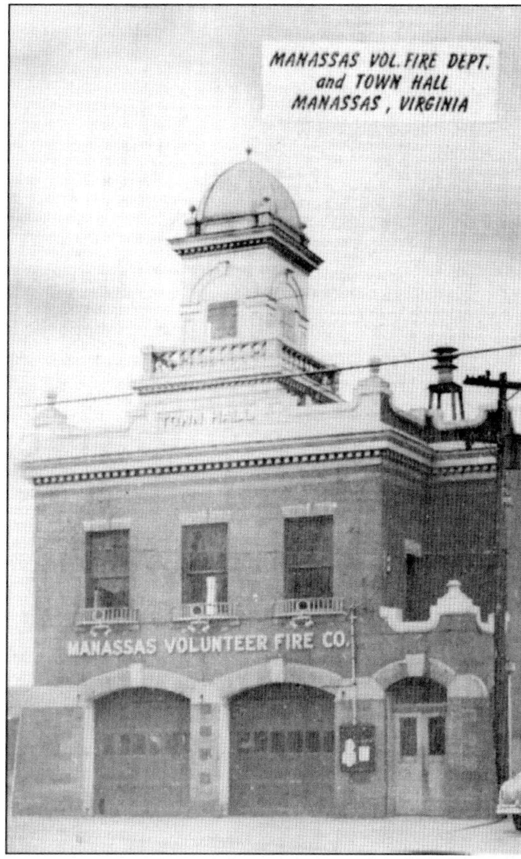

The cupola from old town hall was removed in the 1960s and was not rebuilt and reinstalled until 2002. For a time in the 1980s, its red and yellow brick laid with a thin "butter joint" was covered in white paint. This 1985 image shows a newly refurbished town hall just before most offices moved next door when the new city hall was built in 1987.

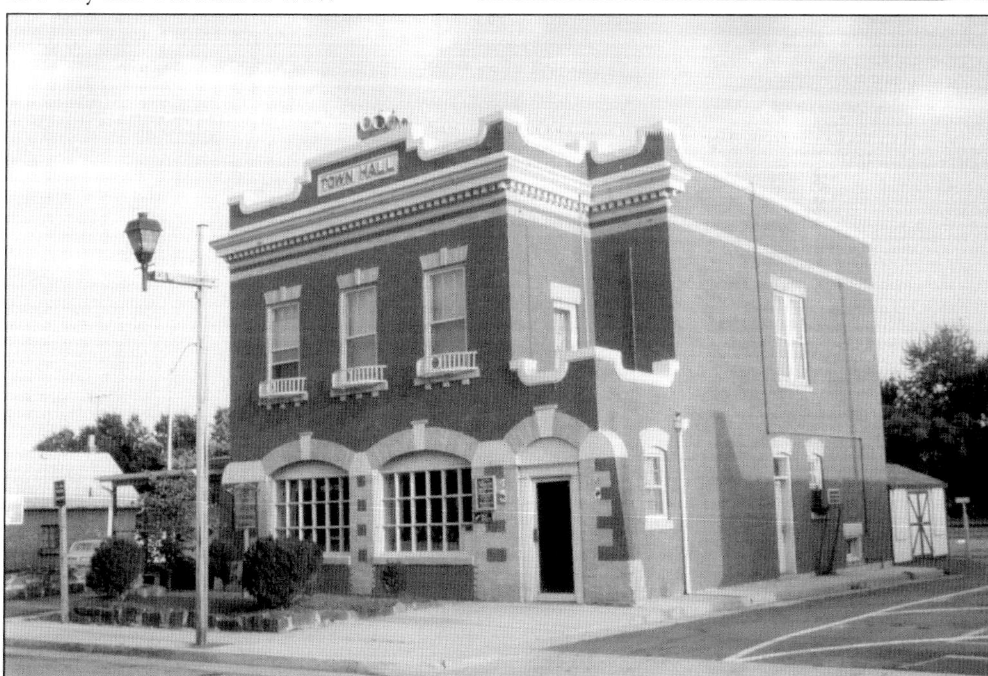

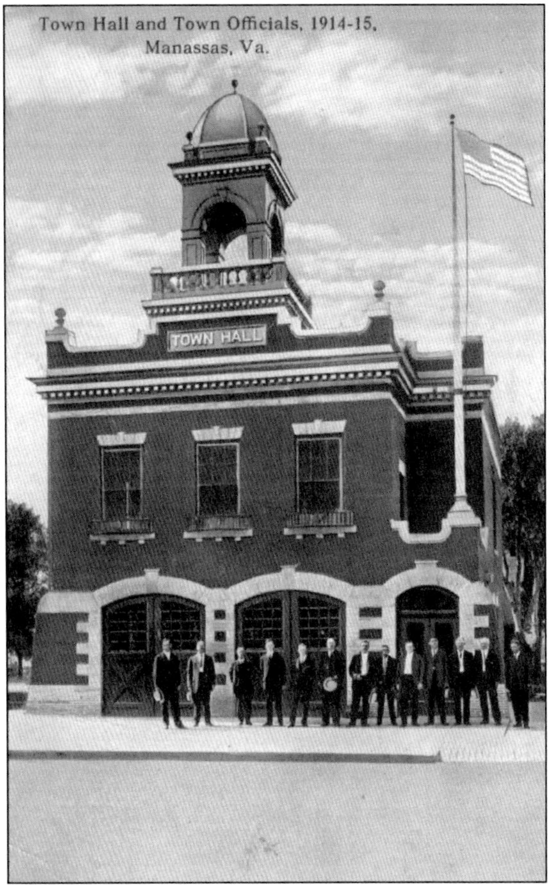

In this image with a flag painted into the background, (from left to right) clerk G.R. Ratcliffe, Dr. C.R.C. Johnson, William Wheeler, E.A. Bland, R.S. Hynson, Mayor W. Hill Brown Sr., Albert Speiden, Daniel Prescott, T.E. Coleman, E.R. Conner, C.E. Nash, James E. Nelson, and Sgt. R.M. Weir pose before the new town hall building in 1915.

Bland's Ford Bridge, a crossing over the Occoquan River near Lake Jackson and present-day Dumfries Road, is first referenced in an 1834 *Journal of the Virginia House of Delegates*, where William Garland was said to be owed $2,300 when the bridge was received. During the 1939 military maneuvers in and around the Manassas battlefields, units from the 28th Army National Guard launched an assault over the bridge.

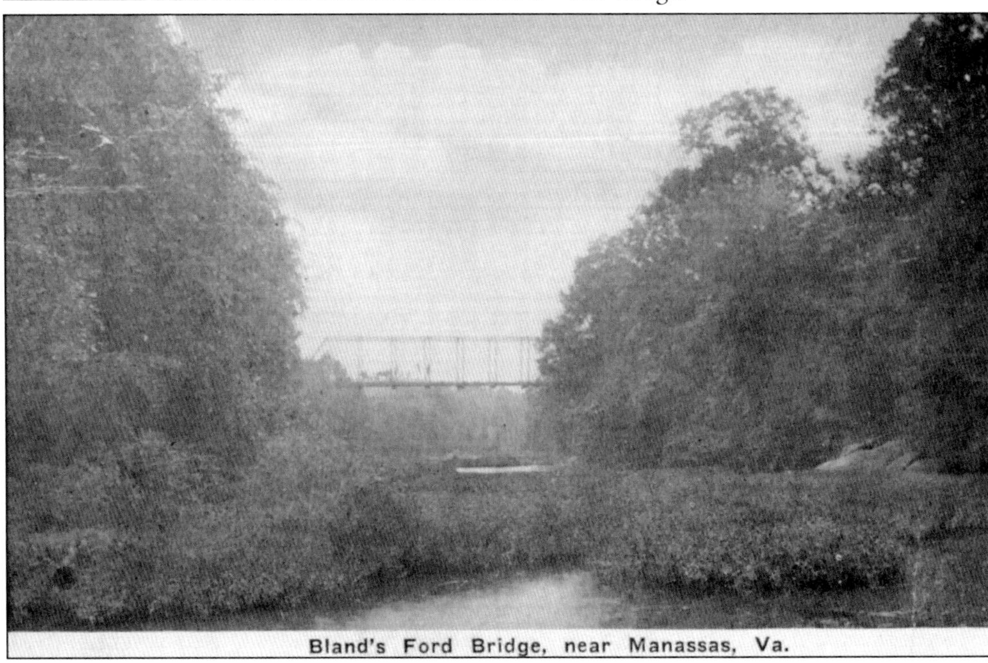

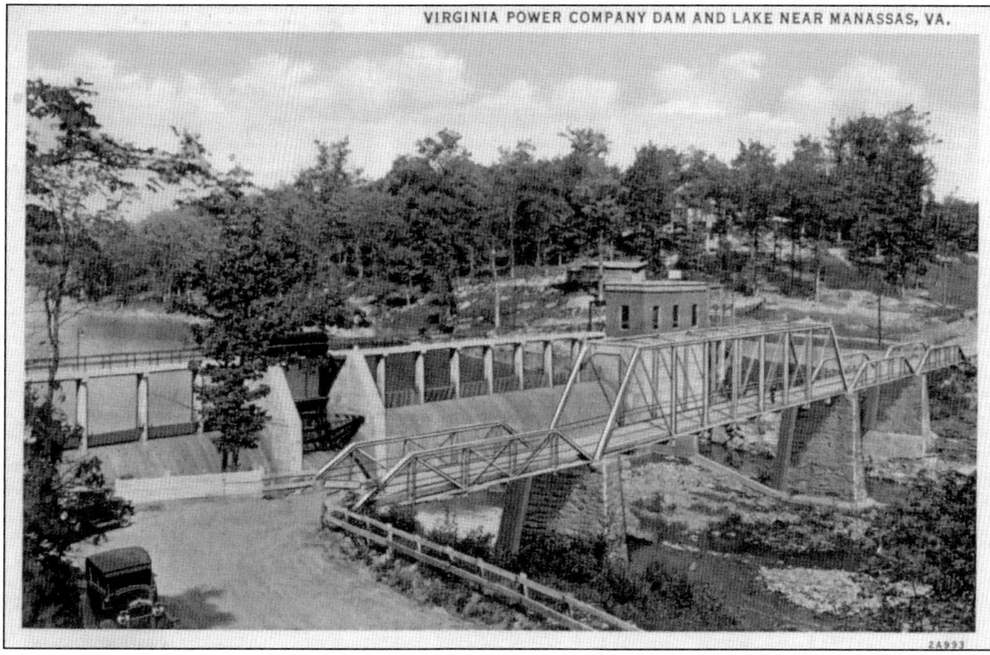

The damming of the Occoquan River at Bland's Ford was completed by Charles Alpaugh in 1929. After local workers built the Lake Jackson dam, Alpaugh sold it to Virginia Public Service, later Virginia Electric & Power Company (VEPCO). The dam produced electricity for the surrounding area until 1955, when it became a booster station providing power when needed.

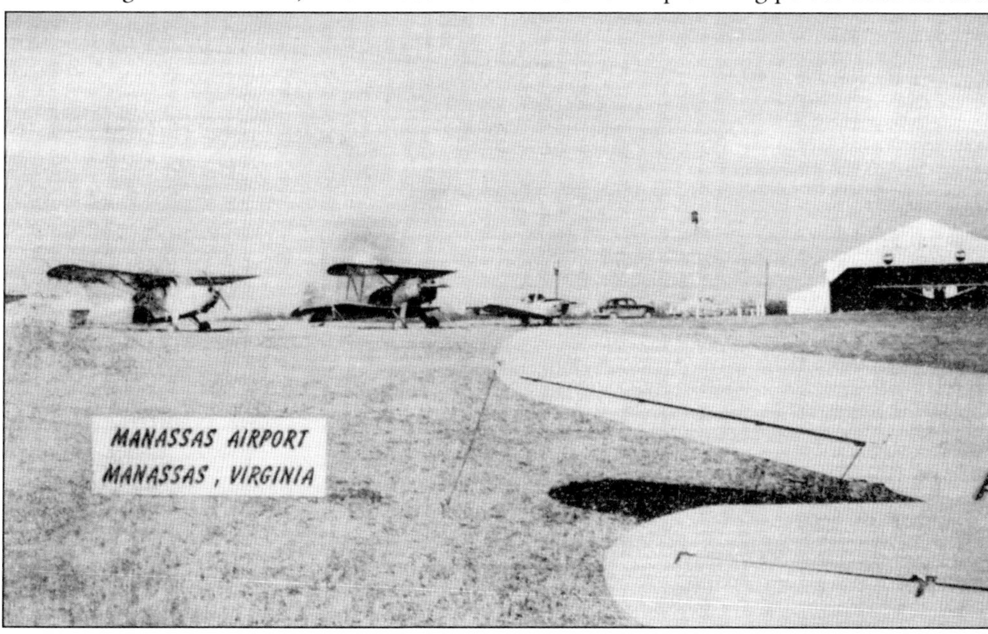

In 1931, seventeen citizens promised to raise funds to purchase land for an airport. The Manassas Landing Field was opened in 1932 on 95 acres of land on Sudley Road. Within two years, another 12 acres were added to extend the runway, and the airport became a stop for airmail service. As the area became heavily developed, the airport, now owned by the town, moved to its present location in 1964.

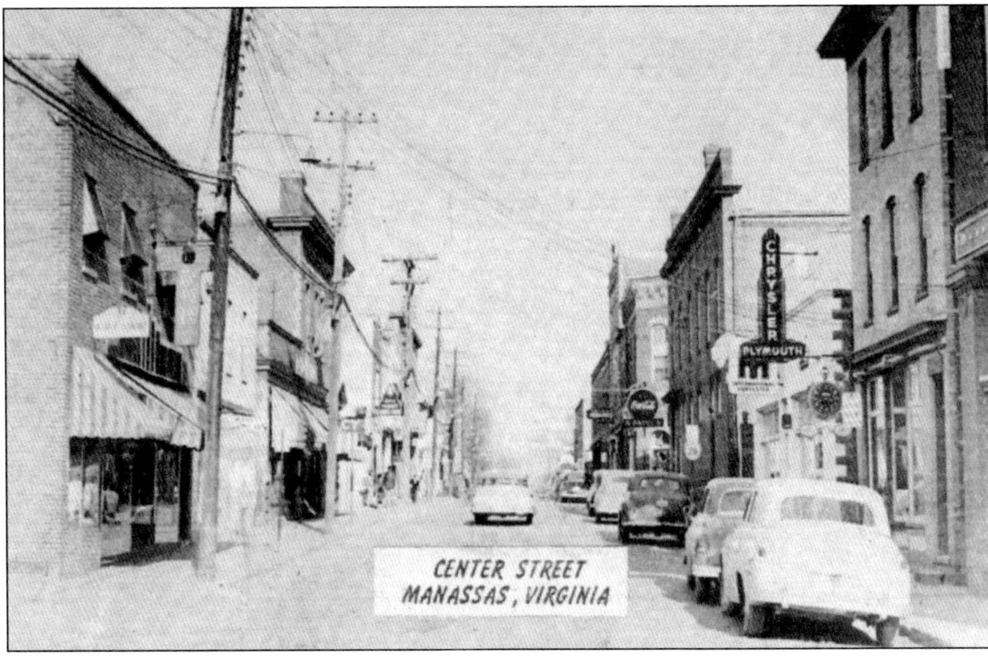

A tire store, car dealer, and soda fountains were among the newer Center Street businesses in these images from the 1940s and 1950s. Caton Merchant's expanded Firestone outlet (below at right) was destined to become a major East Coast tire chain. It was not until the summer of 1929 that the major roads in the town were paved. At that time, there were over eight miles of maintained streets, but only two miles were hard surfaced. "Even though they may be hard and practically free from mud in wet weather, they are generally rough and contrast unfavorably with smooth paved streets, especially in dry weather when the dust becomes annoying," reported town manager William Cocke in 1930.

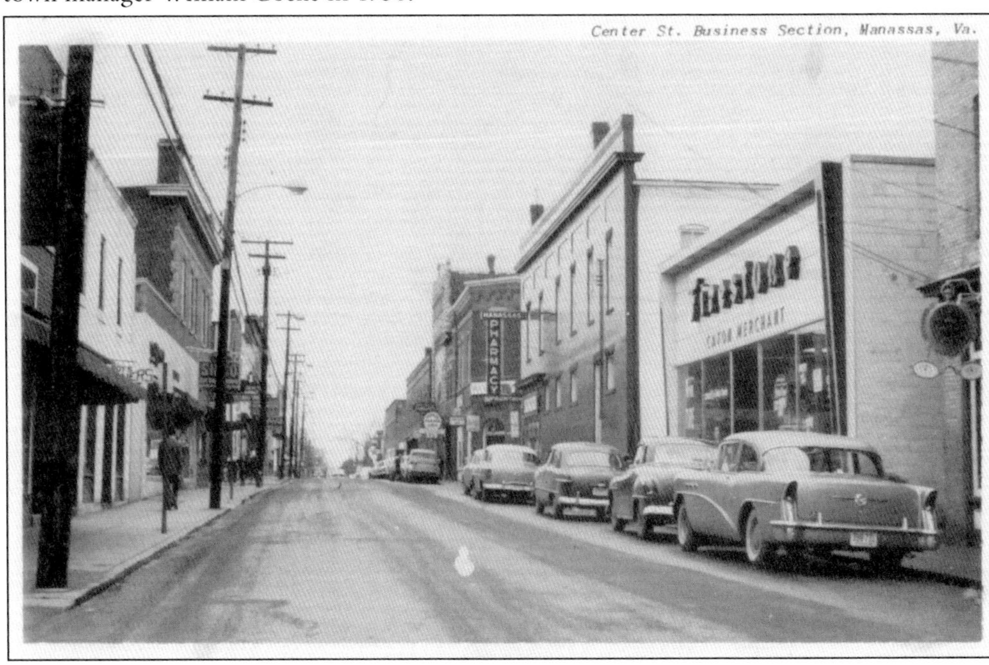

Five

OPEN FOR BUSINESS

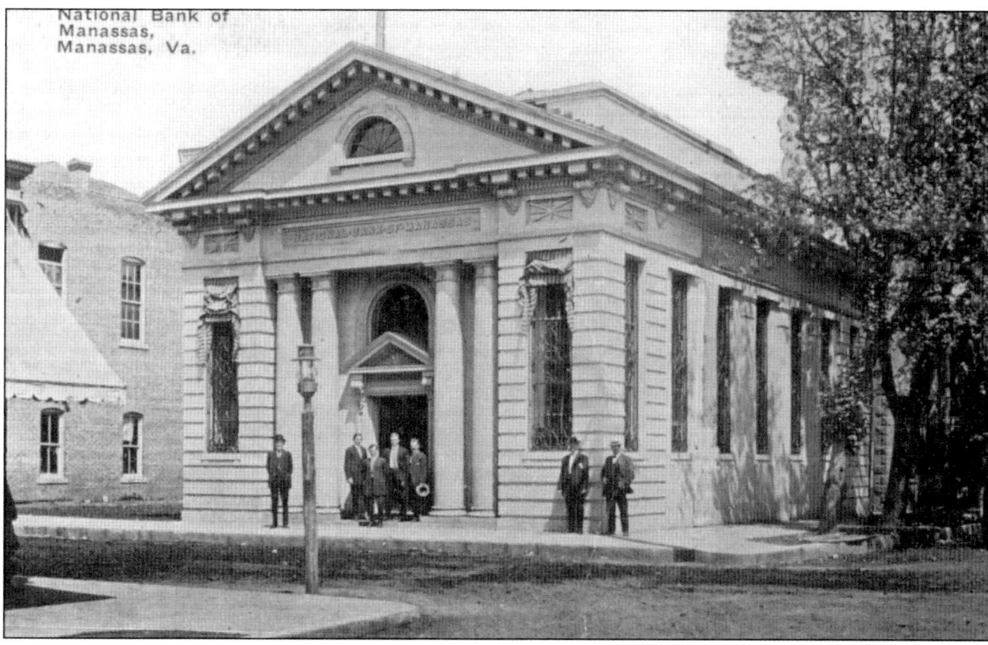

By the turn of the 20th century, enterprising and prosperous businesses included the Mayfield and Yorkshire Brownstone Quarries, Prescott's spoke factory, Taylor and Brown's Planing Mills, Libeau's Brick Works, two nurseries, a gristmill, blacksmith, and lumber mills. The impressive National Bank of Manassas and three hotels by the railroad had a steady business. Hardware, grocery, and beloved department stores likes Hynson's and Hibbs and Giddings made Manassas a shopping destination.

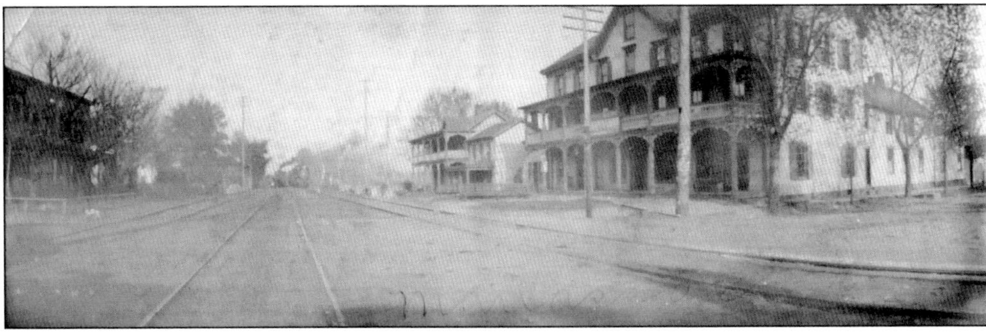

The Goodwin House hotel is at left, and the Keyes House, Eureka House, and Cannon House hotels are at right in this view along the tracks near Main Street. The Eureka House, built by a transplanted New Yorker, and the Manassas Hotel, later known as the Goodwin House, were the first hotels. The Cannon House was renamed the Maine Hotel after the battleship of the same name sank in 1898.

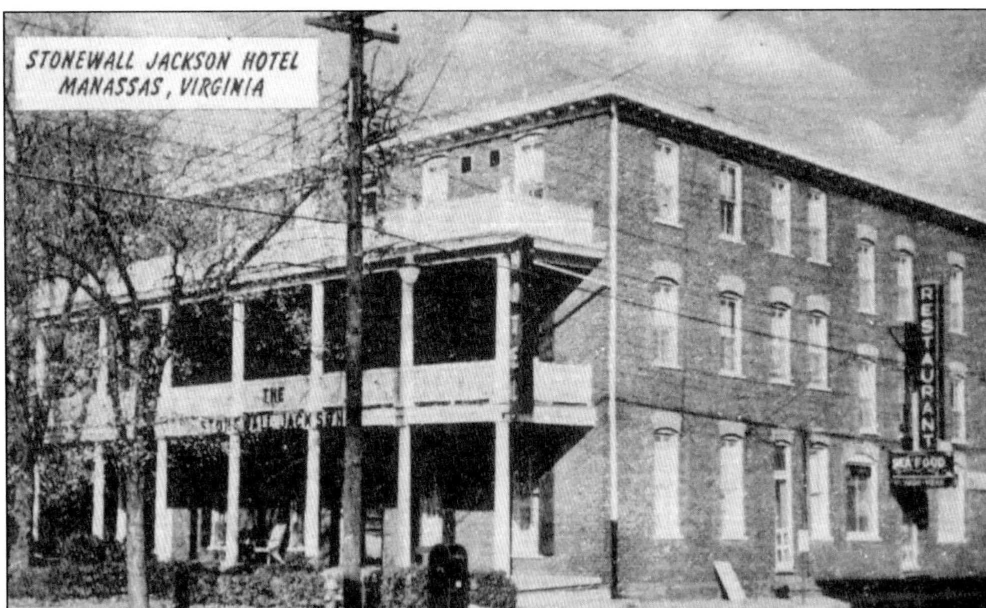

Built in 1912 at the corner of Main and Center Streets as the Prince William Hotel, the Stonewall Jackson Hotel was demolished in the 1960s to make way for the Old Towne Inn. A local resident recalled that after the hotel lost all its keys, it no longer issued keys to guests.

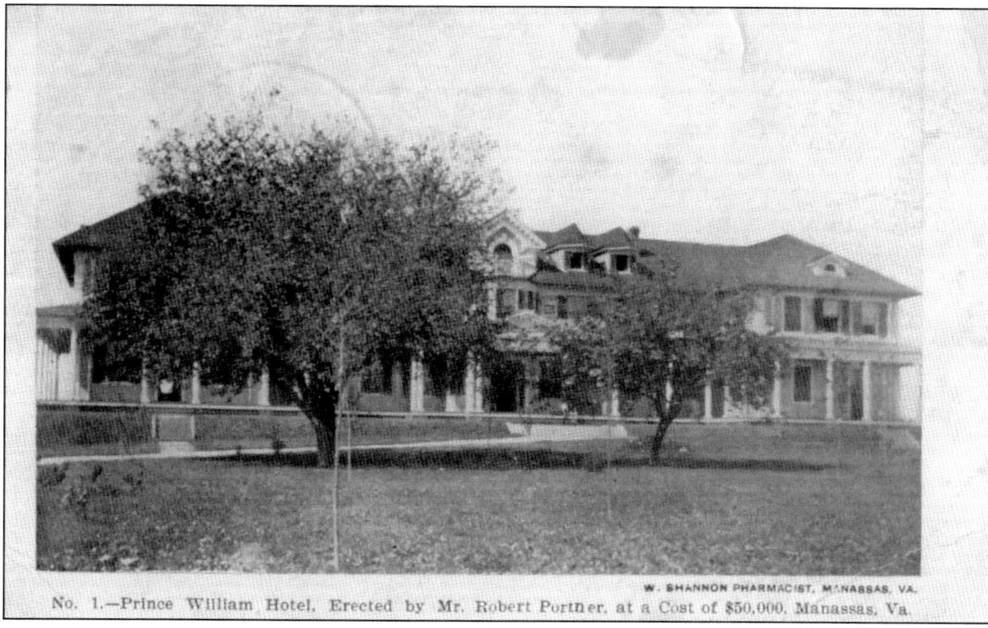

The first Prince William Hotel, pictured above in the early 1900s, opened in 1904 but was destroyed by fire in 1910, like the Manassas and Weaver hotels before it. The hotel was across the street from the railroad depot on the south side of the tracks between Grant Avenue and West Street, where a water tower now stands. Robert Portner, a wealthy summer resident, reportedly spent $50,000 to build the luxurious 45-room hotel as an investment property. A much less grand second Prince William Hotel, later renamed the Stonewall Jackson Hotel, opened in 1912 at the corner of Main and Center Streets.

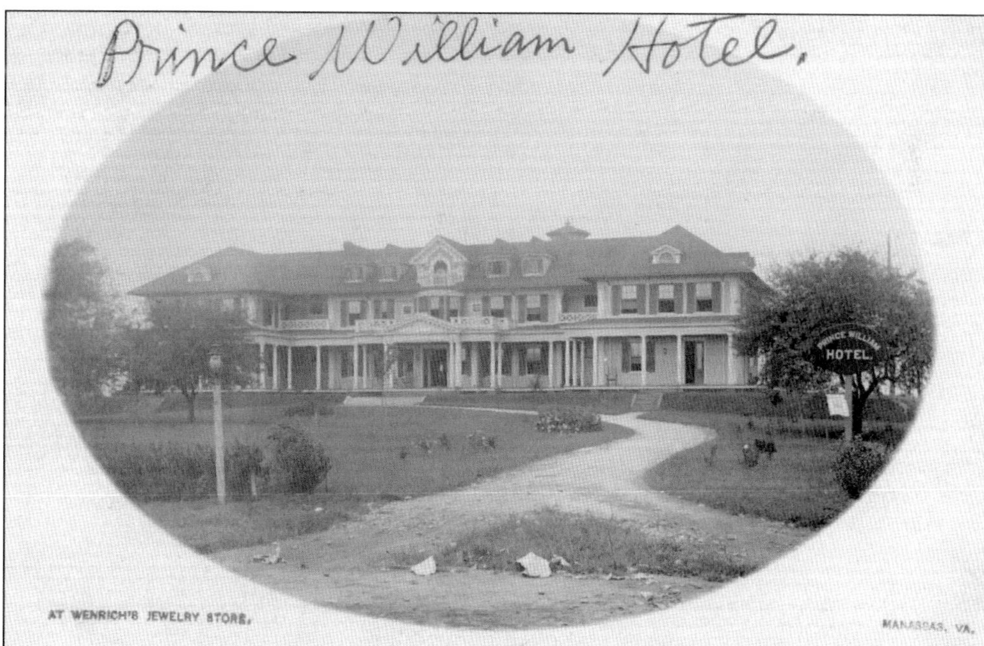

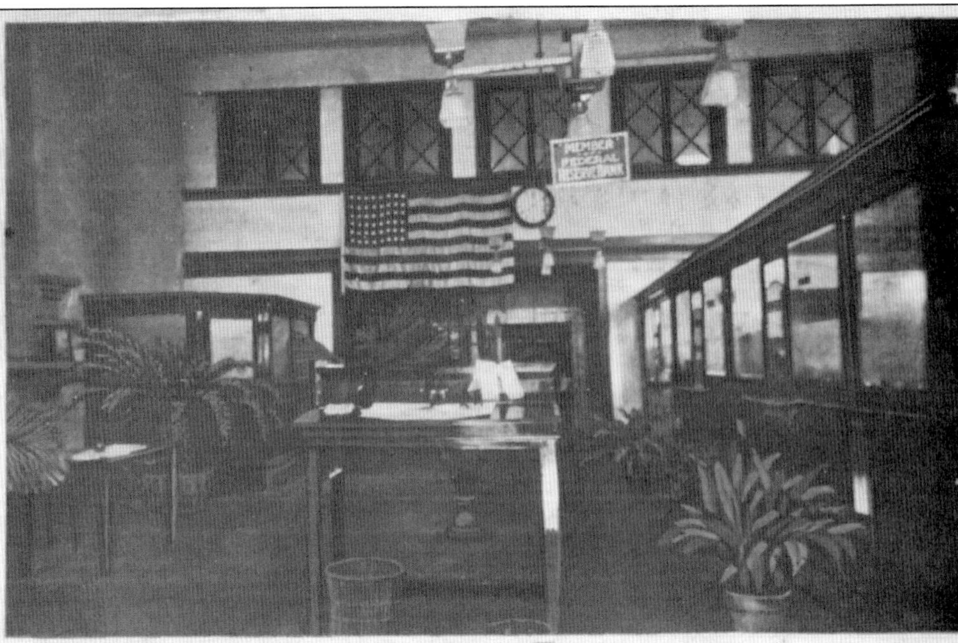

INTERIOR THE NATIONAL BANK OF MANASSAS. MANASSAS, VA.

The National Bank of Manassas was the first bank established in Prince William County. The first meeting of stockholders was held in the office of Judge C.E. Nicols in 1895, and the bank occupied a Main Street location until 1912, when its new building (above) was constructed on the corner of Center and Main Streets. The first cashier at the bank had a salary of $950 per year, the first teller made $35 per month, and employees prided themselves with being "the bank of personal service." It became a First Virginia Bank branch in 1956, and after the branch closed in the 1990s, it has since housed commercial space.

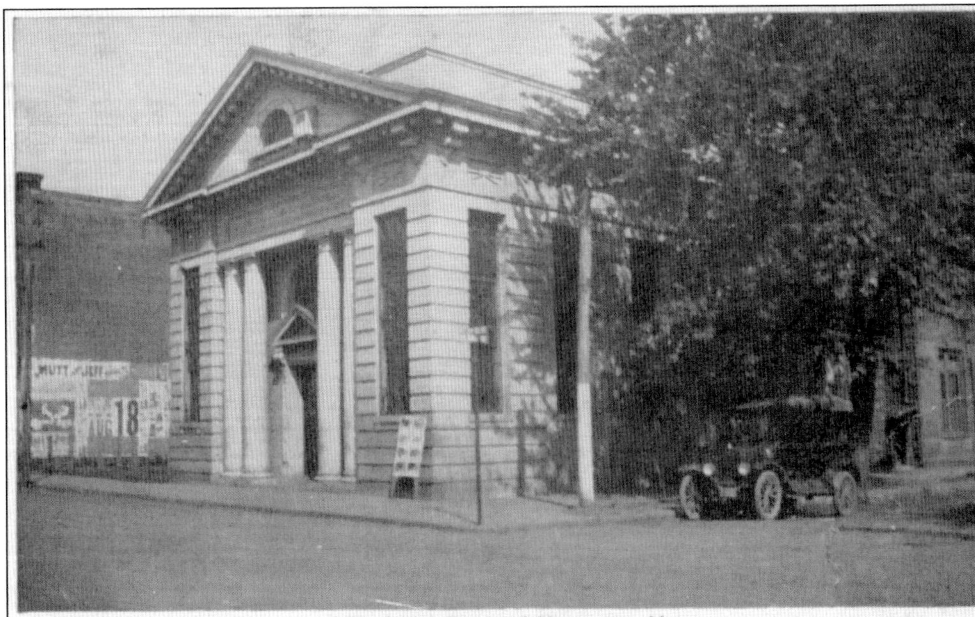

National Bank of Manassas, Va.

The National Bank of Manassas advertised services to make its customers happy and professional expertise to keep their money safe. In 1897, a cashier at the bank proved his ability when he grew suspicious of a swindler trying to sell a bogus note. "He took a hasty departure, boarding a passing train without taking time to purchase a ticket," the *Washington Post* reported of the swindler.

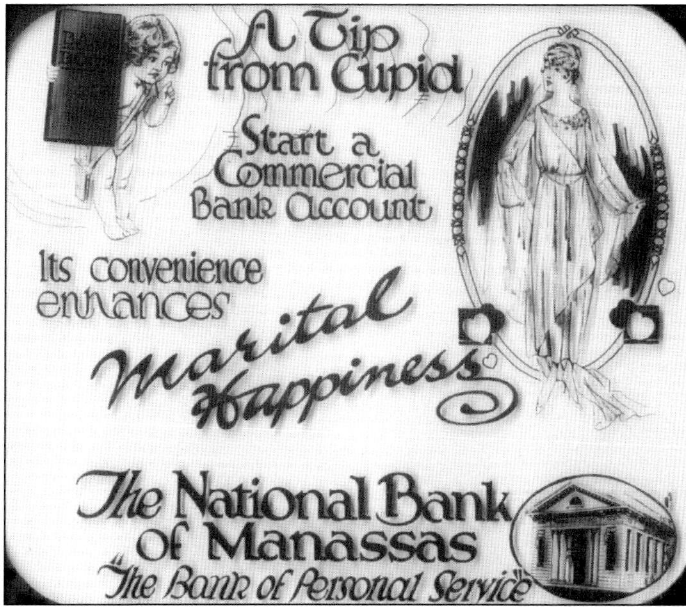

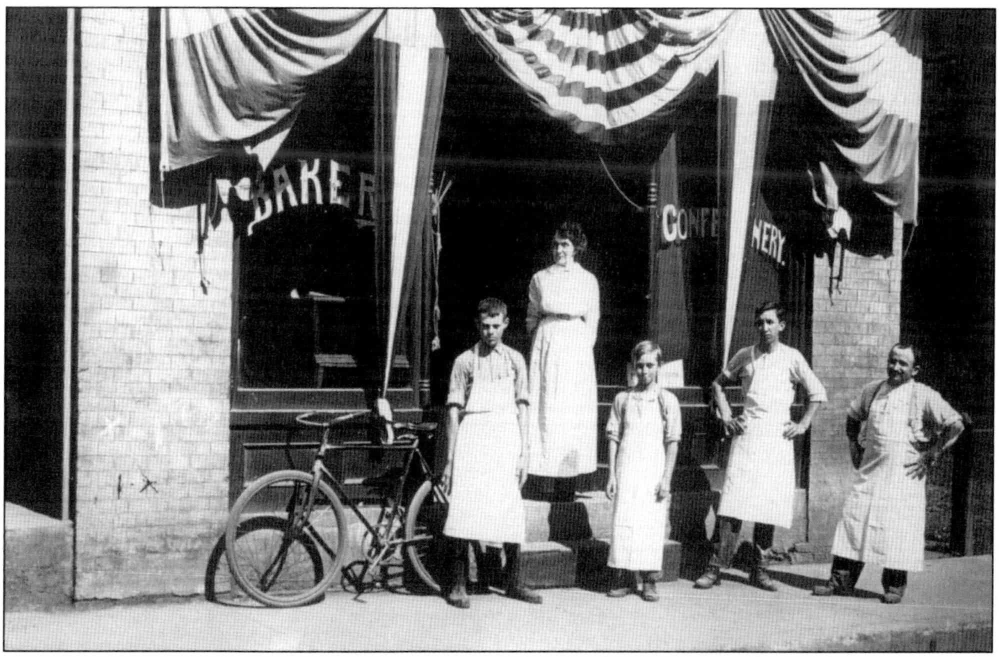

Jesse Bell was the third to own a Battle Street bakery. In this postcard promoting his business, he is at far right, posing before the bakery, which was decorated for the 1911 National Jubilee of Peace. A 1909 advertisement for the bakery reads, "It is a comparatively easy matter to prepare the dinner when you engage us to supply the bread, pastry and other good things."

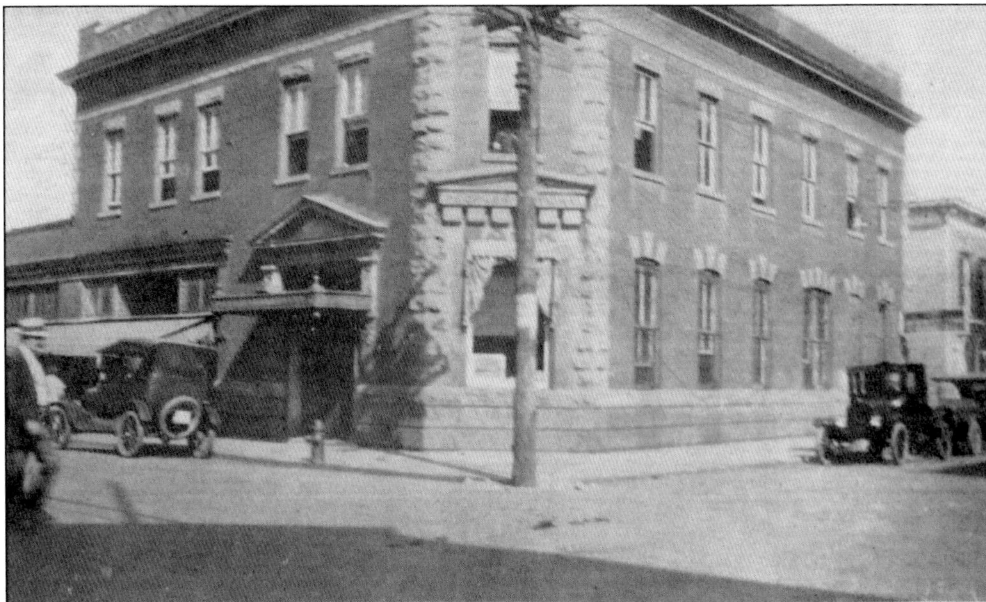

Peoples National Bank, Manassas, Va.

The Peoples National Bank, located at the corner of Center and Battle Streets, was organized in 1903, built in 1904, and survived the Great Fire of 1905 when, legend has it, brickmaker Donation Libeau climbed to the roof to douse flames. The bank had resources of more than a half million dollars in the early 1920s. A newspaper advertisement said of potential customers, "The better he knows us the more likely he is to like us and our business methods." Dowell's Pharmacy opened in the building in 1909, and by 1925, it was also one of five soda fountains in the county.

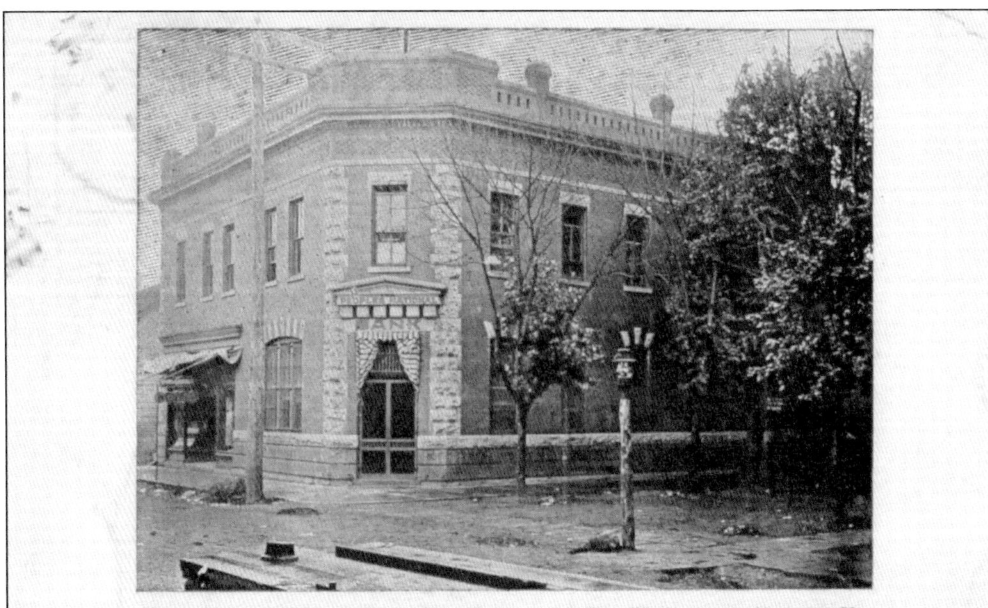

Peoples National Bank, Manassas, Va. Dowell's Pharmacy, Manassas, Va.

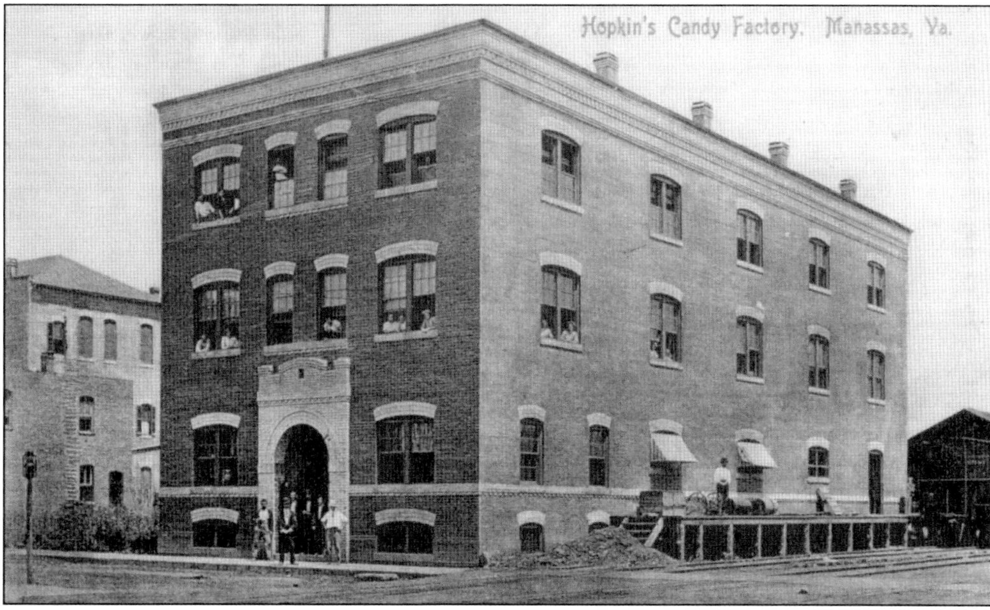

The Hopkins Candy Company expanded to this Battle Street factory in 1908. Proclaimed a marvel of modern industry, the factory shipped five to ten tons of candy annually, including ribbon candy, marshmallows, and chocolates. After the factory closed in 1917, the building housed the Manassas Feed and Milling Company, the Southern States Cooperative, and a tire warehouse until becoming the Center for the Arts.

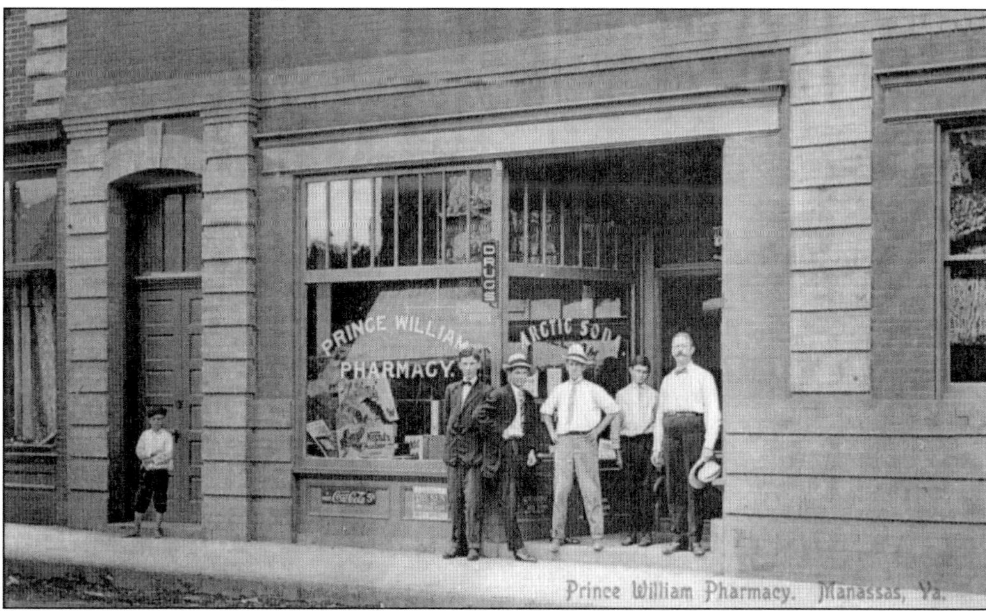

Prince William Pharmacy on Center Street advertised that "a registered pharmacist will compound your prescriptions with the purest and freshest drugs and chemicals," and carried toiletries, garden seeds, ice cream, and school supplies. *The Manassas Democrat* said of the pharmacy's display of candy cartons, "Pretty girls, sweet and irresistible as the confections they exploit, smile bewitchingly upon admiring crowds gazing upon the beautiful display of Hopkins candies in the windows."

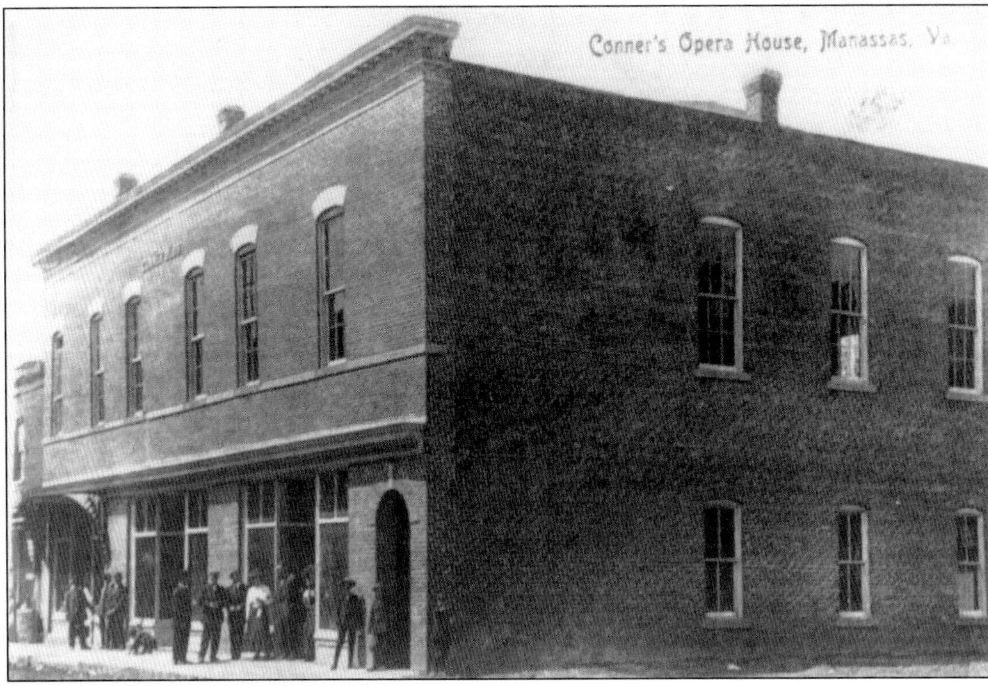

Built in 1906, the Conner Opera House on Center Street was a technological marvel for the small town. E.R. Conner moved his grocery store to the first floor and constructed the ornate Conner Opera House upstairs. In 1910, four years before the town was electrified, Conner built his own light plant. "The lights are excellent and prove conclusively the practicability of electric lighting systems conducted on a private scale," the *Manassas Journal* reported.

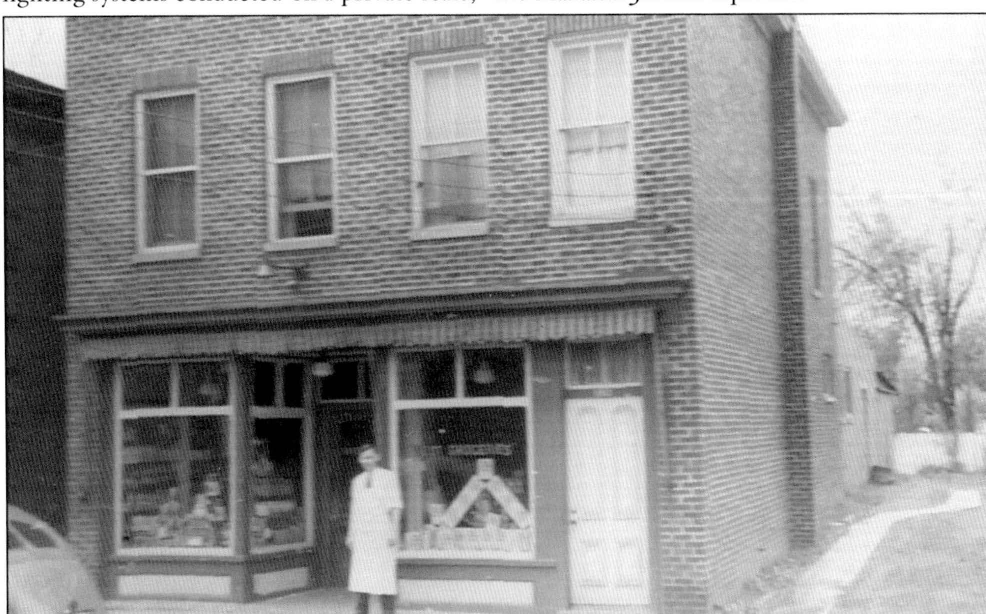

Bushong's grocery was just around the corner on Main Street. J.L. Bushong purchased his first store on Center Street from C.E. Fisher Hardware and moved to this store in 1927. In 1932, customers followed him to a new store on North Main Street, where it remained until 1942.

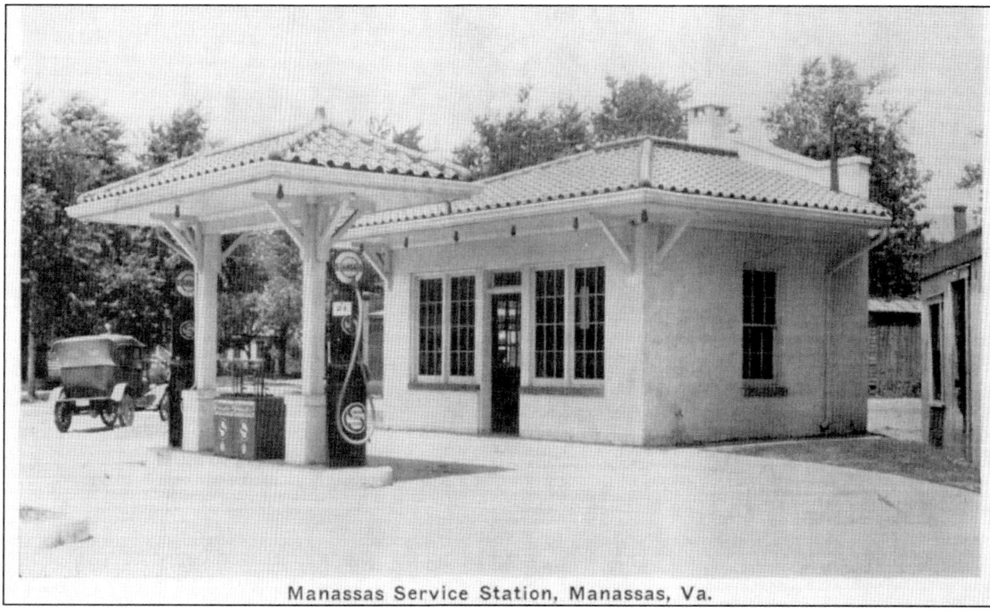

The Manassas Service Station, situated at the corner of Center and West Streets in about 1915, was one of the area's first gas stations and one of six in the downtown area by the 1940s. W. Caton Merchant, who later owned the station, founded the Merchant Tire chain here. A 1921 town ordinance prohibited cars from traveling faster than twelve miles per hour or six miles per hour around corners.

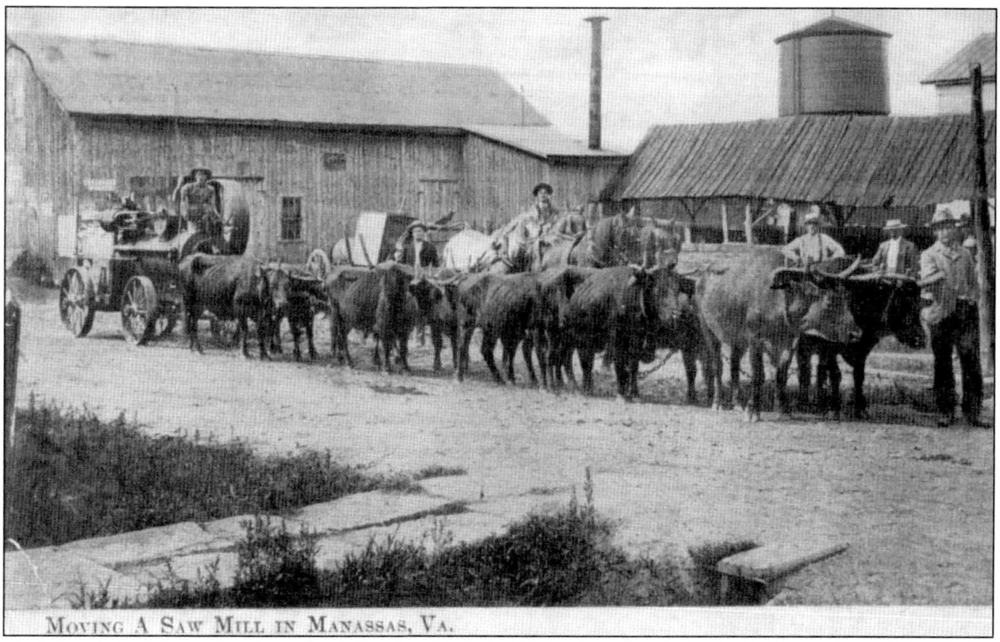

Morey's Saw Mill, located on Center and West Streets, needed to add night shifts to produce enough lumber for the growing town. The mill used oxen to pull heavy loads of wood since horses were often scarce in the area after the Civil War. Morey's produced rough—and not finely finished—lumber, and much of it was used to build churches, barns, houses, sheds, schools, and stores in the area.

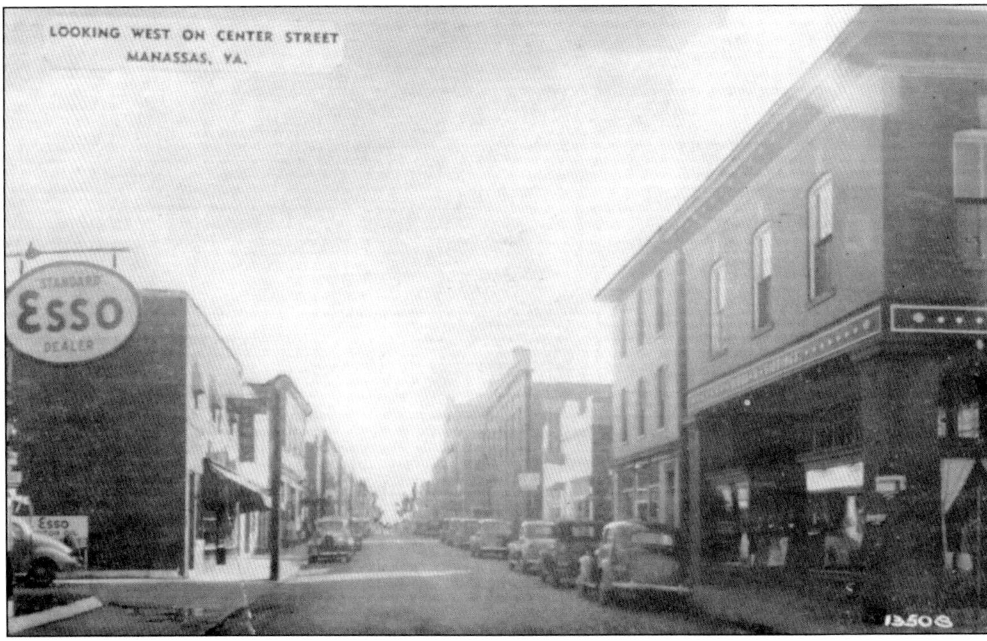

E. Humphrey Hibbs and Eugene B. Giddings opened their fashionable men's clothing store in 1898 and stayed in business for more than 70 years. Shown above to the right on the corner of Center and West Streets in the 1930s, the business survived the Great Fire of 1905 when it was located in the People's Bank building, and moved to this location in 1912. On its first day in business, the store sold $39 worth of merchandise. Known as "the quality shop," Hynson's Department Store, seen below to the left on the corner of Center and Main Streets, sold everything from shoes and gloves to towels and bedspreads for the whole family. To aid a Kiwanis Club effort to post directional signs around town, founder R.S. Hynson had a large sign painted on his roof to aid aviators in about 1930.

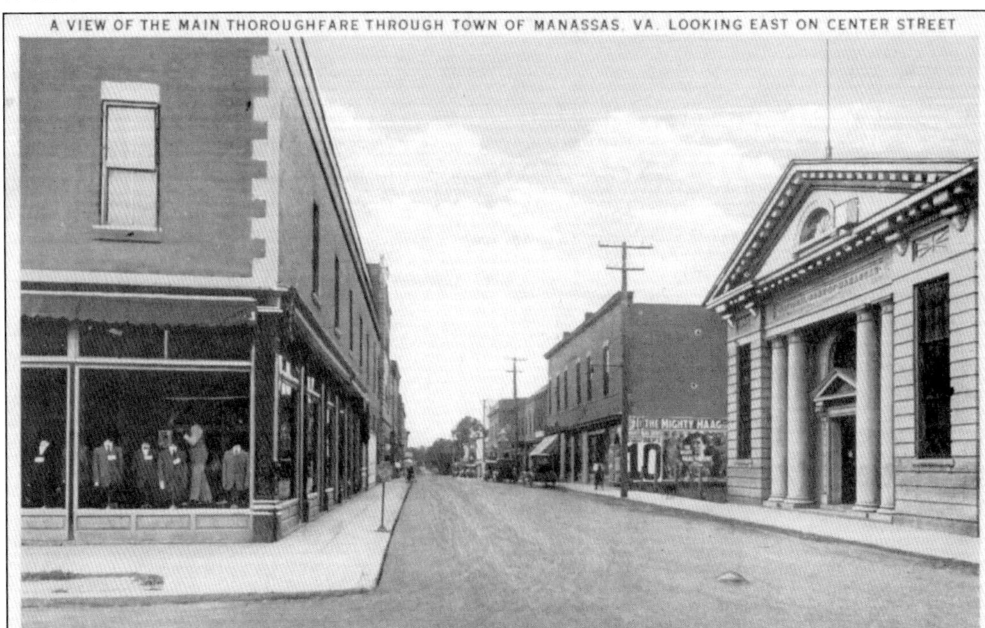

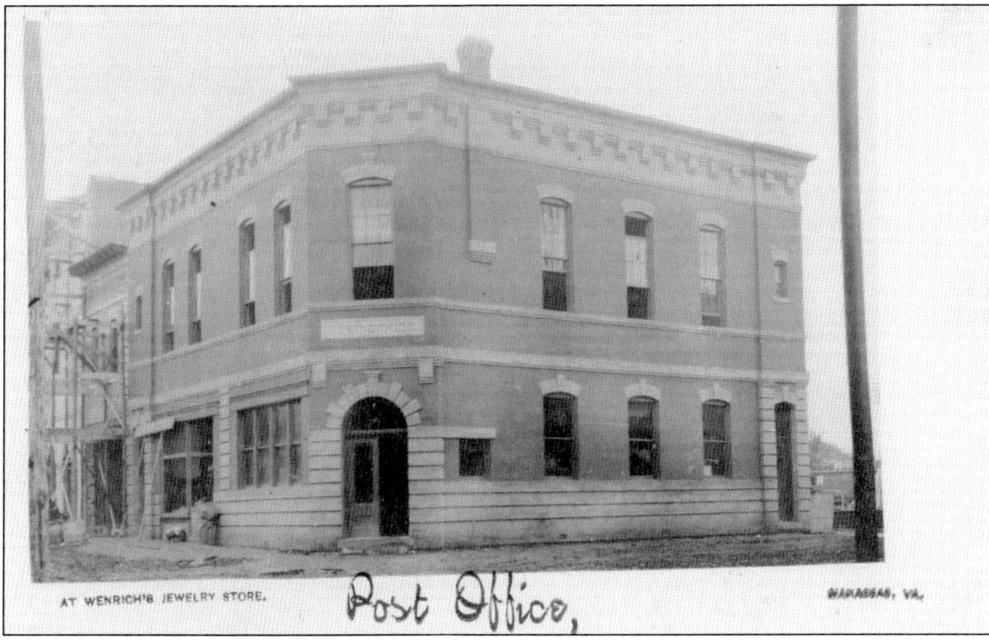

Judge C.E. Nicol took a chance when constructing the post office on the corner of Center and Battle Streets in 1906. Nicol had no promise that the building would be used as a post office but correctly thought its construction would spur further development after the devastating fire of 1905. It was in use until 1923 and has since been prime commercial space. (Nancy Mitchell.)

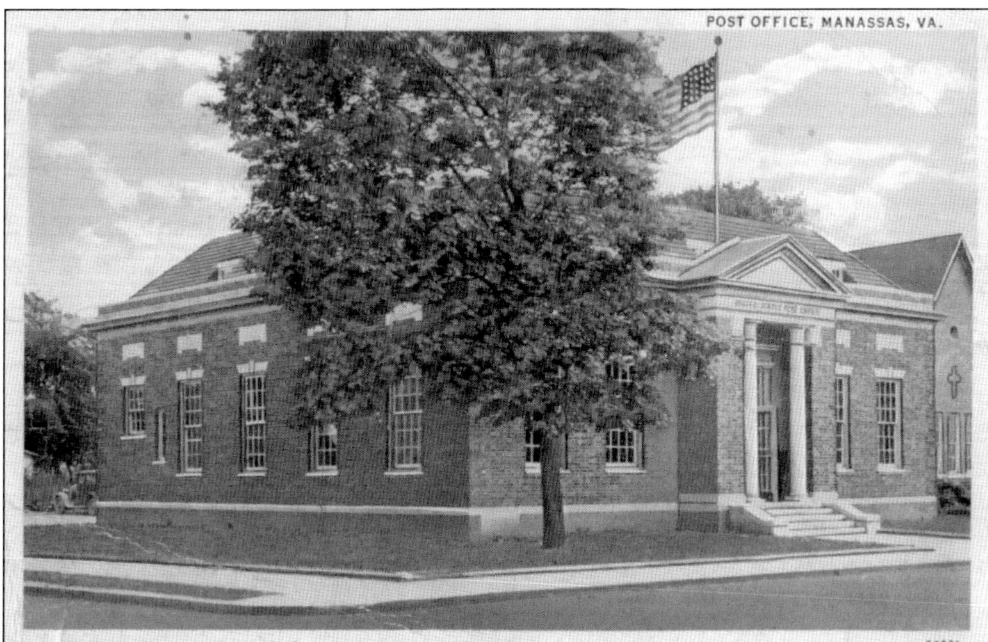

The Church Street post office was one of thousands constructed during the Great Depression in 1932 to help the unemployed and to reinforce the importance of neighborhood post offices. The first Manassas post offices were located at Liberia Plantation, Milford Mills, and the train depot and were housed in various temporary locations.

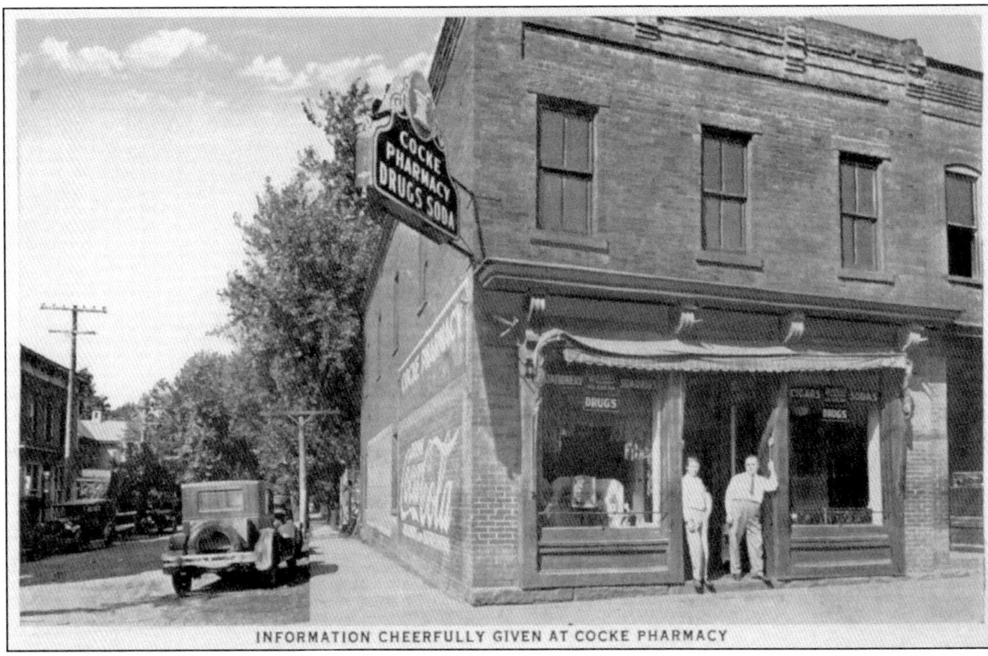

Although this building started life as the Whittington & Company Hardware Store from 1890 till 1895, it was home to Cocke's Pharmacy from 1919 till 1984. In its early years, pharmacist George Cocke advertised free prescription delivery, toilet necessities, cold creams, and vaccines. The store also served as a Trailways bus depot, with daily departures to Washington, Fredericksburg, and Richmond. For decades, Cocke's became a local hangout for teenagers craving a Cherry Coke or for their mothers, who met earlier in the day for coffee and crackers. The building's original plain facade (pictured above) was enhanced by a Mission-style upgrade (pictured below) in the 1920s and included an Art Deco entrance and rear addition. The building has long been home to a restaurant. (Above, Nancy Mitchell.)

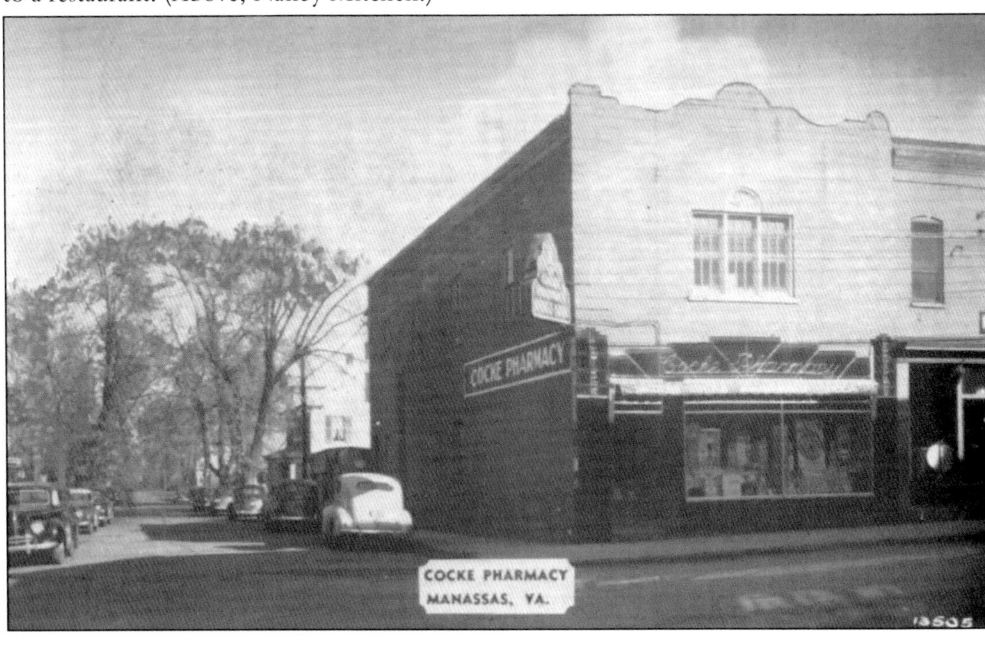

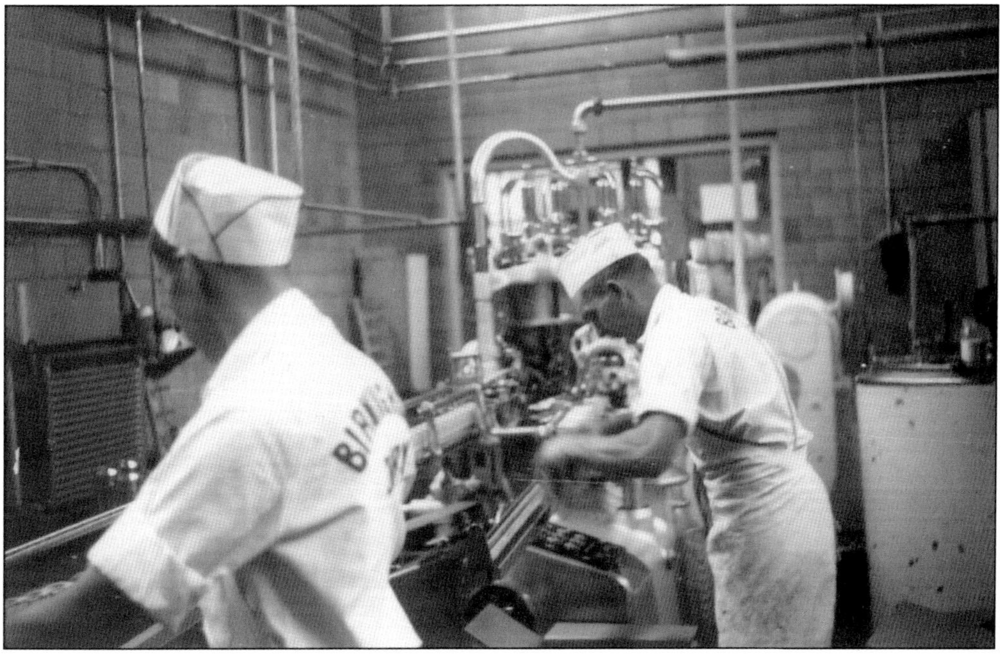

Birmingham Dairy on Centreville Road, shown here in the 1950s, delivered Grade A raw or pasteurized milk, buttermilk, chocolate drink, and cream to area homes and businesses in Fairfax, Fauquier, and Prince William Counties for decades. The Birmingham Milk Bar, open until midnight, was a popular stop for young people craving a late-night hamburger and ice cream.

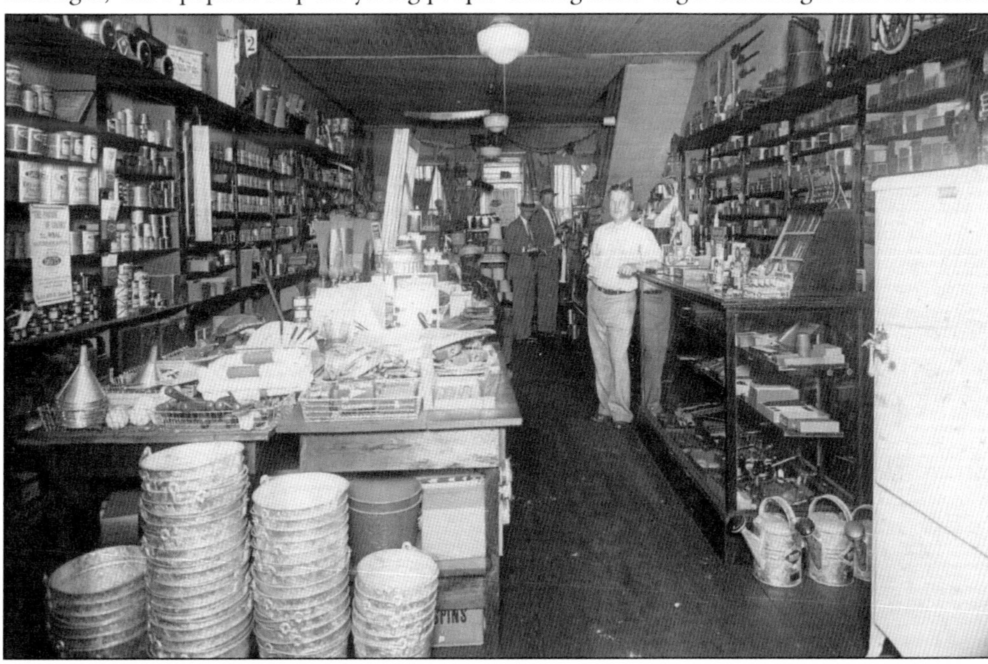

Manassas Hardware Store, shown here around 1933, was a hardware, farming, appliance, garden, and tire store fit tightly into a Center Street space. It supplied—among many other things—stoves, cream separators, tires, glass, harness, garden seeds, and guns. Owner Conroy Seeley (left) and Jack Hutchison are at the rear of the store. The man in the foreground is unidentified.

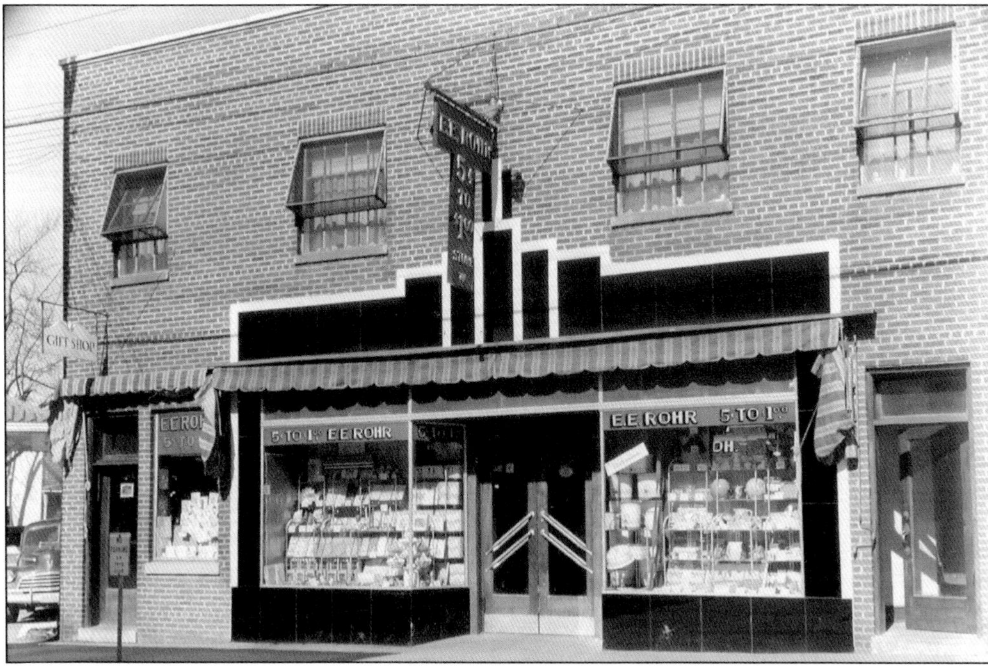

Rohr's 5¢ to $1 Store on Center Street was an important part of everyday life for generations of Manassas residents and visitors from 1934 until 1997. Young shoppers searched for penny candy, while their parents perused overflowing shelves for household goods. Even until the last years the store was open, Rohr's featured such hard-to-find items as washboards, clothes pegs, flycatchers with sticky goo, and strawberry hullers. Children found classic jacks sets, toy rolling pins, and roller-skate repair kits. Edgar Rohr, who served as mayor and councilman, and his wife, Walser, operated a free museum, first on Grant Avenue and later next to their store. It featured Civil War relics, dolls, antiques of all kinds, and cars. Their collection became the foundation of the Manassas Museum.

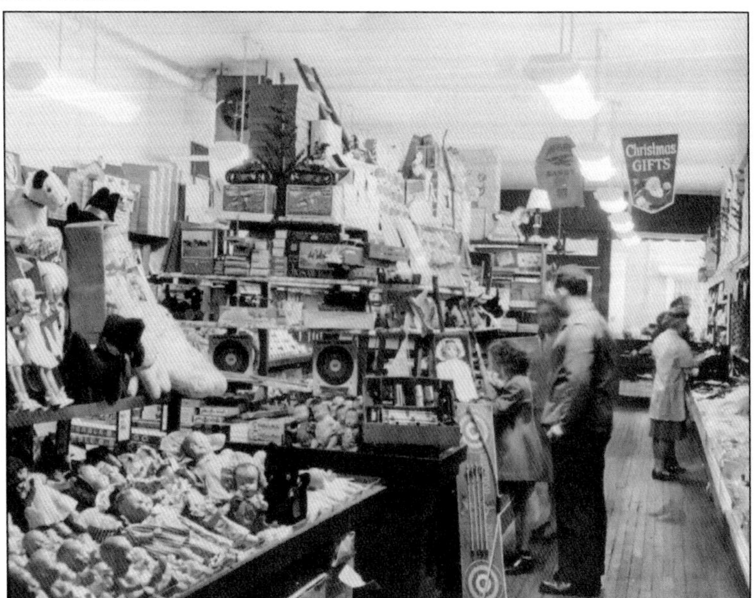

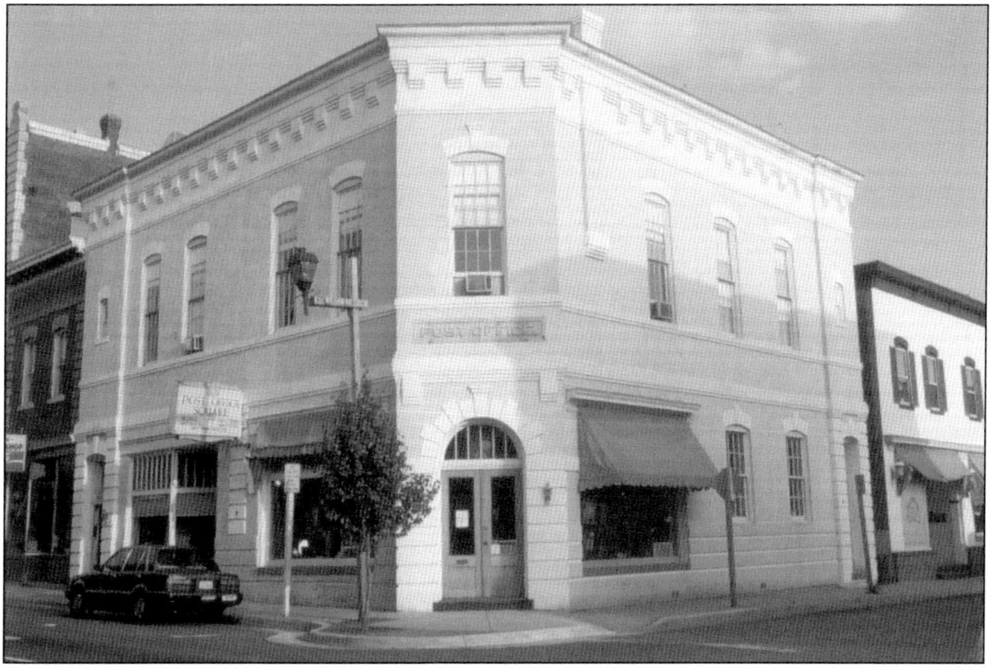

In 1985, the former post office in the Nicol Building at the corner of Center and Battle Streets was home to an antique store. What has long been residential space on the second floor was once Nicol Hall, a meeting space where residents could attend traveling shows, plays, meetings, and dances. The Connor Opera House across the street hosted the prohibitionist Carry Nation and many well-known productions.

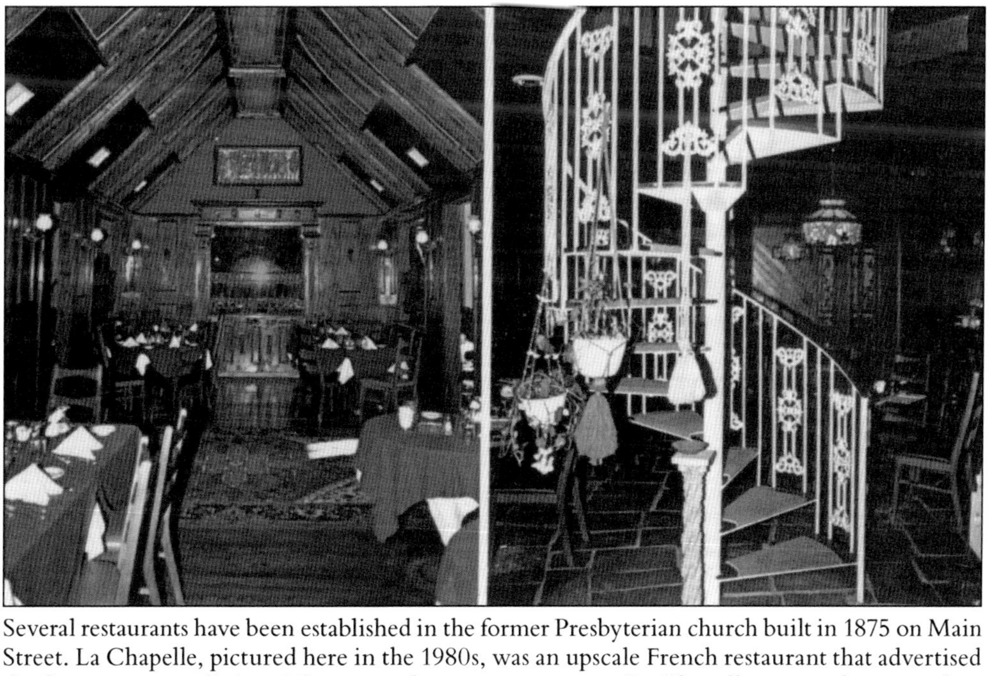

Several restaurants have been established in the former Presbyterian church built in 1875 on Main Street. La Chapelle, pictured here in the 1980s, was an upscale French restaurant that advertised the finest gourmet dining. Like past and present restaurants, La Chapelle set up a basement bar, used the upstairs for events, and advertised the original Tiffany windows.

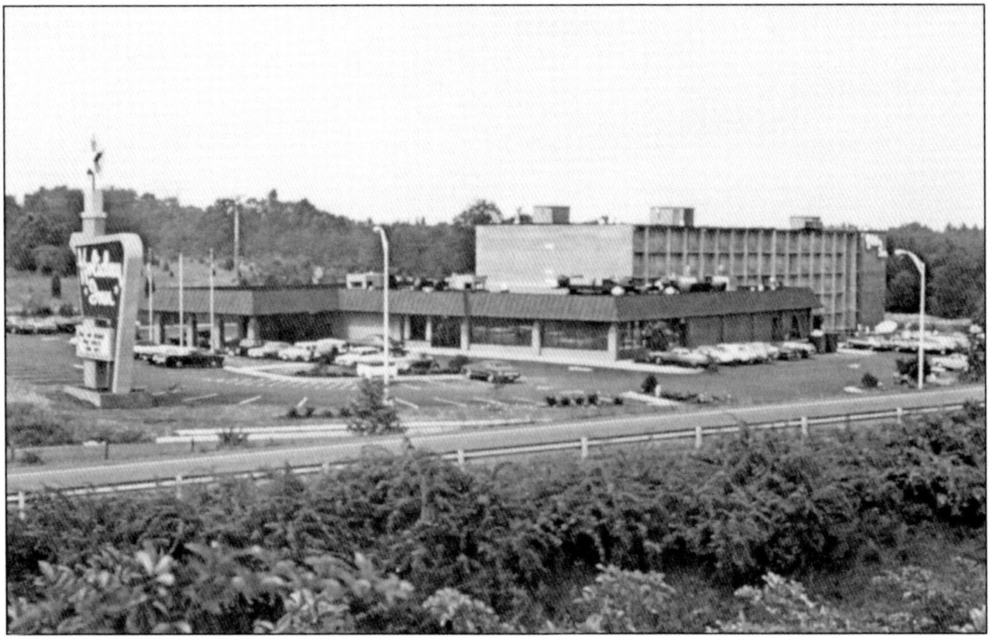

To accommodate a growing number of tourists visiting the nearby Manassas National Battlefield and business travelers visiting the new IBM plant, the Manassas Holiday Inn and many other restaurants and retail stores opened on Sudley Road in the late 1960s and early 1970s. The hotel also advertised its proximity to Dulles International and Manassas Regional Airports. (Author's collection.)

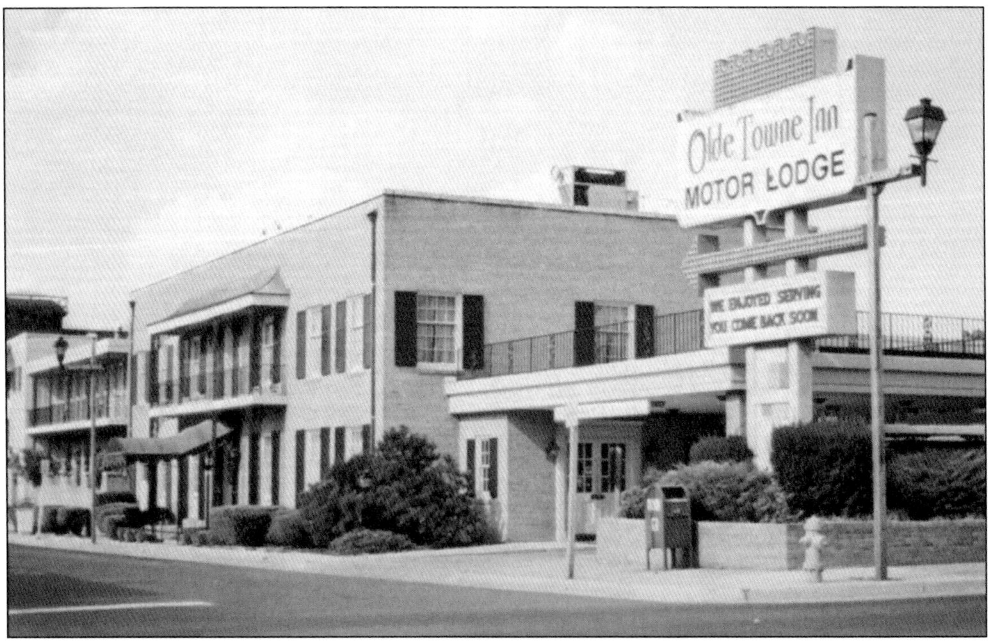

Following a long tradition of downtown hotels, the Olde Towne Inn opened in 1973 at the corner of Center and Main Streets, on the site of the old Pitts Theater and Stonewall Jackson Hotel. The inn has long served tourists and business travelers and has been rumored to be the site of supernatural activity.

Six

Community Diversions

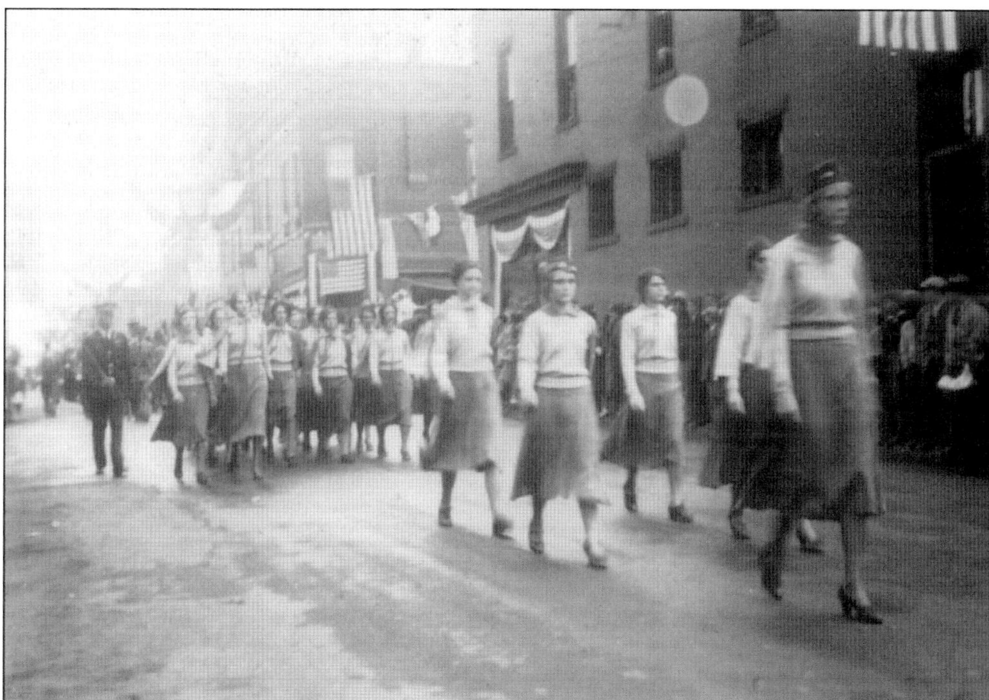

In an age before electronic devices, easy travel, and myriad entertainment options, Manassas families spent their leisure time in town. They enjoyed community events, like the 1935 Piedmont Dairy Festival (pictured), that celebrated the area's agricultural personality, musical and dramatic productions both amateur and professional, and movies, first in neighborhood businesses and then in sparkling new theaters. Citizens also formed clubs both charitable and social that helped bind the community together.

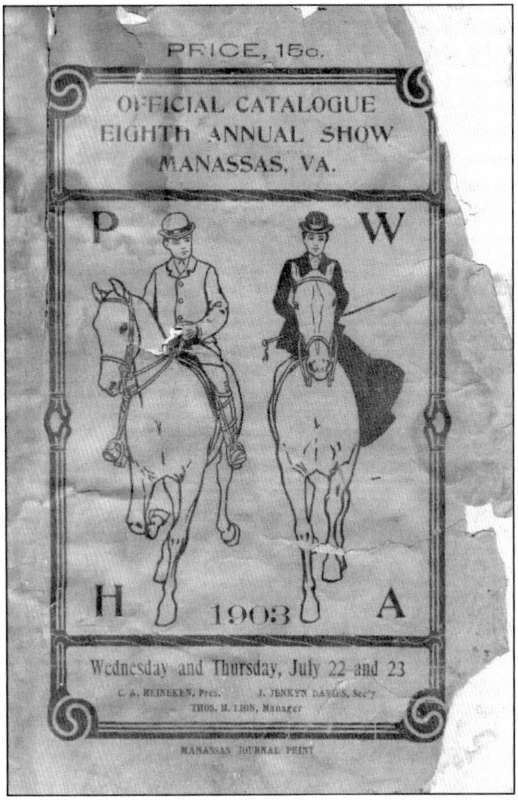

Special trains from Washington carried thousands of visitors to the annual Manassas Horse Show, which was a major social event. The shows continued from 1896 until the early 1950s with few interruptions. In later years, the Bull Run Hunt Club sponsored the show, and some years, it was held at Annaburg Manor. A separate "Colored Horse Show," which ran from 1904 till the 1930s, showcased horses owned by African Americans.

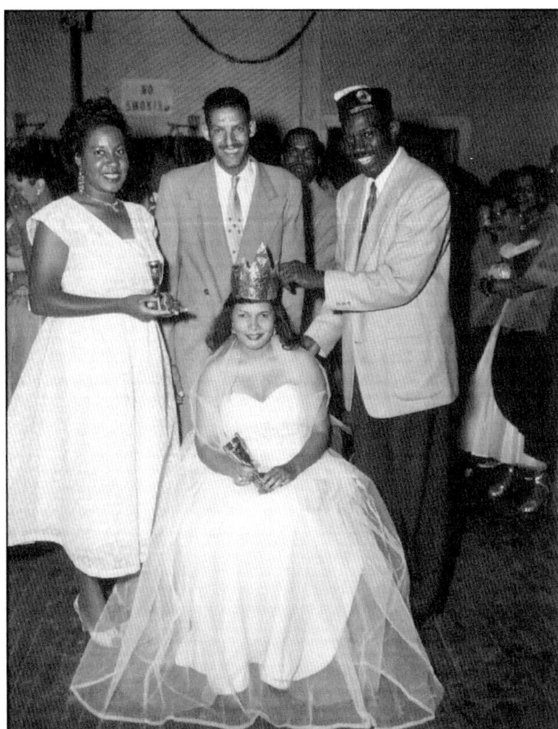

American Legion Post 114 was founded by twelve World War I veterans and four World War II veterans in 1946 when African Americans returned from war and were denied membership in white veterans organizations. Although the African American veterans received a temporary charter as a "colored" post in 1945, the "colored" designation was removed when they received a permanent charter the following year. This queen was crowned during Post 114's 1954 ball.

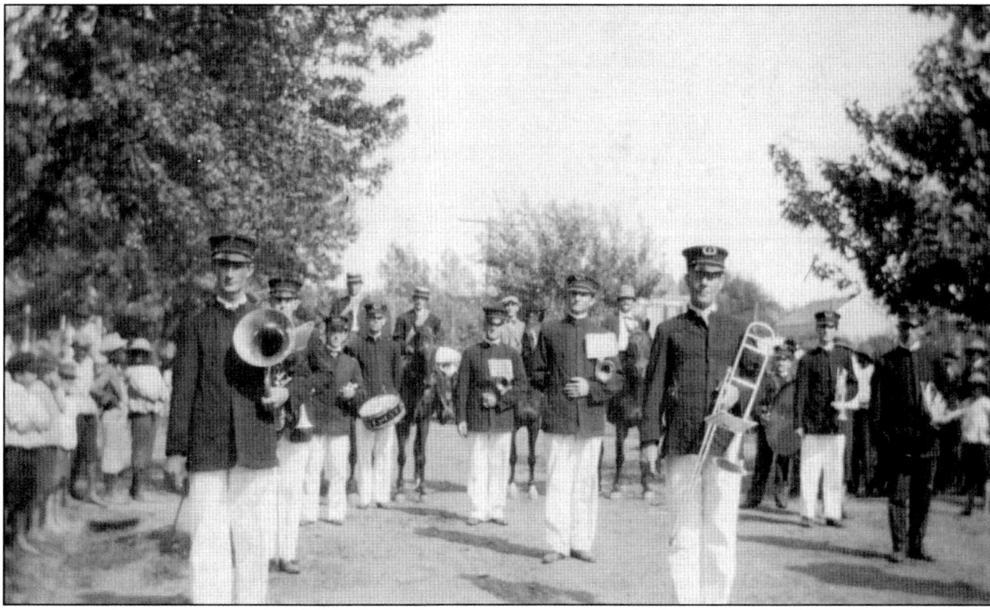

In the early 1900s, young men in the Manassas Band performed on warm summer evenings at a bandstand on the corner of Center and Main Streets. The band played popular songs of the time along with favorite melodies for an appreciative audience until darkness made it impossible for the musicians to read their notes. "The membership in this band was composed of young men who were hard working fellows. After a long day's work on the farm, in the factory, in the store or some other industry, they assembled themselves at night for long hours practicing in Nichol's Hall," the *Manassas Journal* reported. The band's director, Professor Plitt, traveled here by train from Alexandria, where the band often performed, as seen below. The band also represented Manassas in the Alexandria Washington's Birthday parade and at firemen's conventions across the state.

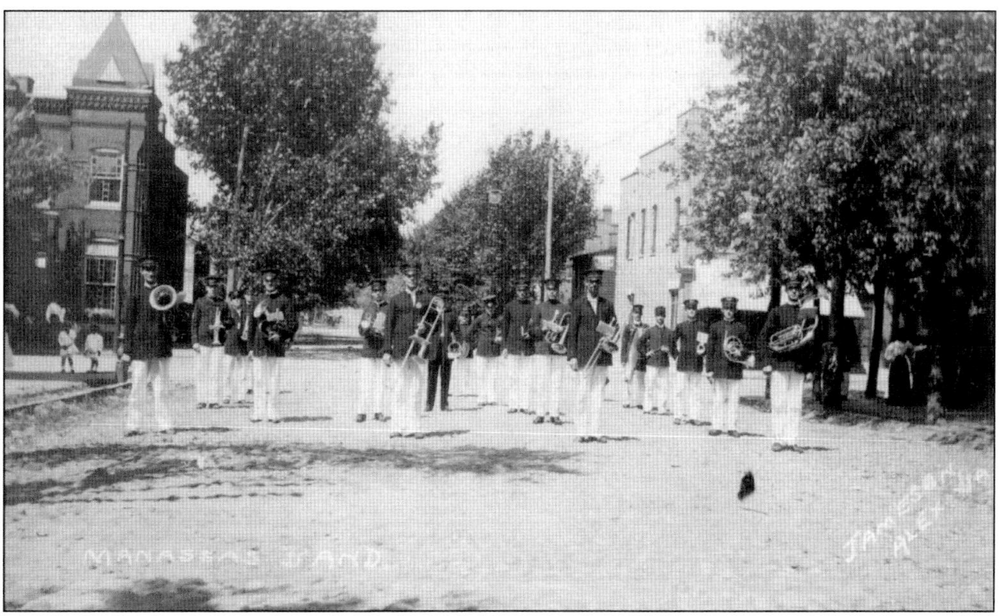

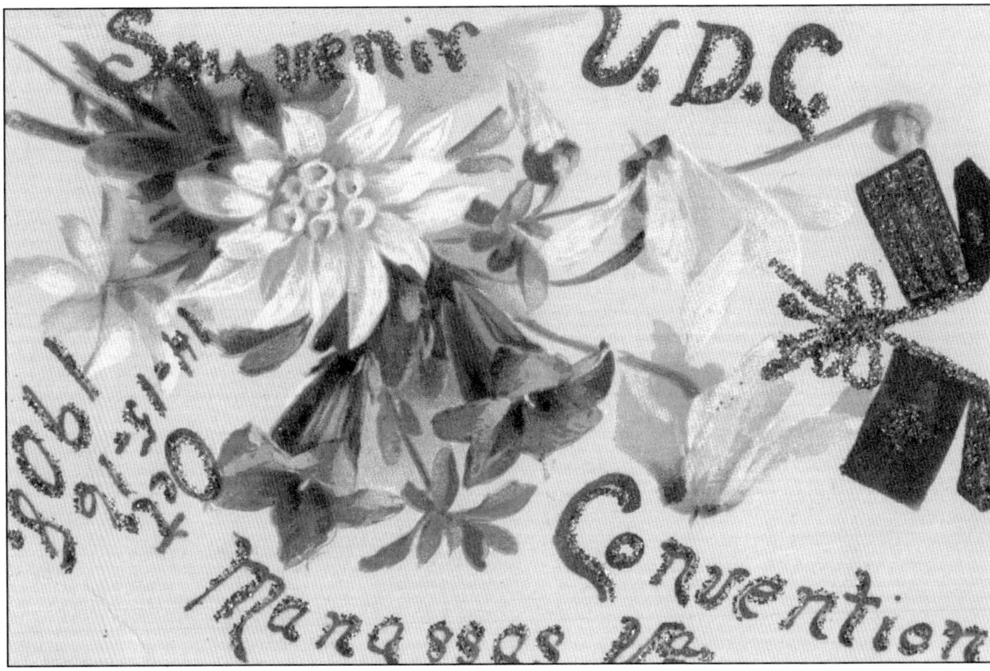

In 1867, the Ladies' Memorial Association of Manassas was formed to care for the graves of Confederate dead. The group succeeded in establishing the town's Confederate Cemetery and in erecting the brownstone monument honoring the soldiers' service, and later became the United Daughters of the Confederacy. In 1908, the chapter hosted the Virginia convention and issued these postcards as souvenirs. The UDC still owns and cares for the cemetery.

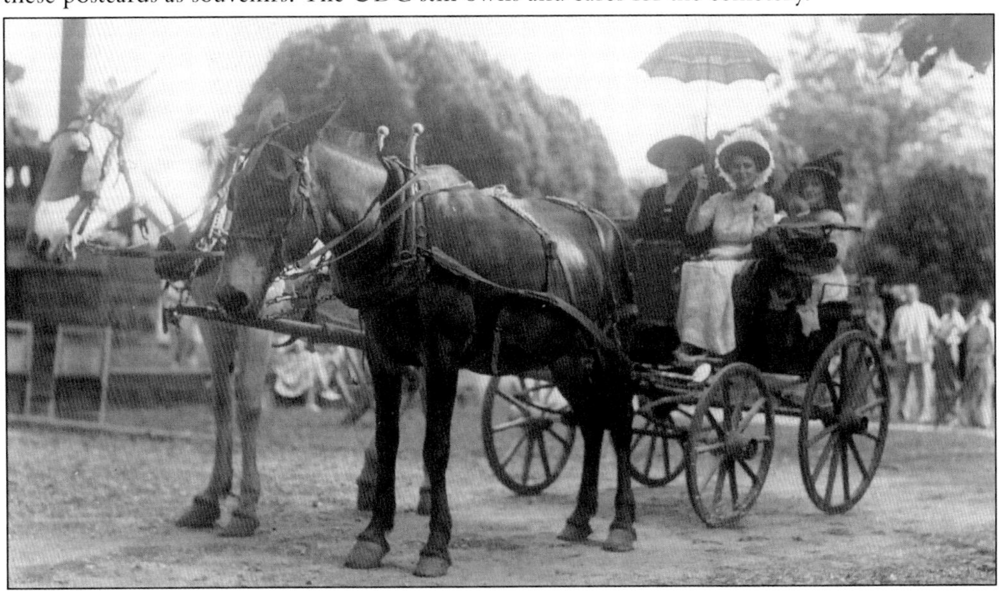

In 1937, the Junior Woman's Club of Manassas held this Gay Nineties party, a theme the club later used for fundraising and entertaining World War II troops. Through the years, women have been just as active as men in supporting community causes, through organizations like the Woman's Club, Volunteer Fire Department Auxiliary, Order of the Eastern Star, Red Cross, PTA, Bethlehem Good Housekeeping Club, and Garden Club.

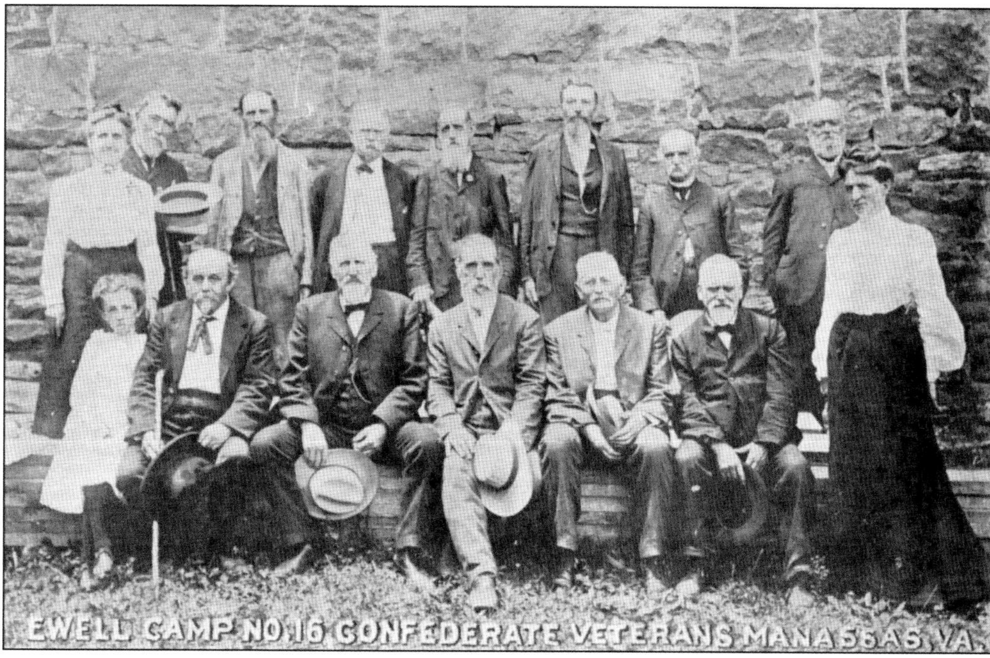

The Sons of Confederate Veterans fraternal organization was formed in 1896 to honor and preserve the history and heritage of Confederate soldiers. The Ewell camp in Manassas, pictured above about 1910, was instrumental in forming the Manassas Battlefield Corporation, which bought and preserved the crucial Henry Hill area of the battlefield. Pictured are, from left to right, (seated) Annie Brawner, John Brawner, Henry Lynn, H.A. Brown, J.P. Manuel, and Lt. B.D. Merchant; (standing) Margaret Barbour, T.O. Taylor, George Johnson, Judge William Lipscomb, unidentified, Westwood Hutchison, Dr. H.M. Clarkson, Robert Hooe, and Florence Lion. The parade seen below rumbles down Grant Avenue on the Fourth of July in 1920. Cars in the parade navigate dirt roads while pedestrians in the background stroll on wooden sidewalks.

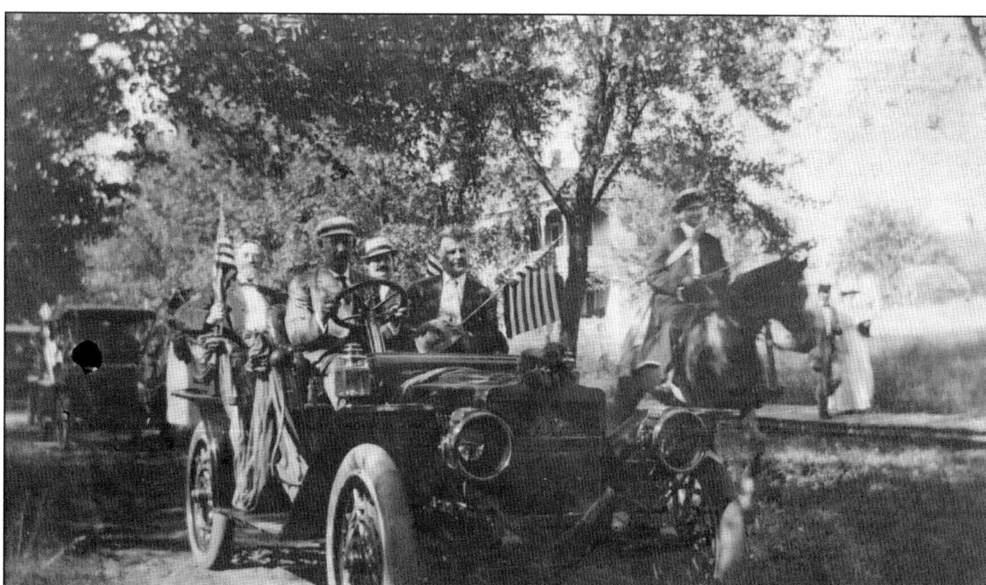

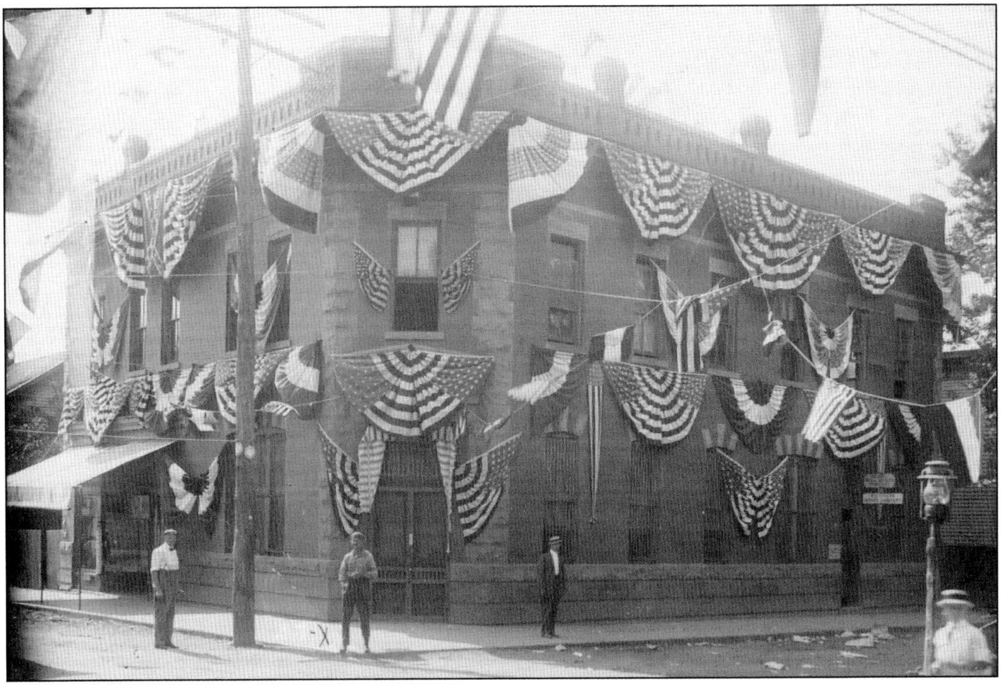

Citizens enlisted the Washington Decorating Company to transform Manassas into a patriotic showcase for the 1911 National Jubilee of Peace. The company came to town laden with flags and bunting for everyone. The *Manassas Democrat* asked citizens for "elaborate decorations on every business and house." Here, the Peoples National Bank is decked out for the occasion.

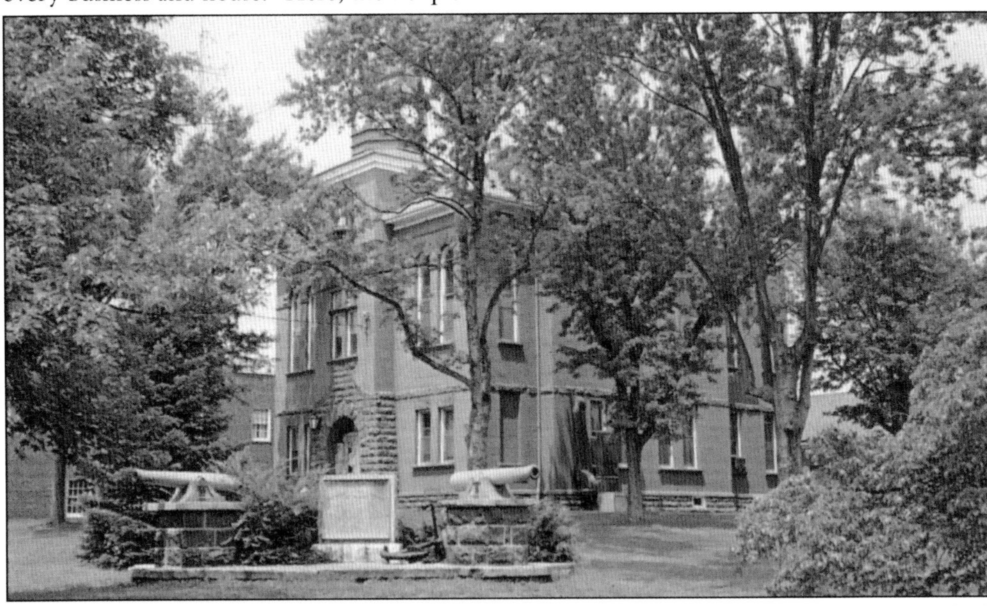

Citizens remembered the significance of the jubilee with the monument pictured here, which was unveiled on the courthouse grounds in 1915. It contains two 400-pound Civil War brass cannon and two anchors and chains from the New York Navy Yard that were donated by the then assistant secretary of the Navy Franklin D. Roosevelt. The base is made of locally quarried red sandstone.

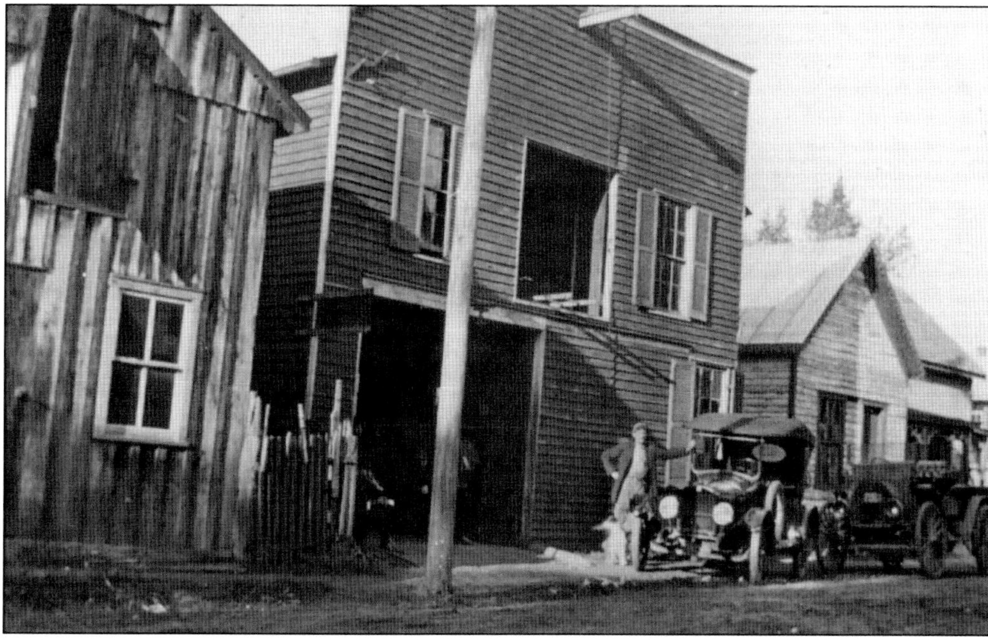

When Model Ts began chugging along local roads and townspeople began venturing to out-of-the-way places, I.J. Randall was ready to help fix their cars. Randall, shown here, was an enterprising blacksmith who began tinkering with cars and opened his garage on the corner of Quarry and Main Streets in 1911.

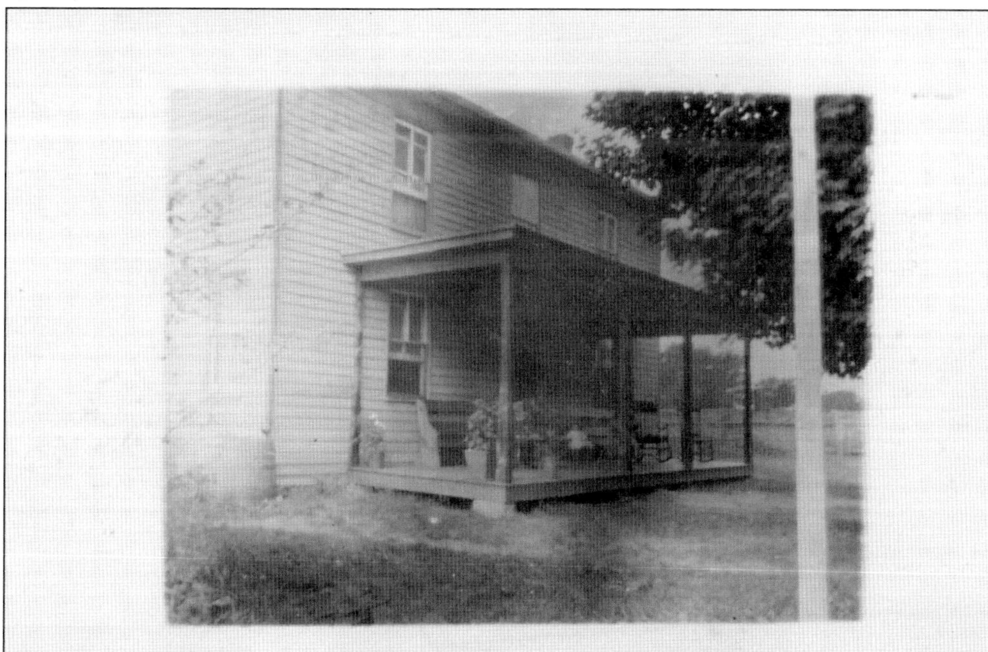

The advent of inexpensive cameras and the invention of new photograph processing in the early 1900s made it possible for amateur photographers to take pictures of their homes or families, have them mounted on a postcard backing, and send them through the mail. This image shows the Sullivan family home near Independent Hill, just outside Manassas on Dumfries Road.

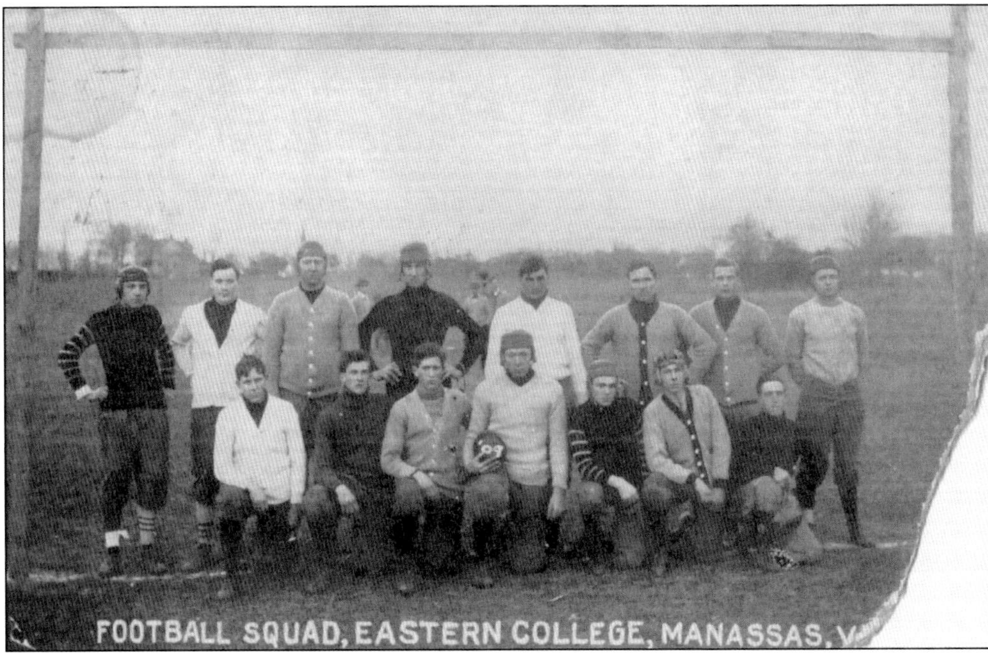

School football games were a popular entertainment and front-page news in the small town of Manassas. This 1909 Eastern College team played against George Washington University, Georgetown University, Mount St. Mary's College, and the Virginia Military Institute in regular-season games and faced the Maryland Agricultural College on Thanksgiving Day.

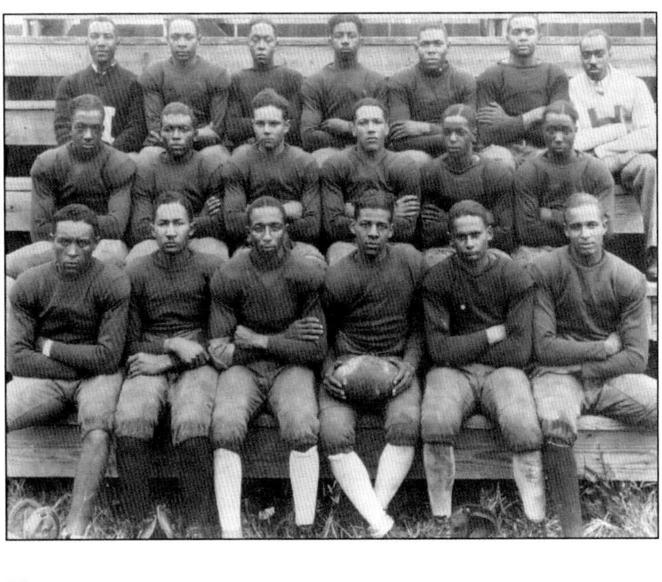

The Manassas Industrial School fielded a football team as early as 1915, and although the town was segregated, the teams earned a loyal following. In the early years, the team played historically black colleges including Howard University and Morgan State University, but this 1927 team and others also played against segregated high schools. Manassas Regional High School, the public regional school for African Americans, continued a strong football tradition.

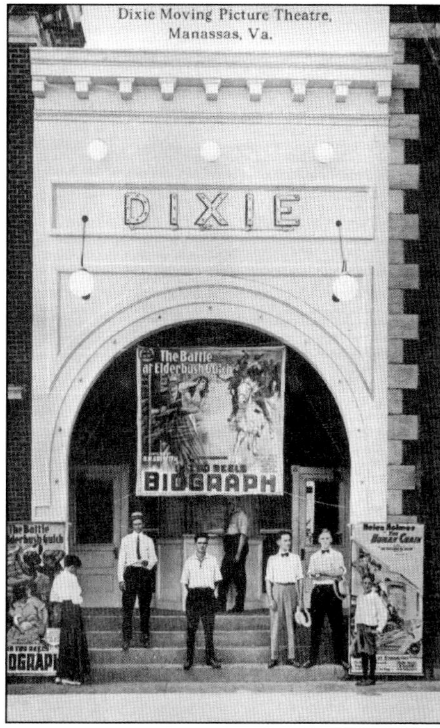

Before the Dixie Theater opened in a narrow Main Street space—where moviegoers sat eight to a row—residents watched films, concerts, and plays at the Conner Opera House. The silent 1913 short Western *The Battle at Elderbush Gulch* was showing when this postcard was sold in about 1915.

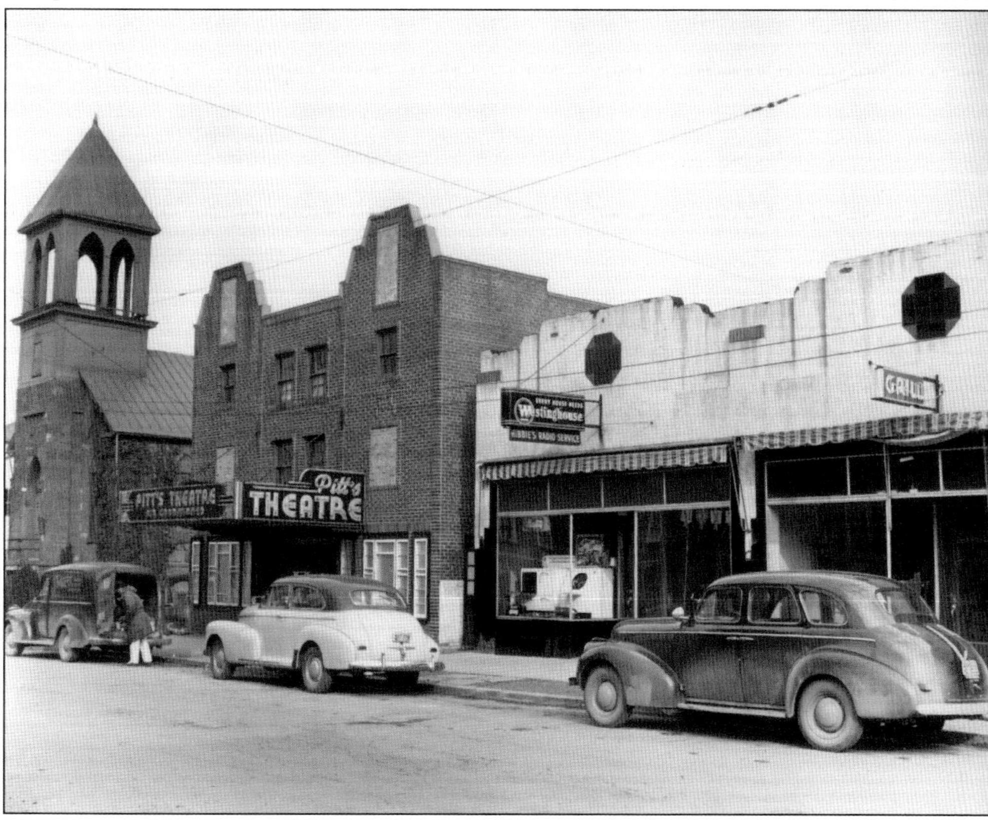

When the spacious new Pitts Theatre opened just up the block on Main Street in 1936, the *Manassas Journal* reported that "it is expected that his new playhouse will draw southward many who have herefore been traveling into Washington where they have millions of parking worries." In 1950, the theater was set on fire by a young man concealing his theft of a Shirley Temple movie reel.

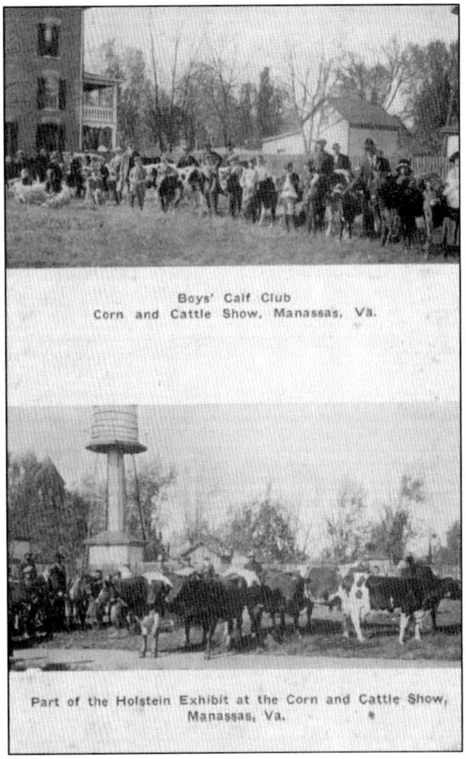

Pictured at left, the first calf club in Virginia was organized by the Agricultural School director and boys first exhibited their calves during this October 1914 show. The *Country Gentleman* magazine reported that "the Piedmont section of Virginia is destined to be a great cattle region and the boys there are going to become great cattle raisers, if the parade of boys and girls and calves thronging the streets of Manassas signal anything." In the photograph below, Louise Carter and Douglas Morris lead a rehearsal parade at Liberia Plantation for the 1936 Piedmont Dairy Festival, an annual event celebrating the county's major industry in the 1930s. The festival crowned dairy princesses and a queen from the 11-county surrounding area, included a "Milk Through the Ages" pageant, a parade along the "Milky Way," a carnival, and a coronation ball.

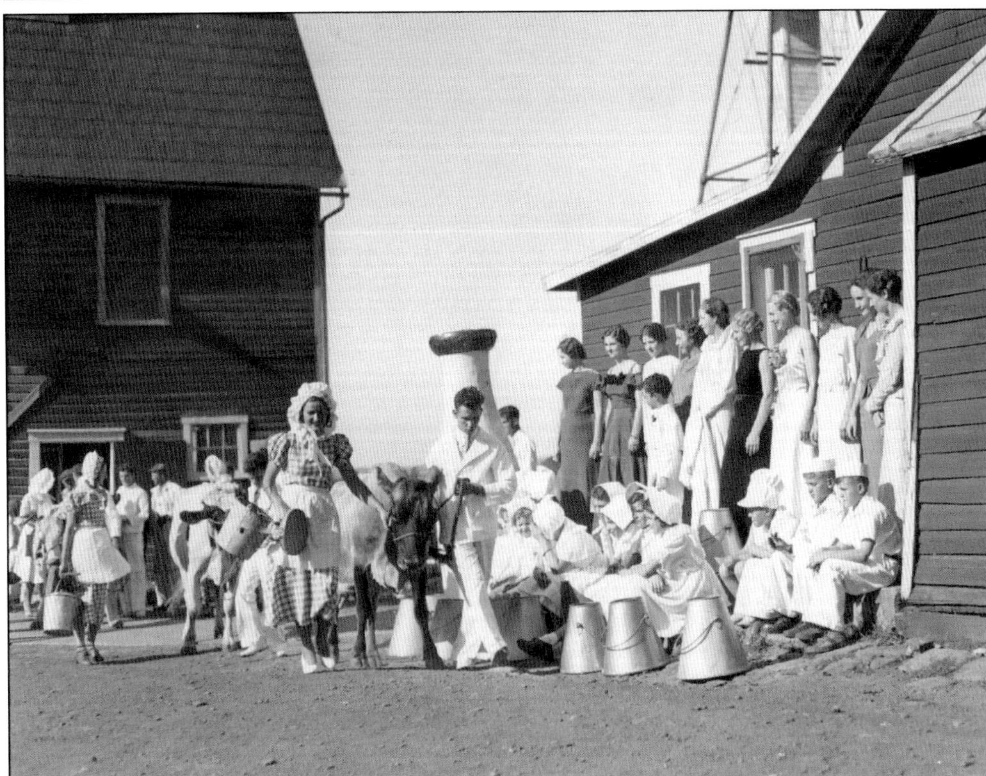

The Manassas Kiwanis Club sponsored the 1935 Constitution Day Tree Dedication, which is pictured at right. The club began in 1924 and has played a part in helping solve many town problems. The group supplied Christmas cheer to the unfortunate, sent a number of crippled and sick children to hospitals, served luncheons to undernourished children in the public school, lobbied for town bond issues, erected highway signs, and entertained farmers.

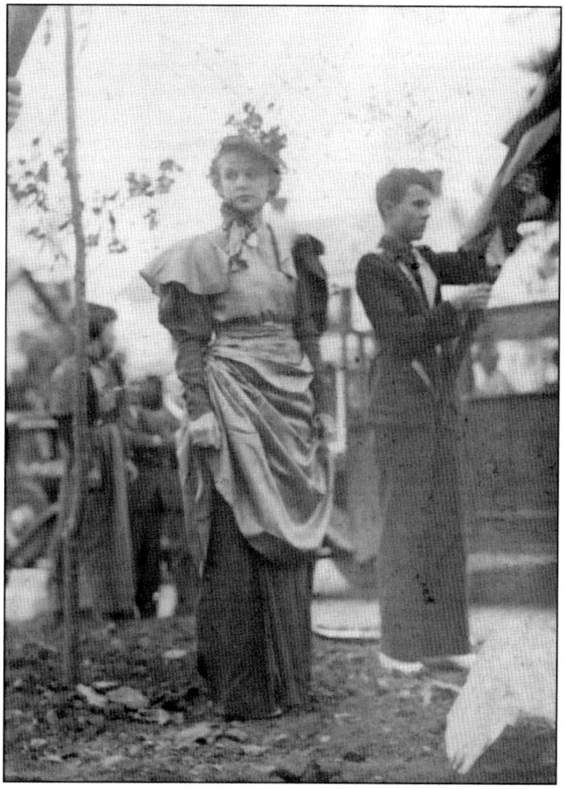

Pharmacist George Cocke and Harry Davis, who served as mayor for 42 years, were among these Knights Templar, whose lodge was formed in 1868; the Knights' purpose was to uphold Christian faith. The Manasseh Freemason Lodge was chartered in 1875, and after the town's 1905 fire destroyed its meeting hall, wealthy Alexandria brewer and Manassas philanthropist Robert Portner donated $5,000 to construct a new lodge on Center Street.

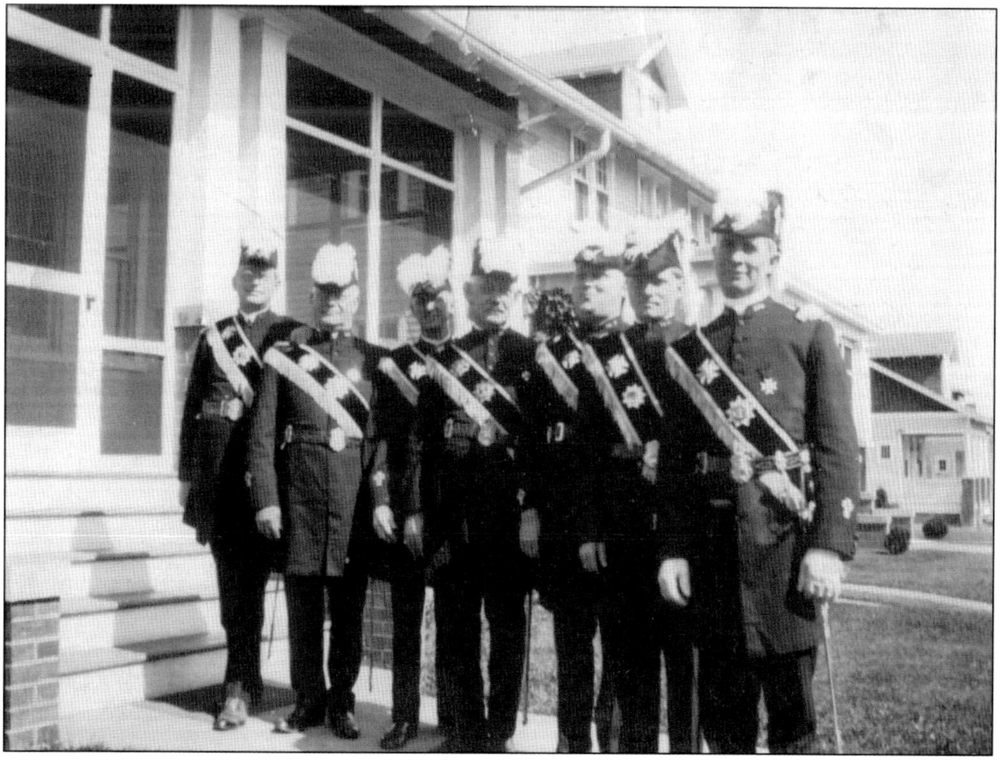

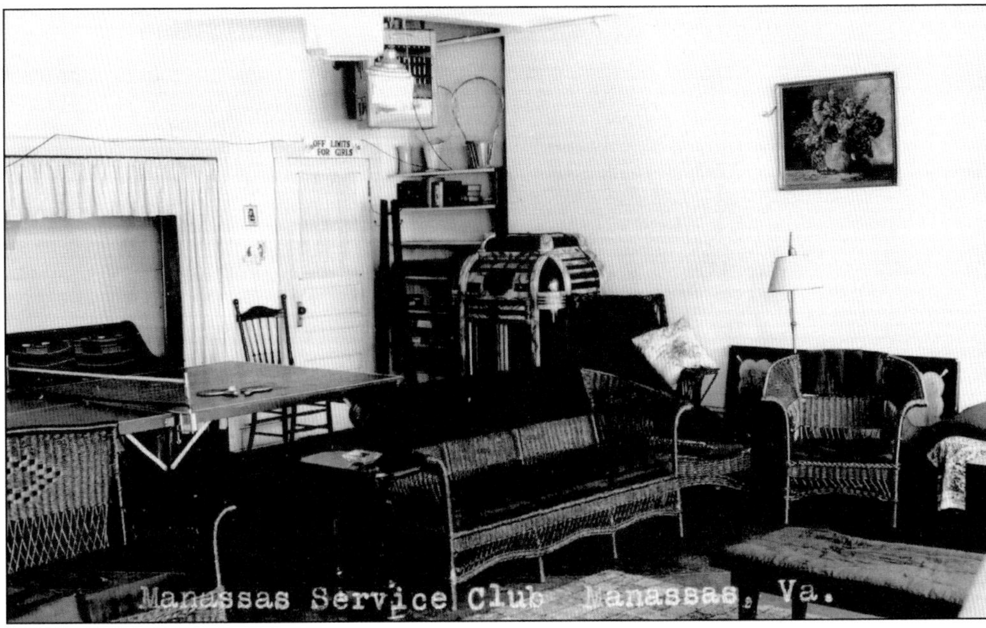

Walser Rohr, whose husband, Edgar, owned Rohr's 5¢ to $1 Store, formed the Manassas Service Club during World War II. The group was a branch of the United Service Organizations, which still provides programs, services, and live entertainment to US troops. The club used this Main Street lounge to offer food and companionship to service members far from home who were either stationed nearby or passing through on the train.

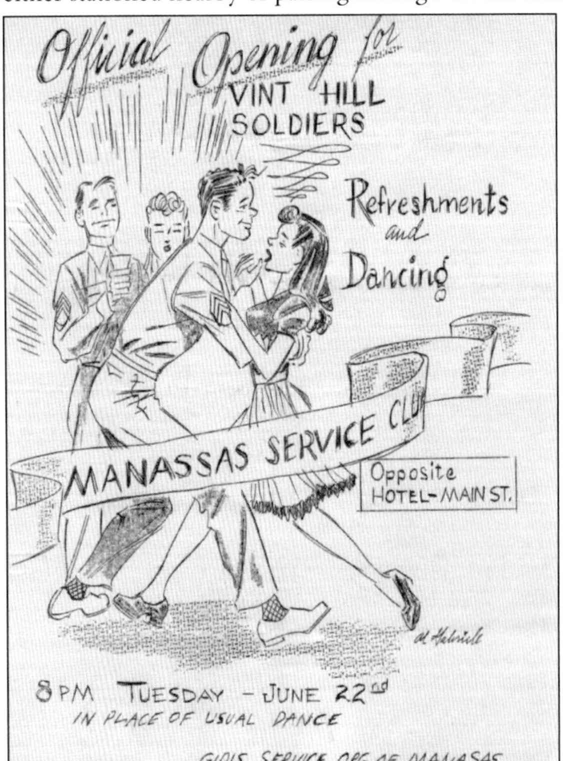

The Girls' Service Organization, open to younger members of the Service Club, assisted with events like these World War II dances. Dances were often geared toward soldiers from nearby Vint Hill Farm Station, where 2,000 US Army personnel and civilians intercepted and interpreted coded messages during the war. The station's groundbreaking work was a model for intelligence gathering until it was closed in the 1990s.

Seven

SUNDAY STROLLS

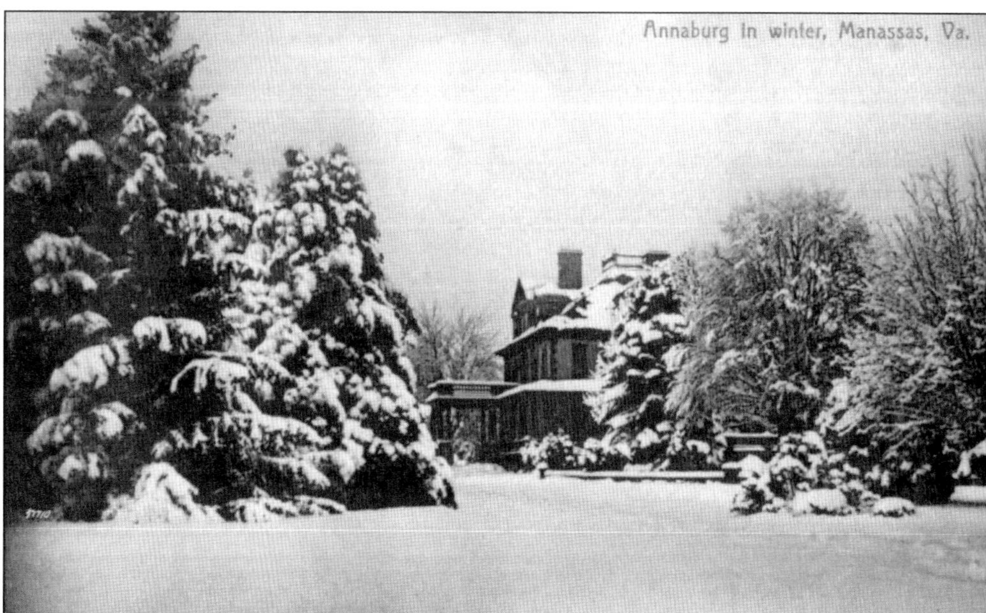

In the days when a skate on a frozen pond or a romantic stroll by the swan pond were the ultimate in entertainment, Robert Portner's Annaburg estate was a frequent destination for townspeople. Portner's generosity enabled many of his neighbors to enjoy what was essentially a cultivated town park long before public parks existed in the area.

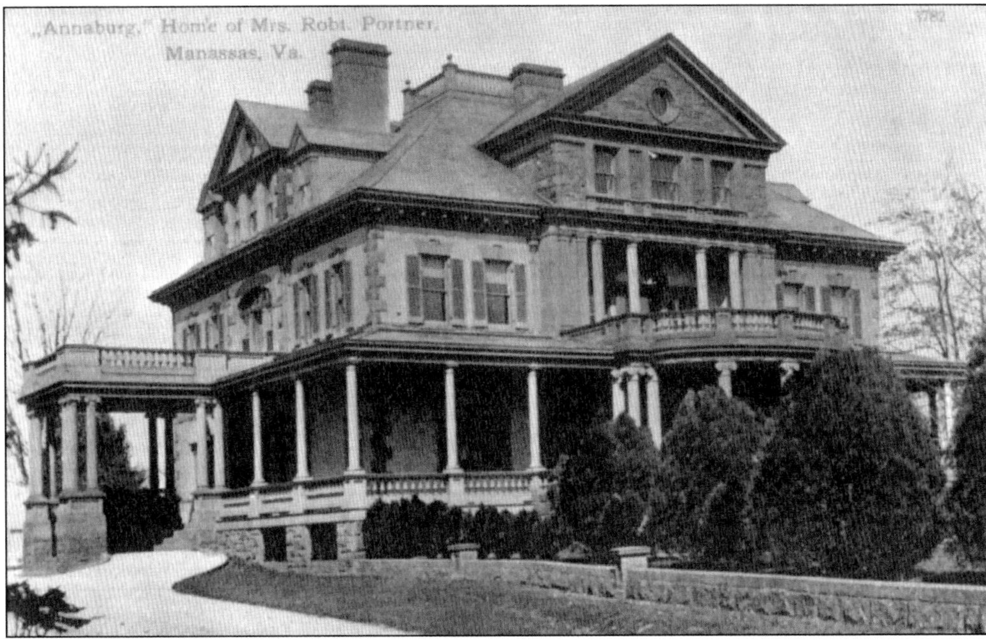

While visiting the Mathis family in Manassas, Robert Portner, the Prussian-born entrepreneur and founder of the Portner brewery in Alexandria, decided to purchase property and build Annaburg, a legendary summer retreat named for his wife, Anna. He considered the 1892 house—with its 35 rooms, electricity, and mechanical air-conditioning of his own invention—his escape from the city. Twenty-five landscaped acres and a park of luxurious trees, some of which still stand, surrounded the house on Maple Street. The 2,000-acre estate included a deer park, fountains, a greenhouse, a vineyard, a swimming pool, and the 1825 Liberia Plantation, which he operated as a dairy farm. In the 1960s, two wings flanked the house when it became a nursing home, but they have since been removed. The original gatehouse, now a private residence, stands one block away.

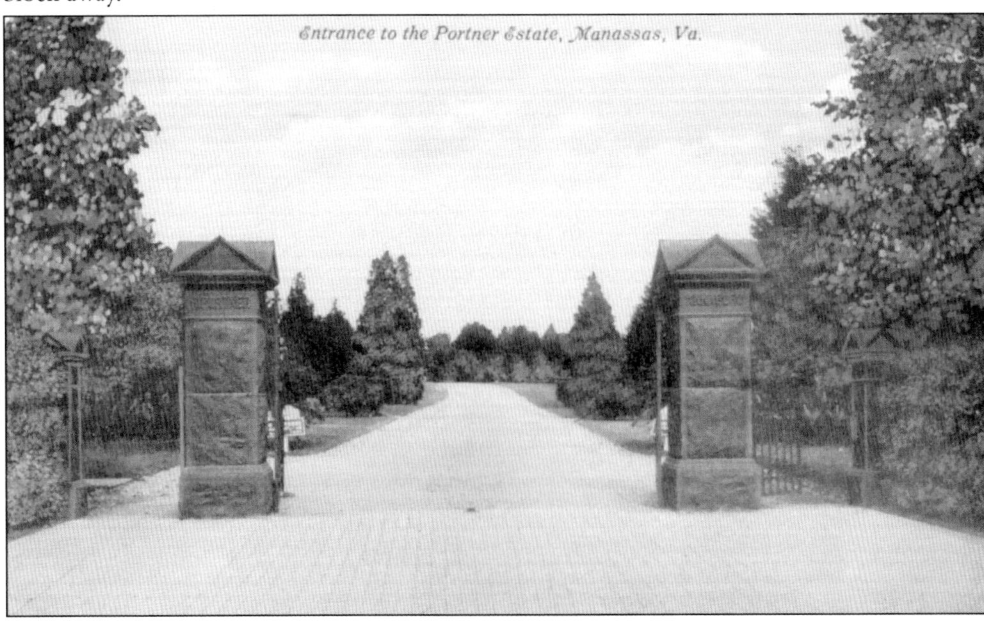

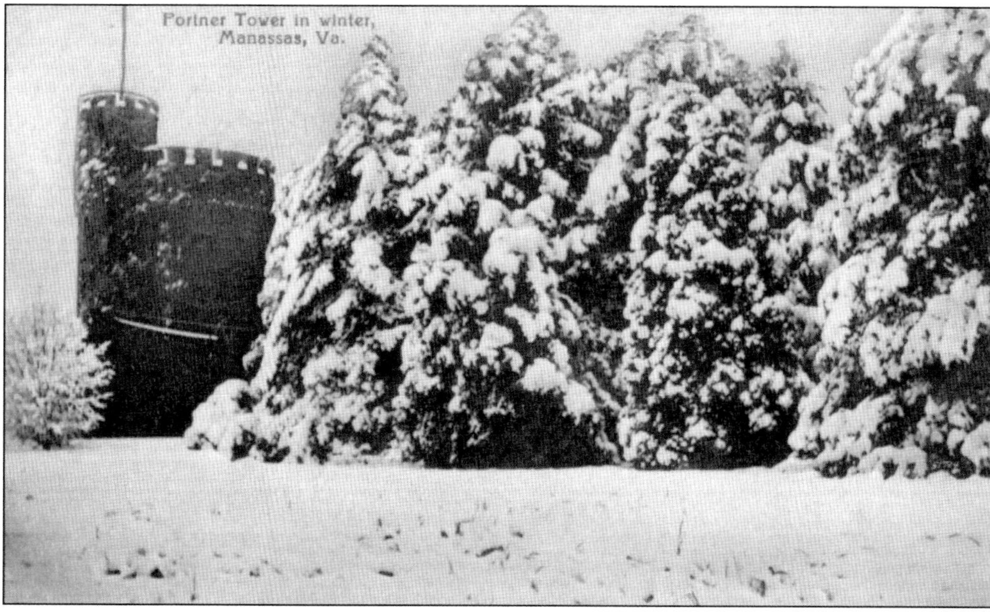

Annaburg hosted the town's Piedmont Dairy Festival for many years, and invited guests might enjoy Fourth of July fireworks, a peek inside its horse stables or greenhouse, or even church baptisms in the pond. The setting often inspired romance as well. "Boy and girl would stroll through the park and maybe hide away in the summer house for a little romance," Ethel Byrd remembered years later.

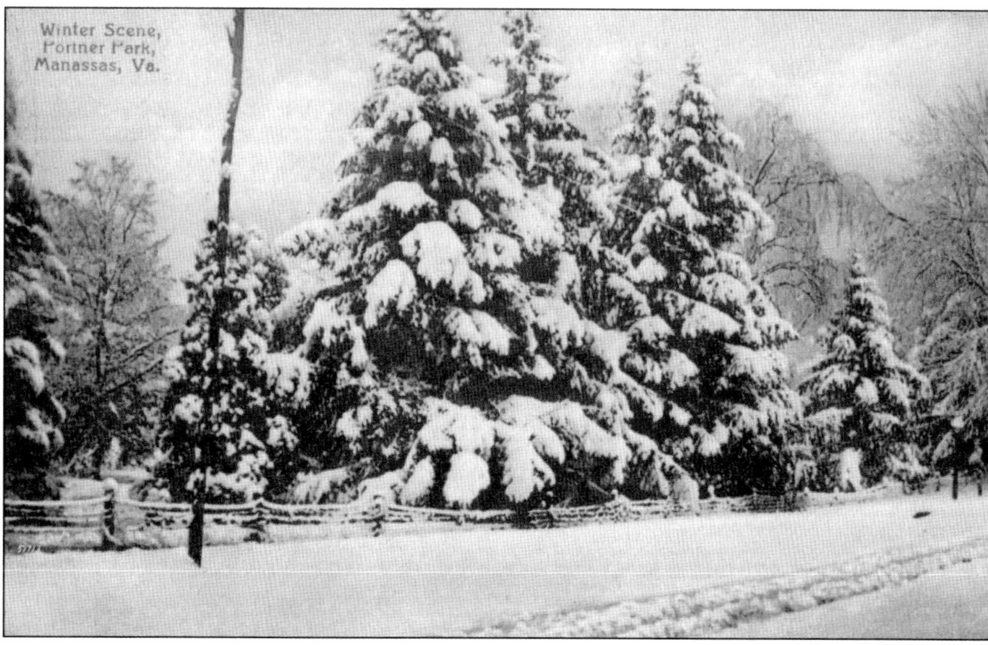

The caption on this c. 1915 image describes Annaburg as a park, rather than a private home. Although the Portner family had always welcomed friends and neighbors to their estate, its grounds were a popular destination after Robert and Anna Portner passed away and the house was no longer occupied. Residents recalled the grounds as a place to stroll, take photographs, and skate on the frozen ponds in winter.

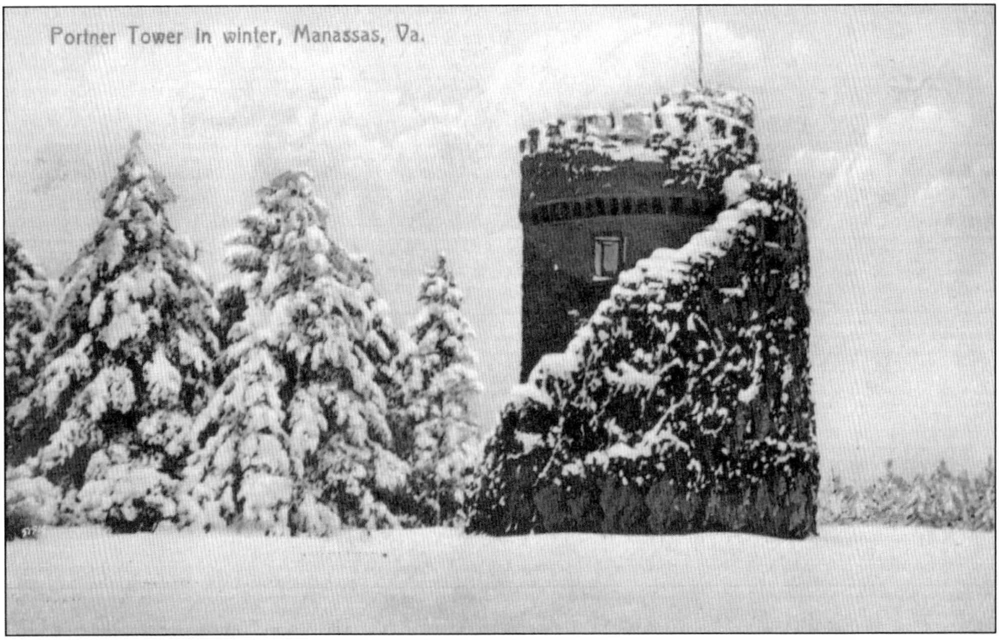

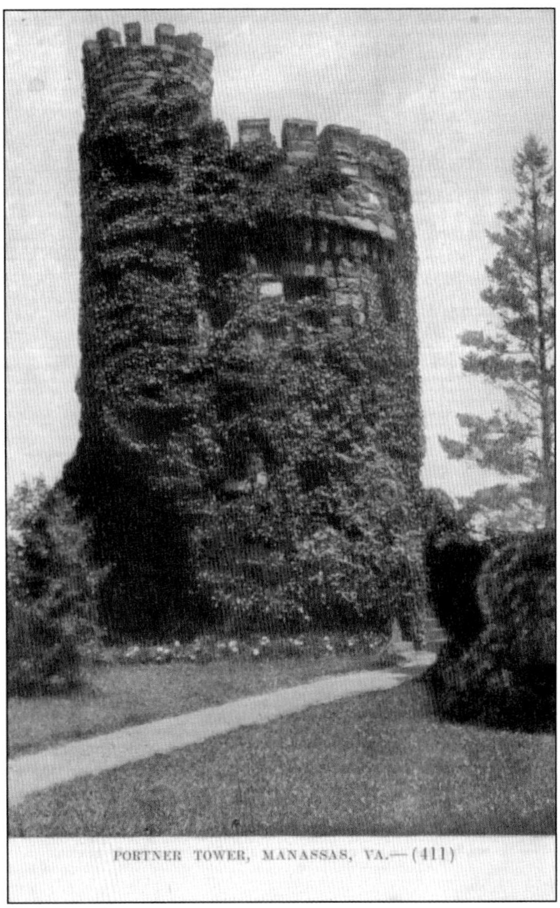

The ivy-covered stone tower, resembling a medieval stone folly or ruin, was a landmark on the Annaburg estate. The *Washington Post* reported that it was a replica of an old tower Anna Portner admired on her many trips to Europe with her husband. Thirty feet tall and completed even before the mansion, it served "mostly as a museum," housing "bits of cannons and cannon balls and other residue of the battlefield near-by which had been dug up by farm machinery," but its top was "sought as an elevated beer garden" during the summer. Other accounts say the tower was used to store wine produced from the estate's vineyards, mugs, and curios. The tower was demolished in the late 1970s.

Robert Portner's casket lies inside Annaburg before a family portrait. When Porter died in 1906, he left a $1.9 million estate and generous contributions, including $5,000 to the Manasseh Lodge of Masons to build a Masonic Hall, $5,000 to improve Manassas streets, and $5,000 to a trust fund charged with caring for the poor, with a provision that one-third of the money should go to "the poor colored citizens."

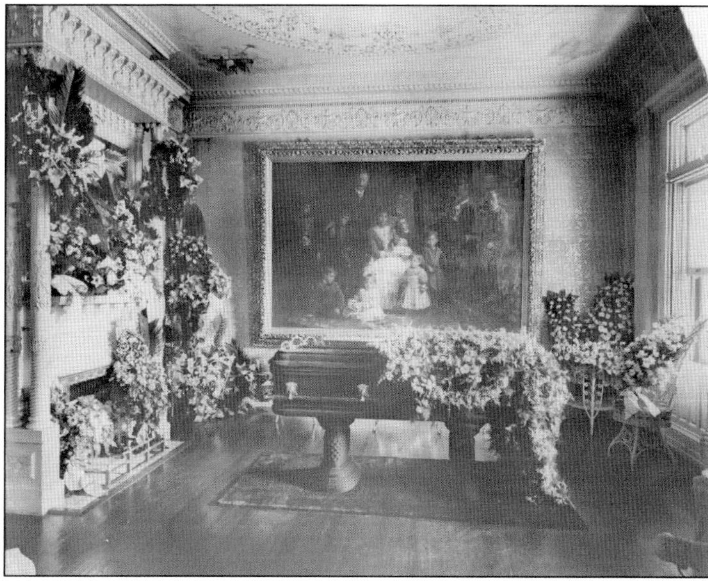

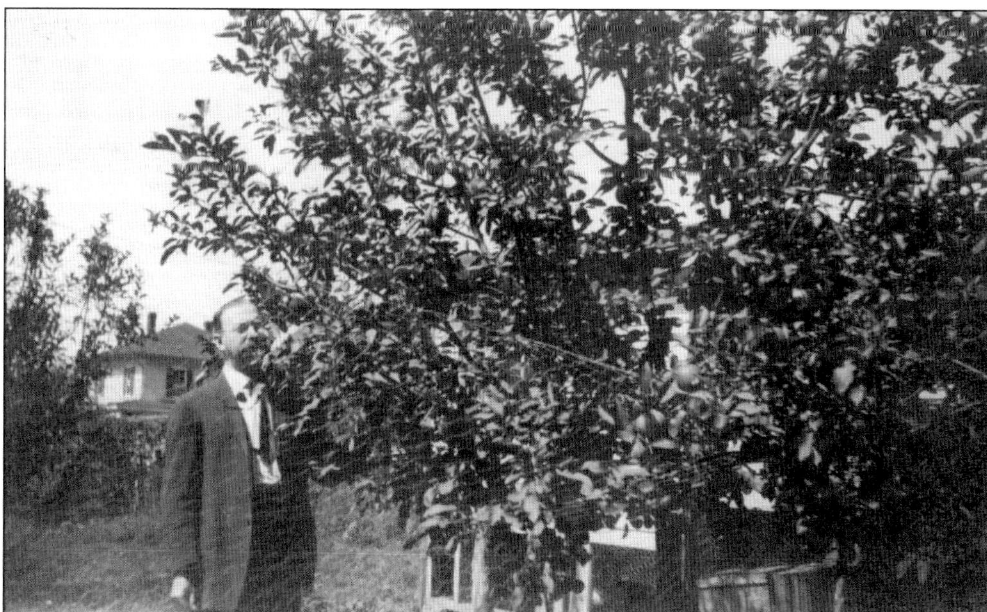

Clover Hill, the Johnson family farm, was established in 1770 in what is now the Wellington area and first grew grains before becoming a well-known dairy farm in 1900 that later shipped milk to Washington. The family farm was sold to developers in 1987, but the slave quarters and family cemetery remain. Here, the third of five Joseph Johnsons in the family works in his fruit orchards in 1913.

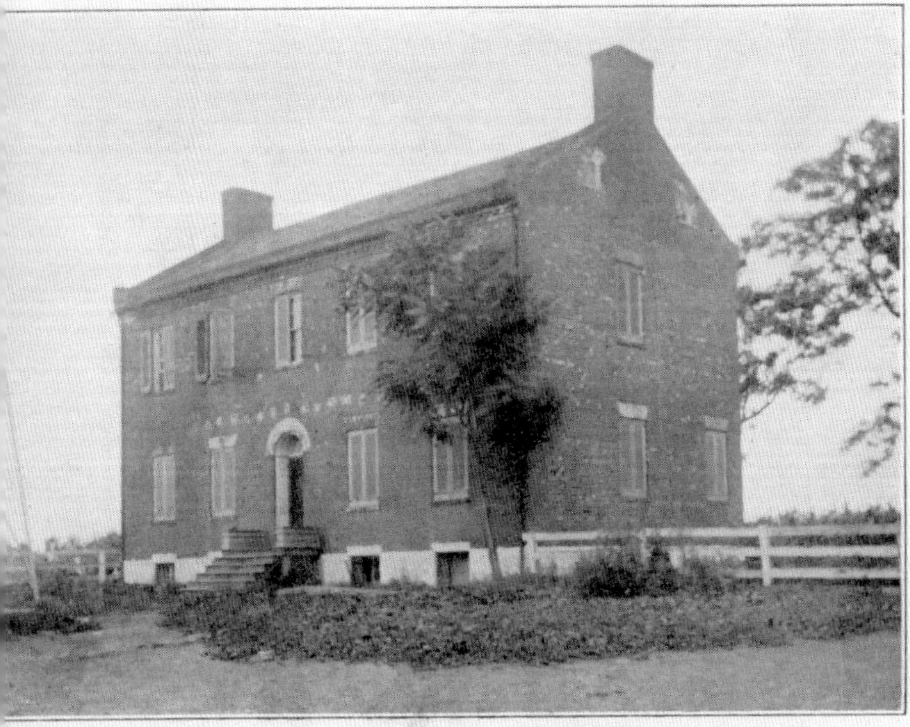

IBERIA MANSION, MANASSAS, VA., GEN'L BEAUREGARD'S HEADQUARTERS, JULY '61.

By about 1910, when this postcard was produced, Liberia was known as the dairy farm on part of Robert Portner's Annaburg estate, but the house held a long and significant place in history. Built in 1825, Liberia was a successful 1,600-acre plantation that cultivated corn, wheat, and oats and had a post office, store, and boarding school for boys on site. By the time the Civil War began, Liberia was the largest slaveholding plantation in Prince William County, with nearly 90 slaves. Confederate general P.G.T. Beauregard and his troops occupied the house in 1861, when Confederate president Jefferson Davis visited. Union general Irvin McDowell and his troops occupied the house in 1862 when President Lincoln visited. After its time as a dairy farm, Liberia became the home of I.J. and Hilda Breeden, who donated the house and land to the City of Manassas in 1986. Located between Portner and Mathis Avenues, the house is open for special events.

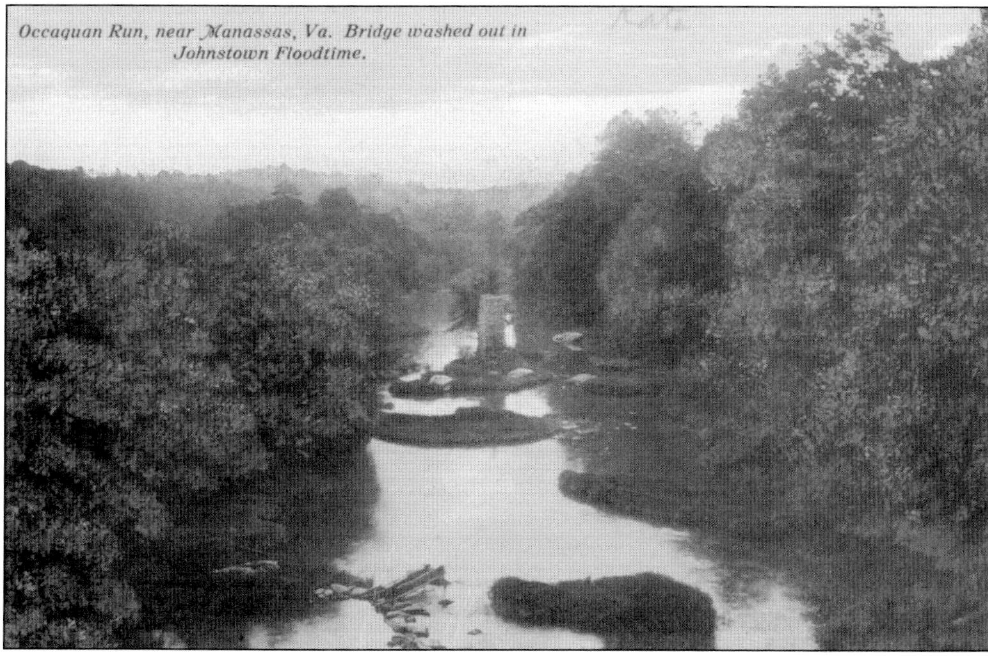

Known as the Johnstown Flood for the Pennsylvania town ravaged by several fatal floods, the March 1936 flood also caused substantial damage in Virginia. The area experienced heavy snowfalls that year, and the snowmelt, combined with six inches of rain in two days, caused the Occoquan River to overflow and wash away a wooden bridge.

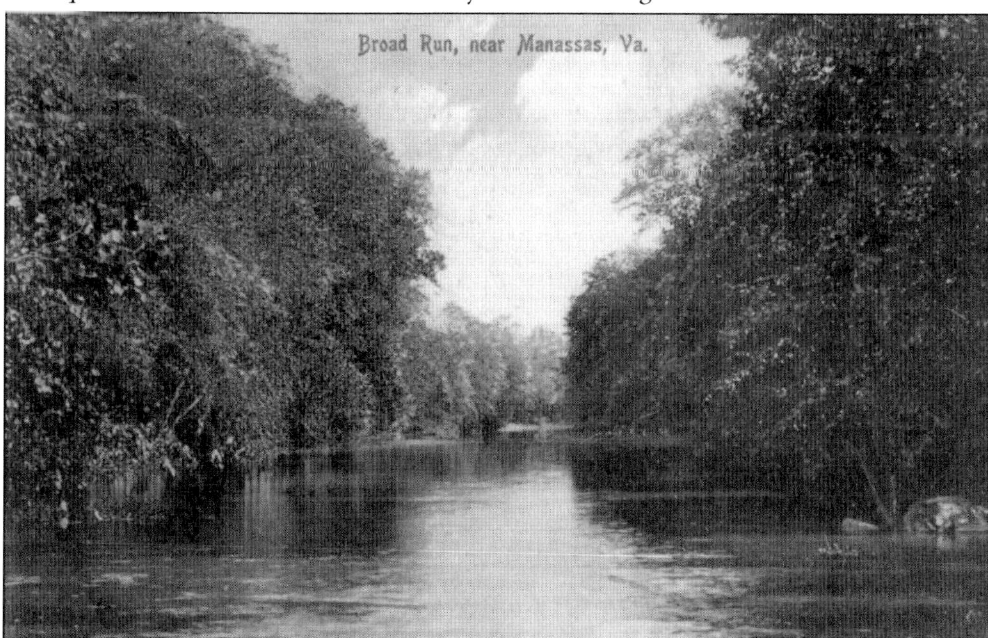

The waters of Broad Run powered Milford Mills, its banks sheltered camps, and its proximity to the Orange & Alexandria Railroad line made it a heavily guarded waterway during the Civil War. In later years, the stream that flows from the Occoquan River and winds through Manassas, Bristow, and Brentsville became a popular spot for fishing and church baptisms.

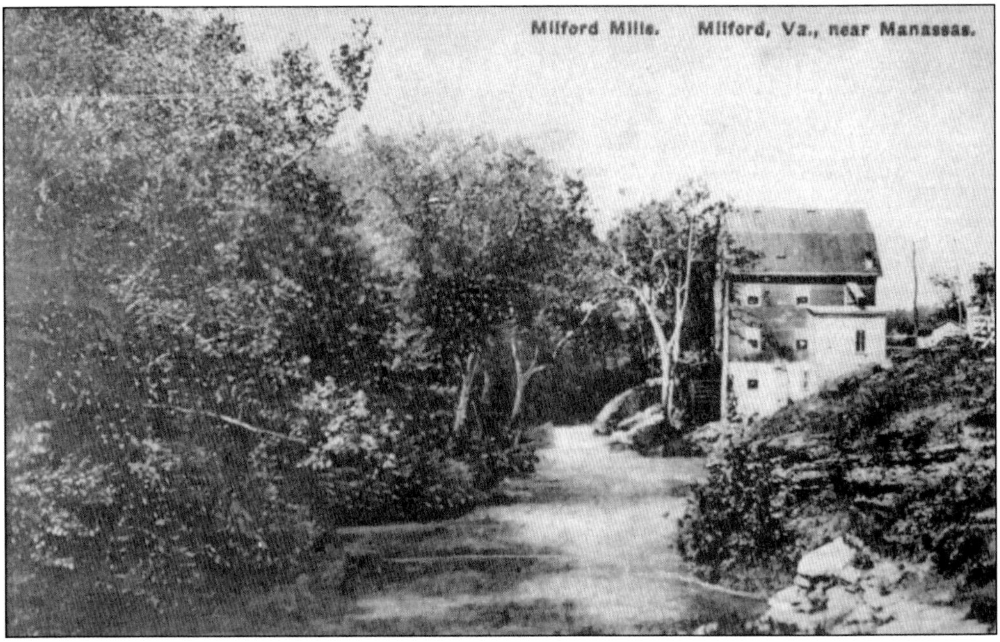

Where the Broad Run stream naturally pooled—near present-day Route 28 in Bristow—enterprising millers harnessed waterpower to build a gristmill in the 1770s. William Weir of Liberia Plantation bought Milford Mill in 1839, ran its post office until 1852, and supervised the mill's production of as much as 110 barrels of flour, 10,125 bushels of meal, and 6,500 pounds of animal feed each year. During the Civil War, Weir's daughter Julia stored her household goods there until they were carried off by Union troops. The Union army later promised not to destroy the mill so slaves could continue grinding cornmeal for their food. The mill prospered after the war until its last owner, the Manassas Milling Company, sold the property in the 1930s, and it became a family farm. The mill was torn down in 1960.

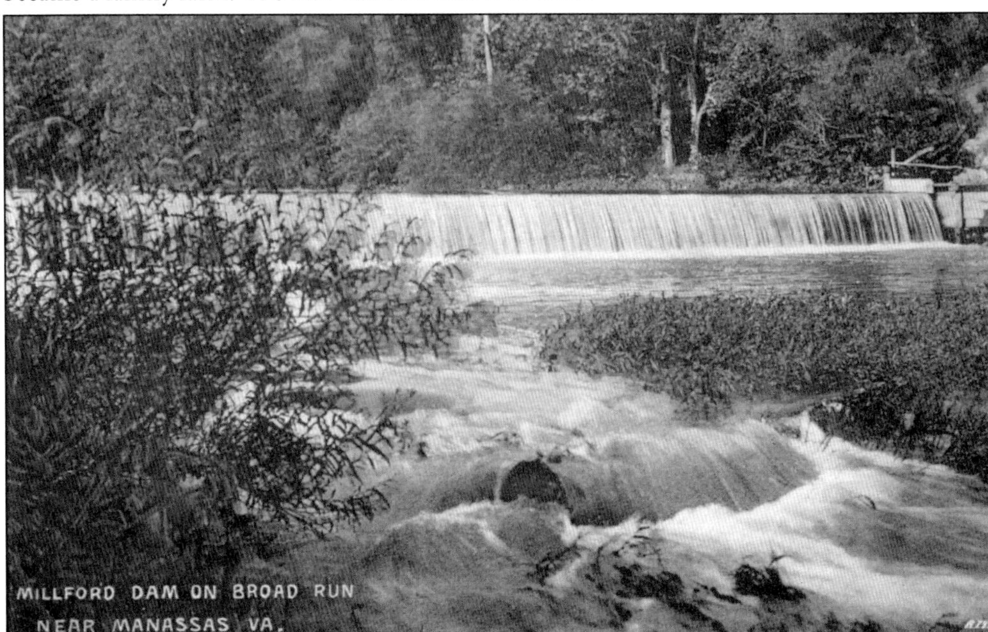

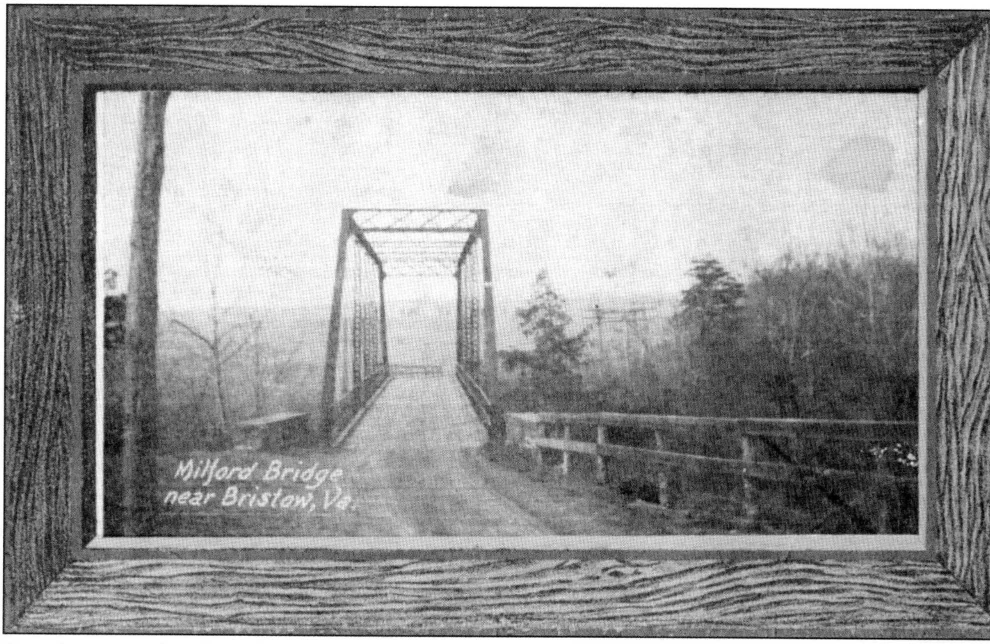

Seen here crossing Broad Run near present-day Route 28 and Piper Lane, the historic Milford Bridge no longer exists. Various bridges crossed Broad Run since the 1700s along this well-traveled route. In 1962, the town of Manassas purchased 250 acres surrounding the bridge for Harry P. Davis Field, now the Manassas Regional Airport.

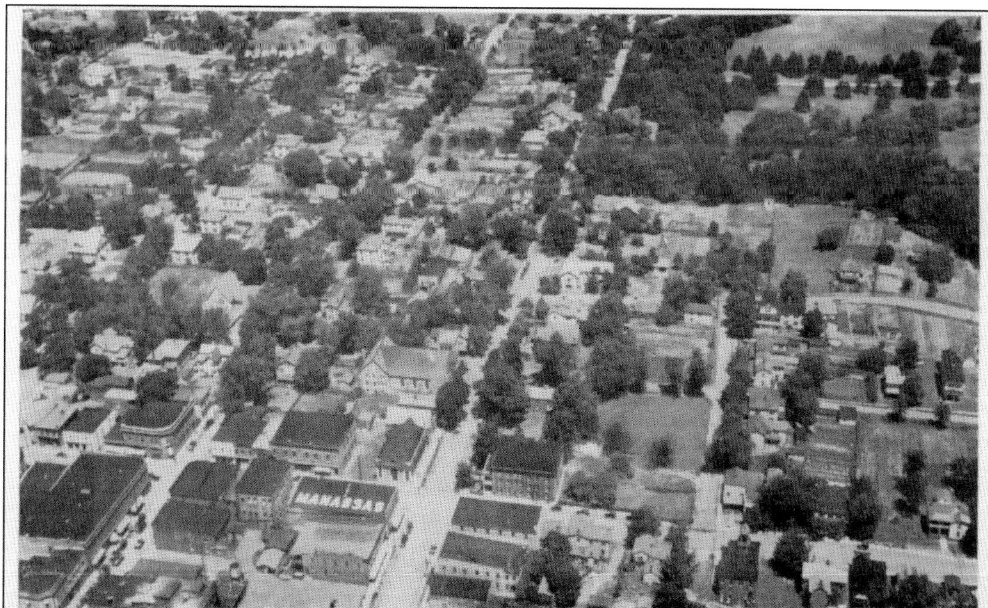

AIRPLANE VIEW OF TOWN OF MANASSAS

Manassas is clearly identified in the sign on the Hynson's Department Store roof that aided aviators in this 1930s aerial view of the town. Hynson's is located on the corner of Center and Main Streets, in a cluster of still-familiar commercial buildings. What is now Church Street was then a largely residential area. The wooded area at top right was part of Annaburg, the vast Robert Portner estate.

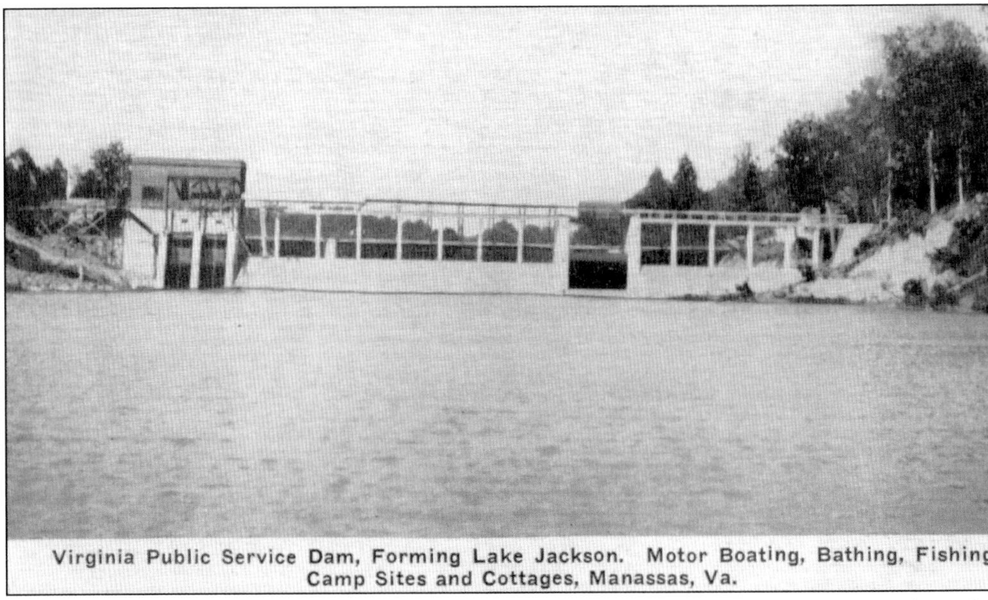

After Charles Alpaugh sold his interest in the Lake Jackson Dam, he concentrated on the development of Lake Jackson. His goal was to turn what then surrounded the newly formed lake—rundown farms, gristmills, sawmills, and moonshine operations—into a summer escape for Washington residents. He began with constructing a replica of the Custis Lee Mansion, now known as Arlington House, for his own home there.

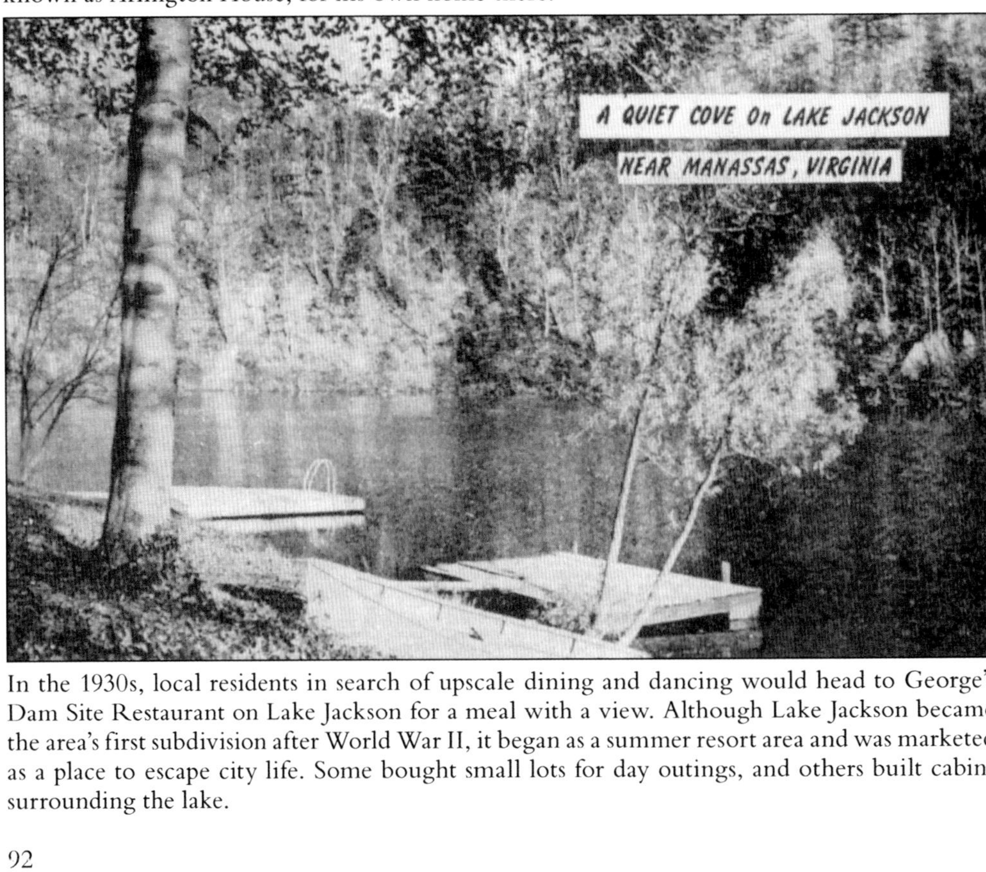

In the 1930s, local residents in search of upscale dining and dancing would head to George's Dam Site Restaurant on Lake Jackson for a meal with a view. Although Lake Jackson became the area's first subdivision after World War II, it began as a summer resort area and was marketed as a place to escape city life. Some bought small lots for day outings, and others built cabins surrounding the lake.

Eight

A Place of Pilgrimage

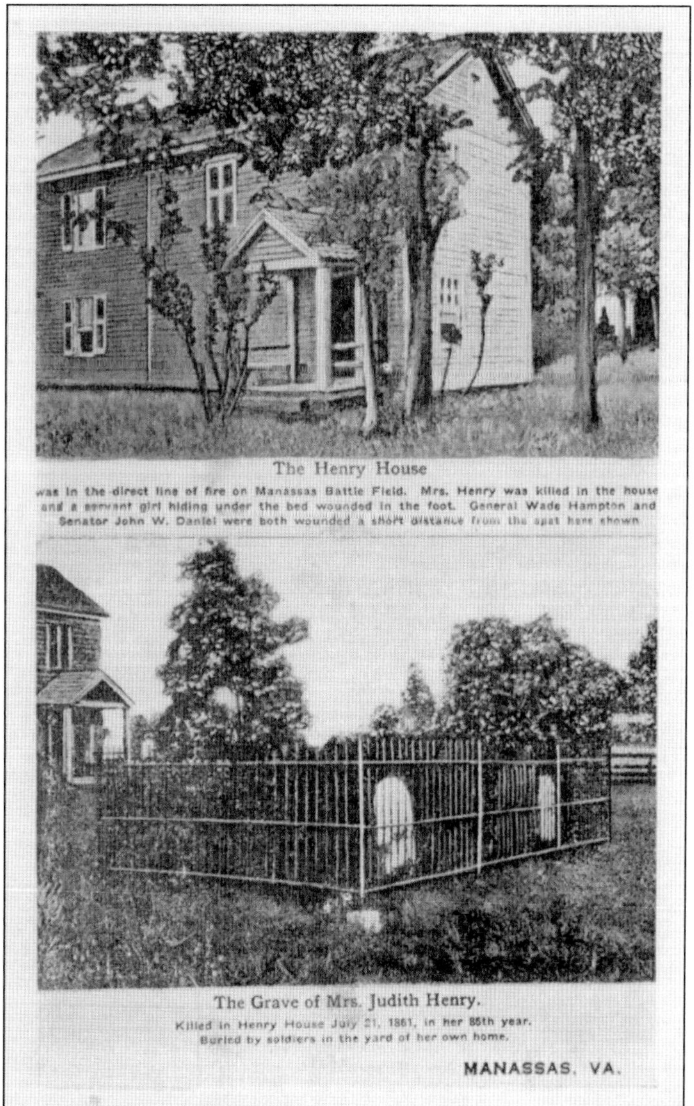

The Manassas/Bull Run battlefield was for locals a sacred place of carnage that had profoundly changed their lives and inadvertently made their town's name known across the land. For farmers who owned the scarred land, it was a place where bullets and bones littered fields after rains or plowing. And for a growing number of curious from across the country, it was a place of pilgrimage.

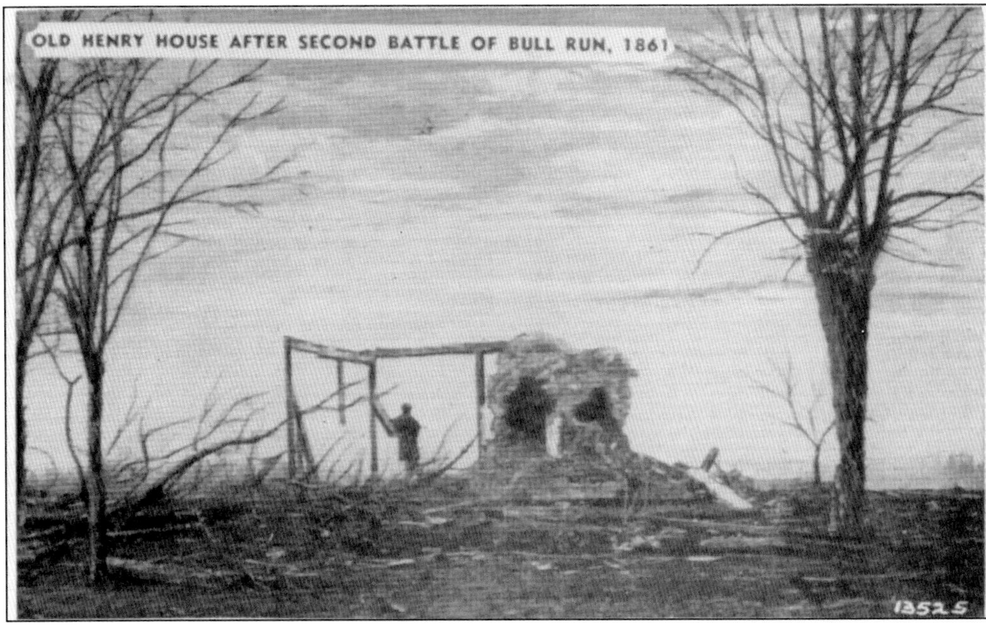

The Henry Farm, situated on the infamous Henry House Hill, was surrounded by warring armies during both the Battles of First and Second Manassas. Although the house survived the first battle, this 1862 image, reproduced on a 1930s-era postcard, shows the home in ruins after it had probably been stripped for wood. The Henry family built a larger house on the same site in the 1870s that still stands.

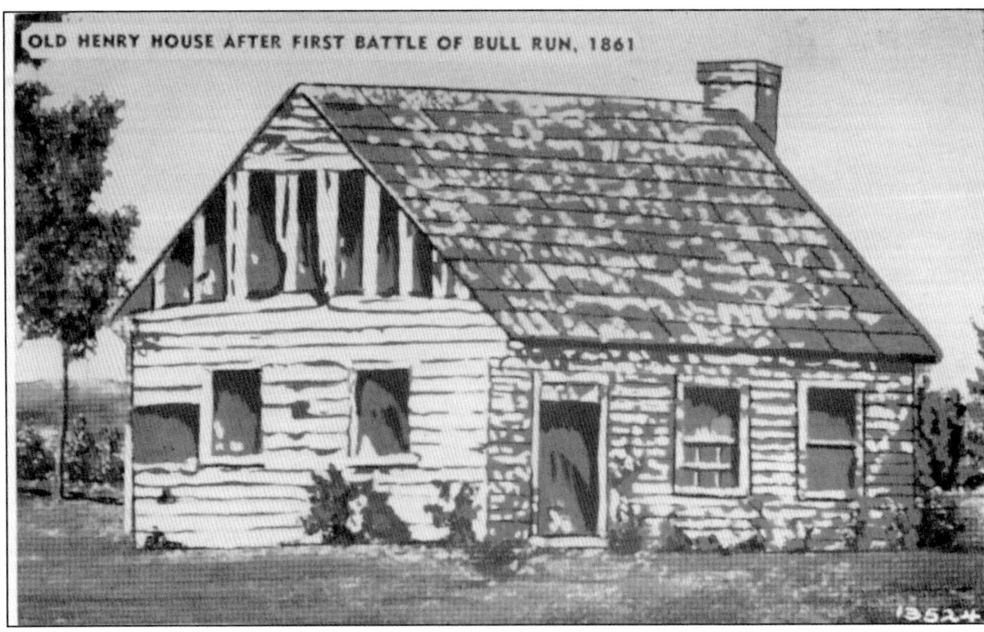

When the Battle of First Manassas raged around her, 85-year-old invalid widow Judith Carter Henry refused to leave her home. Confederate snipers and artillery batteries took up positions around the house, and when Union batteries began bombarding her home, Henry was hit by a shell that tore through her bedroom wall. She died four hours later and was the only civilian casualty of First Manassas.

Even before the Civil War ended, the Manassas battlefield was a destination for the reverent and the curious. While he was stationed at Fairfax Court House, signal officer Albert Seip told the *Washington Star* that he "frequently escorted parties from Washington visiting these famous fields, which at that time abounded in skulls and other human bones."

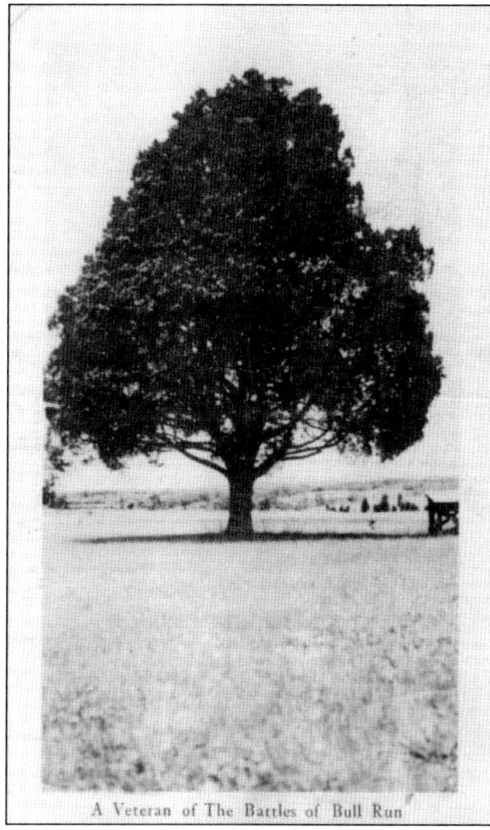

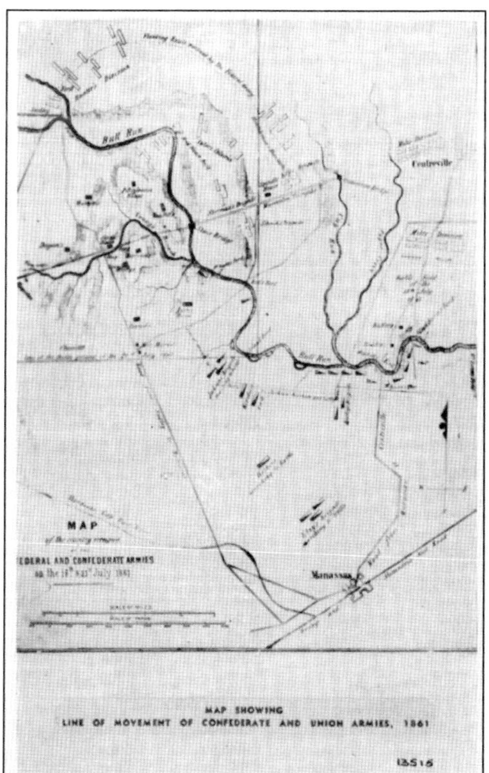

Relic hunters, longing to bring souvenirs home from the battlefield, dug bones, bullets, buttons, artillery shells, and even long-forgotten bodies from the sacred ground for years. It was not until the battlefield became a national park that penalties for such relic hunting were instituted. The removal of these artifacts has made it more difficult for historians to determine battle lines like those depicted on this 1930s-era postcard.

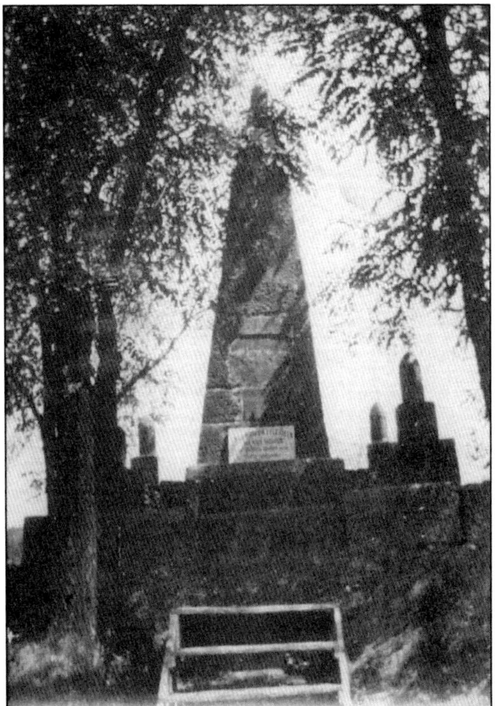

The Monument at the Henry House in 1905. dedicated June 11th, 1865. The trees around the Monument were set out by U.S. Soldiers, June, 1865.
Near Manassas, Va.

Unlike other Civil War monuments, the first federal battlefield monuments on Henry Hill were built by soldiers who had not yet been mustered out. "The stone was hauled in government army wagons and dressed with axes and hammers furnished by the quartermaster department. The lime and cement were brought from Washington and also the large rifle shells used in the ornamentation of the monuments. Every stroke of the work was done by soldiers enlisted and paid by the government and the entire work from beginning to end was under the direction of United States Army Officers," *the Washington Star* reported in 1914.

FIRST MONUMENT OF CIVIL WAR

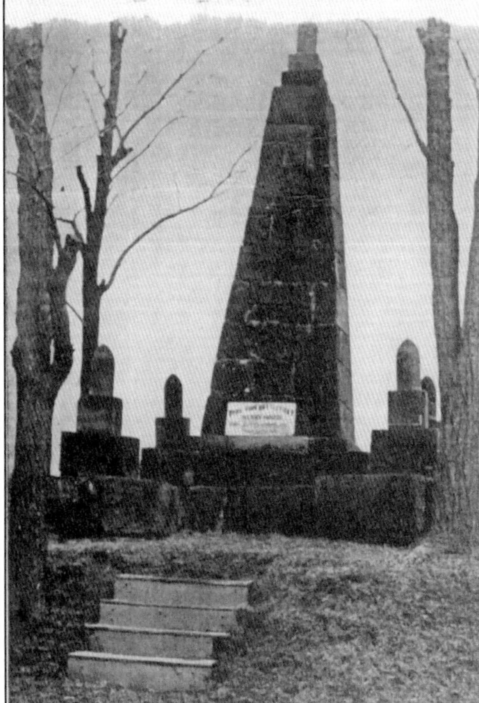

DEDICATED WITH IMPOSING CEREMONIES BY ARMY OF POTOMAC, JUNE 11, 1865

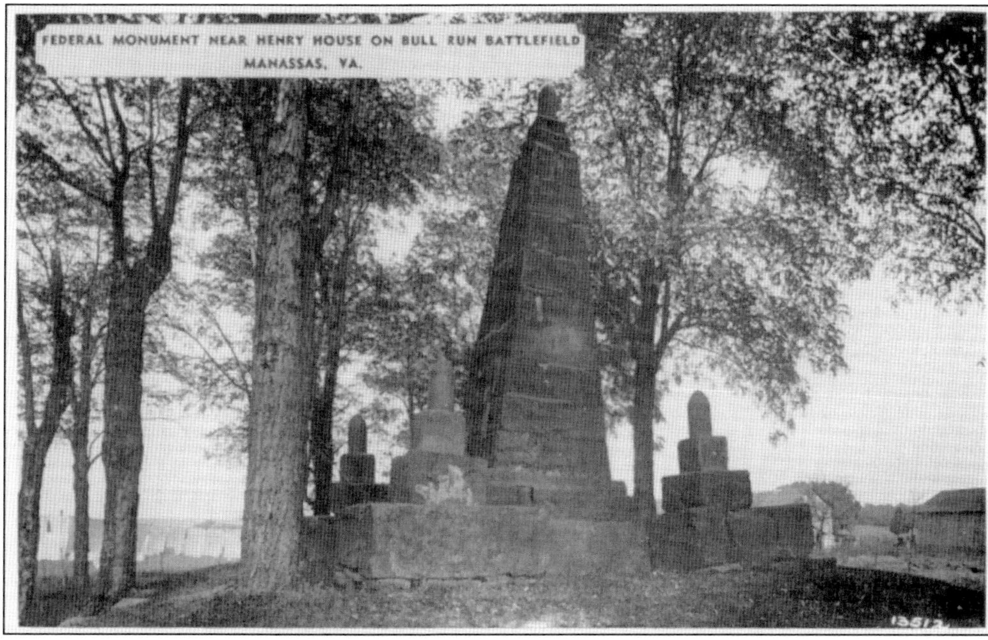

Dignitaries traveled by government train from Washington to Fairfax Station, and 60 army wagons and ambulances then brought them to Henry Hill and Groveton for the elaborate dedication ceremony of the first monuments on June 11, 1865. Inscribed "In Memory of the Patriots Who Fell," the Henry Hill monument was ornamented with five 200-pound shells.

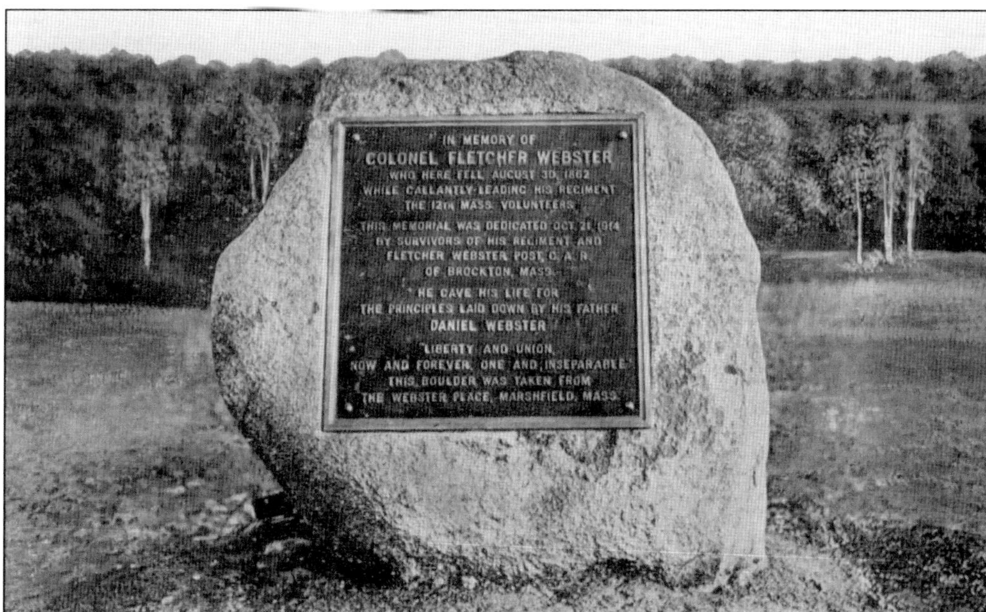

The 12th Massachusetts Regimental Association purchased the spot on which Col. Fletcher Webster, the son of Daniel Webster, was killed on August 30, 1862, during the Battle of Second Manassas, and dedicated this monument in 1914, using a boulder taken from Webster's home. *Harper's Weekly* reported that "Colonel Webster had always been considered a good officer, but was also remarkable for his quiet, unambitious temper."

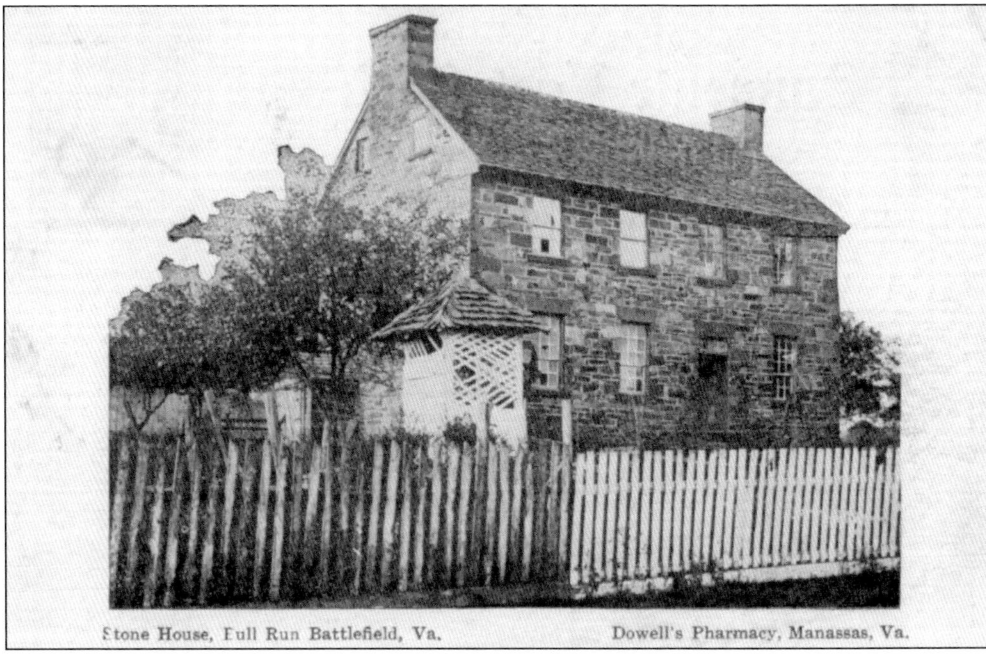

Veterans were the first to visit Civil War battlefields, often while participating in reunions. George C. Round was one of the original tour guides, and organized an excursion to the Manassas battlefield during the 1892 Grand Army of the Republic (GAR) Washington reunion. Realizing the benefit of tourism income, he enlisted Manassas farmers to hire out their horses and wagons to transport veterans from Manassas to the battlefield. Concerned that the farmers might be taxed on their proceeds, he sought the opinion of the Virginia auditor of public accounts, who assured him that farmers would be free from taxation and not need livery licenses. As veterans and the curious continued to visit, they bought souvenir postcards like this 1907 image of the Stone House (above) and the 1910 image of the Henry House (below).

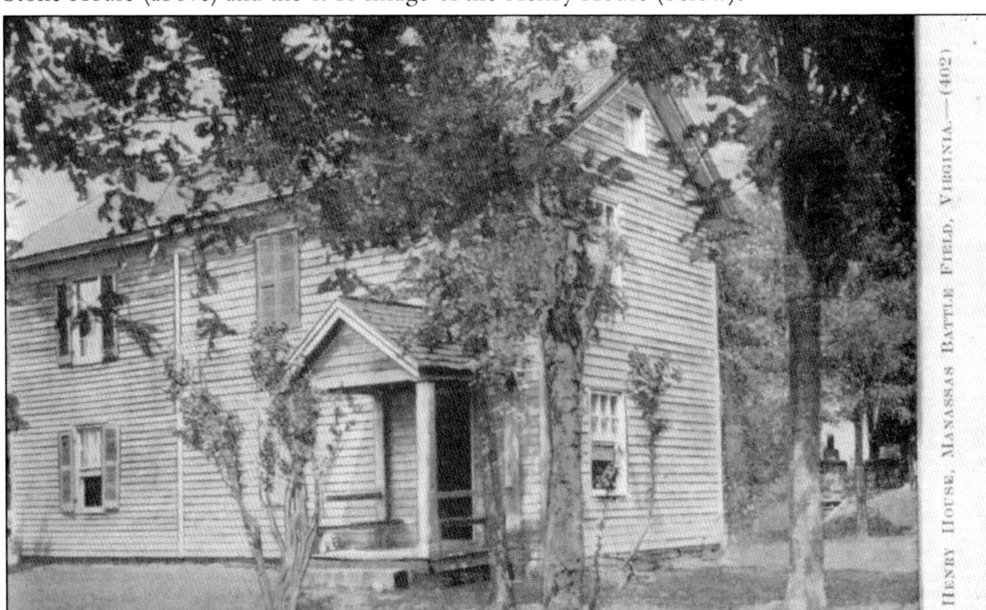

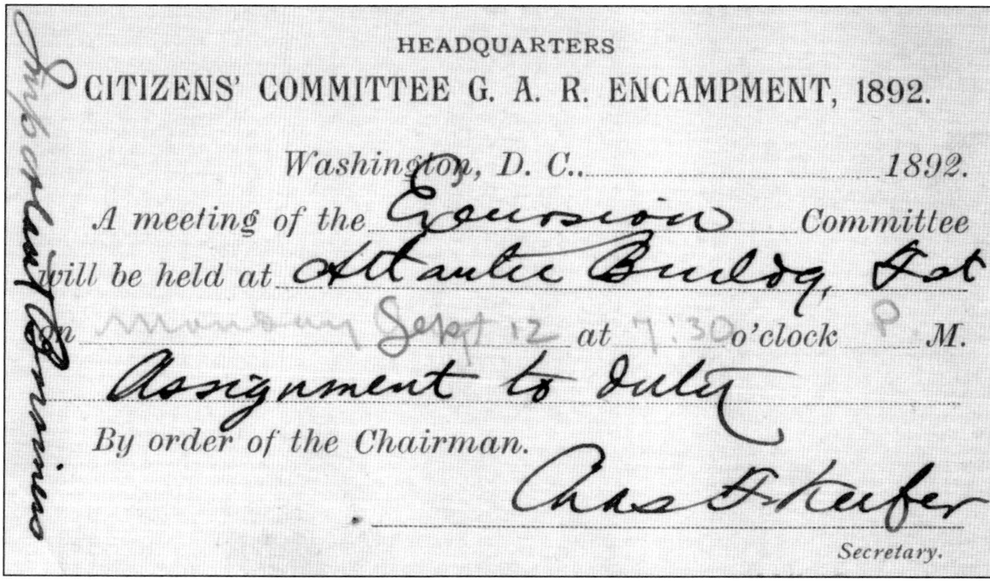
HEADQUARTERS
CITIZENS' COMMITTEE G. A. R. ENCAMPMENT, 1892.

Washington, D. C., ... *1892.*

A meeting of the Excursion *Committee will be held at* Atlantic Bldg, *on* Monday Sept 12 *at* 7:30 *o'clock* P *M.*

Assignment to duty

By order of the Chairman.

Chas F. Kiefer
Secretary.

George C. Round received this postcard invitation to a meeting of the excursion committee for the 1892 Grand Army of the Republic reunion in Washington. Round not only organized the reunion's trip to the Manassas battlefield but also helped organize reunions for the Army of the Potomac and Signal Corps veterans throughout the early 1900s. He is best known for organizing the 1911 Manassas National Jubilee of Peace.

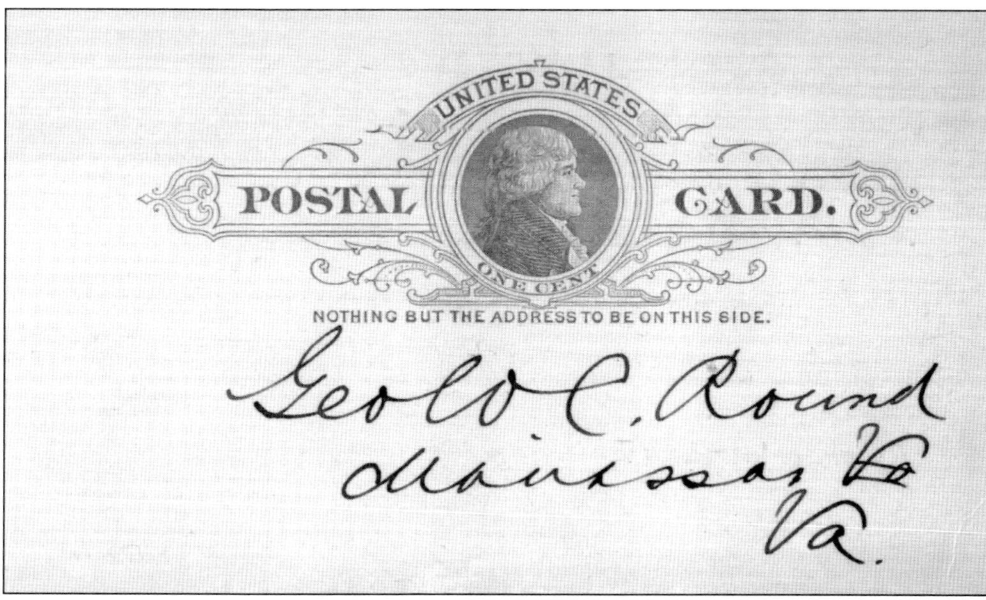

The front side shows a government postcard with preprinted postage, an inexpensive form of correspondence at the time. Round also heard from a veteran inquiring about the 1892 battlefield excursion, noting that he read about it in Round's "little Manassas paper," perhaps referring to a local newspaper. He also wrote that the ladies of his church planned to sell refreshments at Henry House during the reunion.

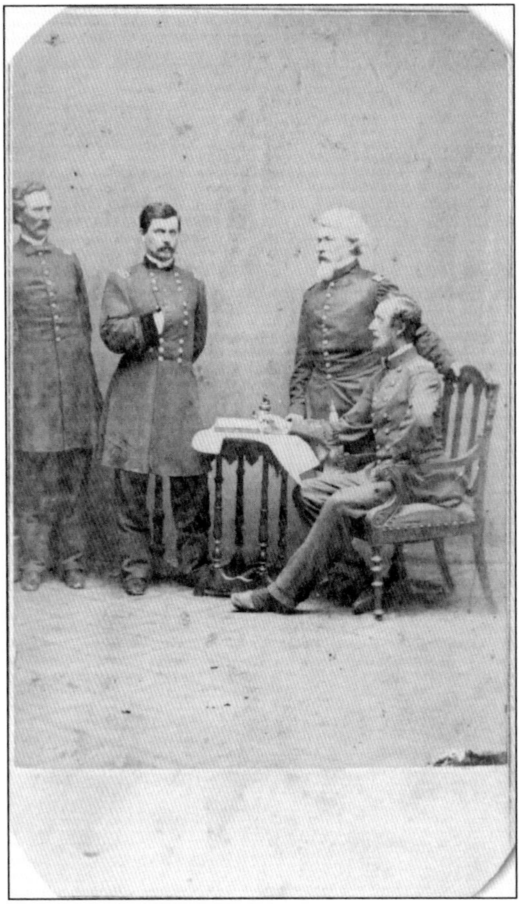

These very early postcards—or cabinet cards as they were known in the 1880s—had replaced the much smaller cartes de visite that resembled today's wallet-sized portraits. Cabinet cards almost always featured portraits of either ordinary people or of celebrities mounted on stiff cardboard to prevent the thin photo paper from curling. The E. & H.T. Anthony Company in New York produced many cabinet cards featuring both Confederate and Union generals. Northerners who moved to Manassas would have been interested in collecting or mailing cards like this one picturing Gen. George McClellan. Although the card attributes the photograph to Mathew Brady, the Library of Congress found only an unverified caption on the negative's sleeve, which reads: "McClellan and staff. L to R: Capt. Clark, Gen. McClellan, Capt. Van Vliet, Maj. Barry."

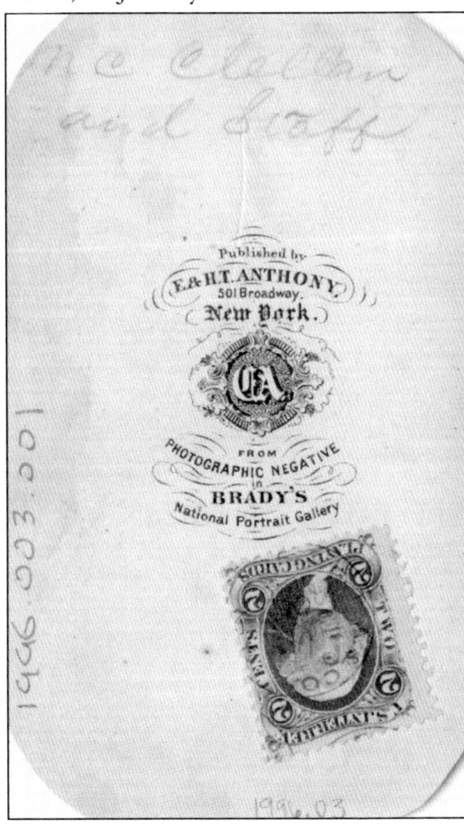

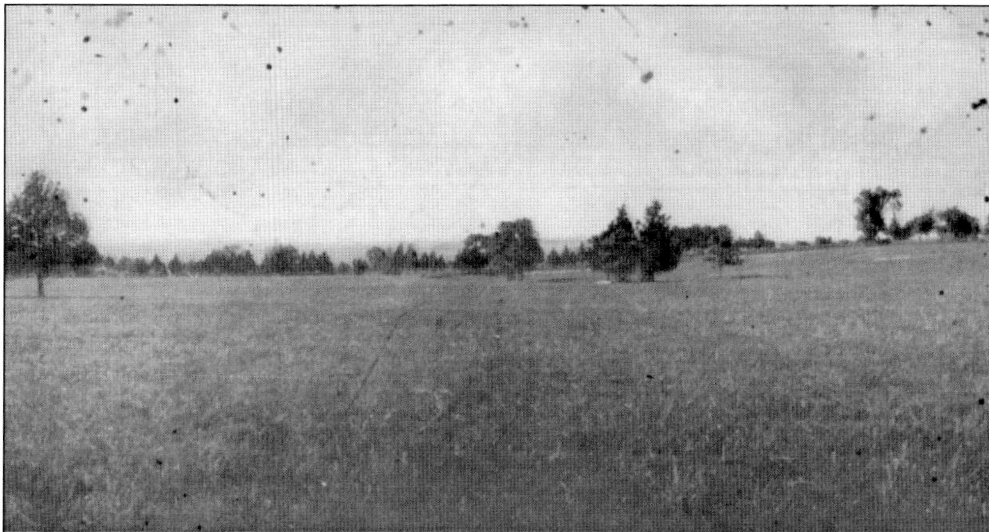

THE CENTER OF COMBAT, MANASSAS BATTLE FIELD, VIRGINIA.—(301)

"If you have but one hour at Manassas," George C. Round writes in his *Around About the Battlefield, A Guide to Strangers*, "you can get a fair idea of the campaigning ground, of which Manassas is in the center, by going to the Ruffner School House or even to the elevation on which the Court House stands. Place your back to the R.R. and look Northward. Leesburg is 30 miles to your front and Fredericksburg 30 miles behind you, while Washington is 30 miles on your right and Culpeper the same distance on your left, Gettysburg is 90 miles to the North and Richmond 90 miles to the South." Round wrote the guide in response to the large number of people visiting the battlefield. These 1909 (above) and 1940s-era (below) vintage postcards were produced for visitors.

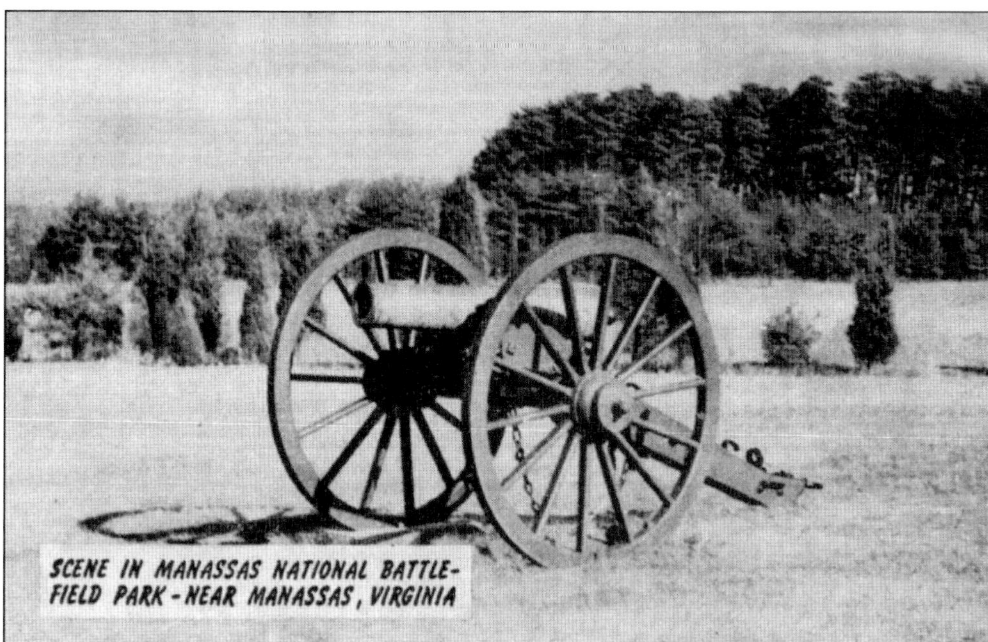

SCENE IN MANASSAS NATIONAL BATTLE-FIELD PARK - NEAR MANASSAS, VIRGINIA

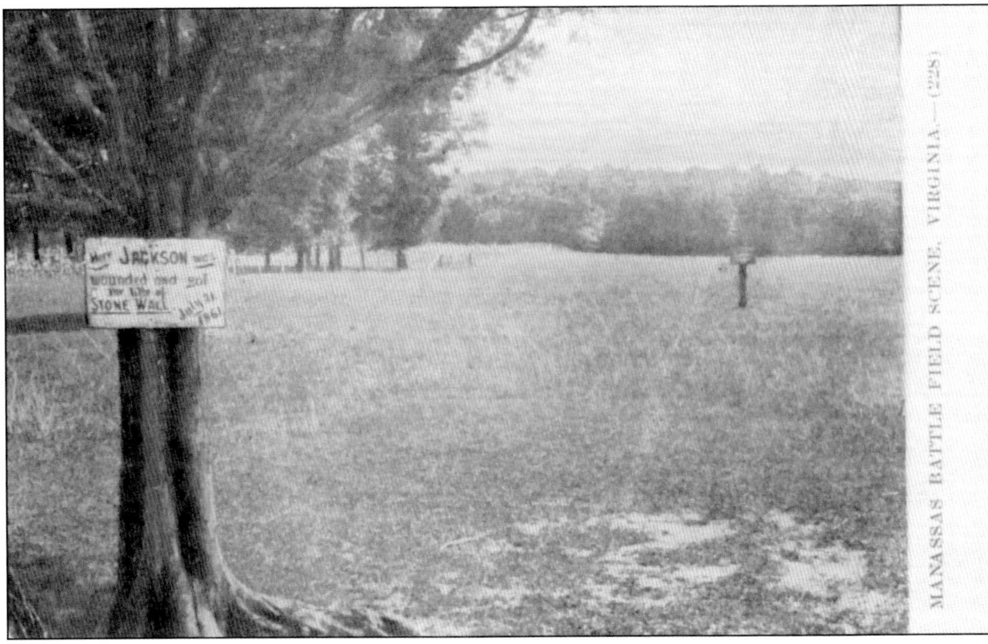

Before other monuments were built, hand-lettered signs marked places on the battlefield where prominent officers fell, as these images from about 1908 show. Above, an early sign marks the spot where Gen. Thomas Jackson was wounded and inspired Gen. Barnard Bee to describe Jackson as a "stone wall." The sign in the image below honors Col. James Cameron, who led the 79th New York Volunteer Infantry into battle on Henry House Hill, where he was mortally wounded on July 21, 1861. Cameron's brother was President Lincoln's first secretary of war, Simon Cameron. The postcard calls the battleground "Bull Run Battlefield," as it was known in the North, where battles were named after waterways or natural features. In the South, battles were named after the nearest town.

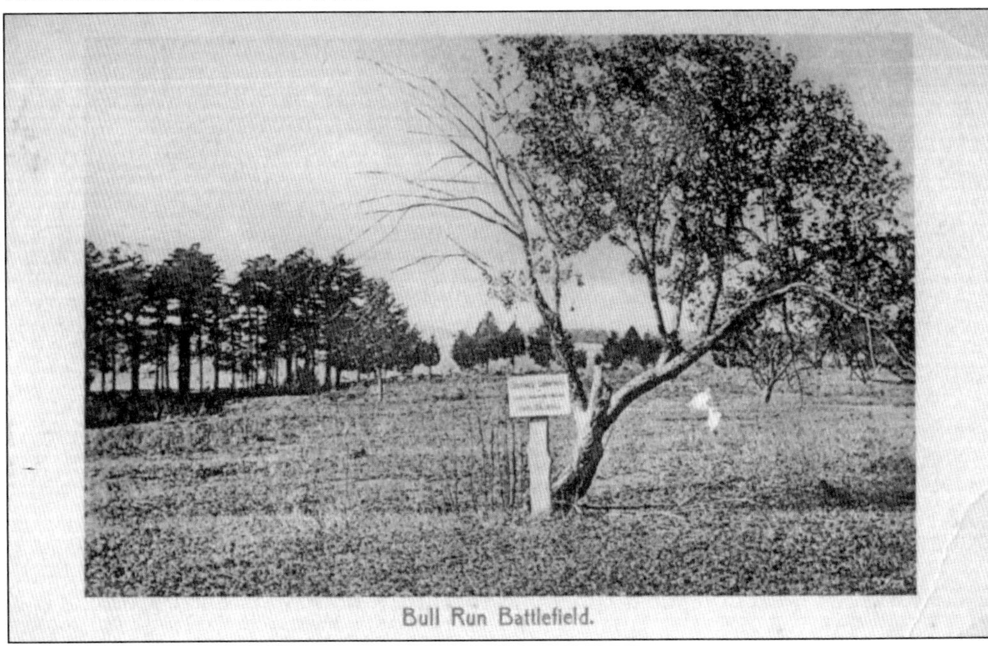

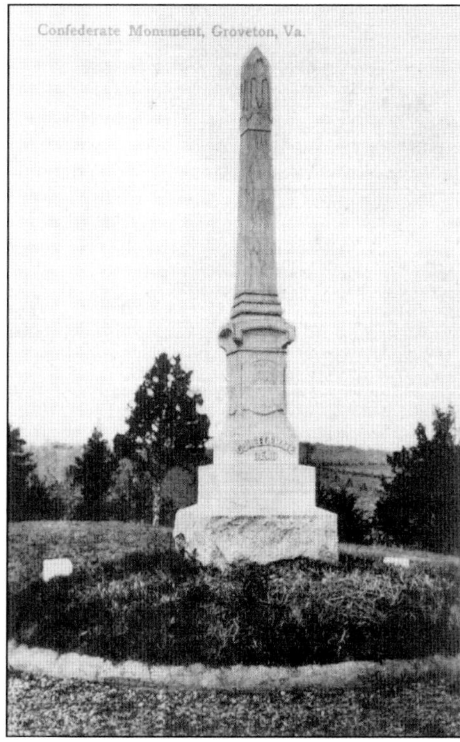

The Bull Run Chapter of the United Daughters of the Confederacy (UDC) erected this Confederate monument in 1904 in the Groveton cemetery, which had been instituted by local women in 1866. When the Groveton cemetery was established, only two bodies were identified out of 266, but the UDC listed the names of others thought to be buried here. Most of the Union dead were reburied at Arlington National Cemetery. The UDC became an umbrella organization for Ladies Memorial Associations that were formed by women in response to federal efforts to disinter Union dead for reburial in national cemeteries. Although the associations began in Virginia, they soon spread across the South, where women established their own cemeteries like those at Groveton and Manassas to honor Confederate dead and permanently mark battlefields.

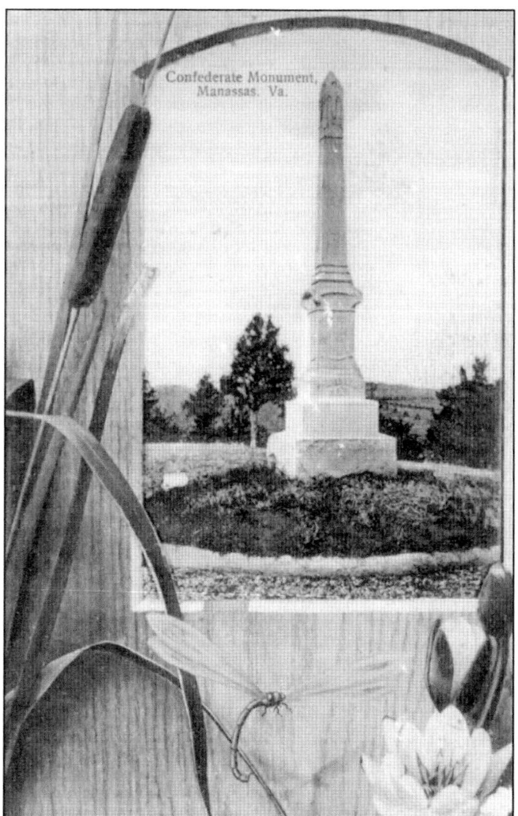

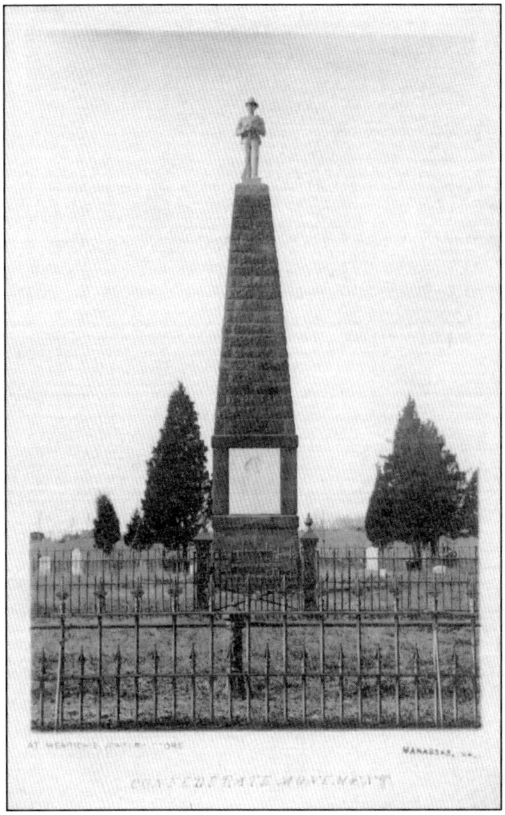

The Ladies' Memorial Association of Manassas (later to become the United Daughters of the Confederacy) created the Confederate Cemetery in 1867 on one acre of land donated by former Confederate colonel William Fewell. The land was given to hold the remains of Confederate soldiers "scattered over the Plains." The nearby Bull Run Ladies Association reburied the remains of soldiers found on the battlefield in the Groveton Cemetery, but there were many other remains recovered throughout Manassas. Soldiers who had died in camp, hospitals, or farmhouses were recovered and reburied. In 1911, the association placed a bronze statue of a Confederate soldier "at rest" on the brownstone monument that had been dedicated in 1889. Legend has it that the soldier faces east to guard against attack from Washington. The cemetery, on Center Street, is still owned and maintained by the UDC.

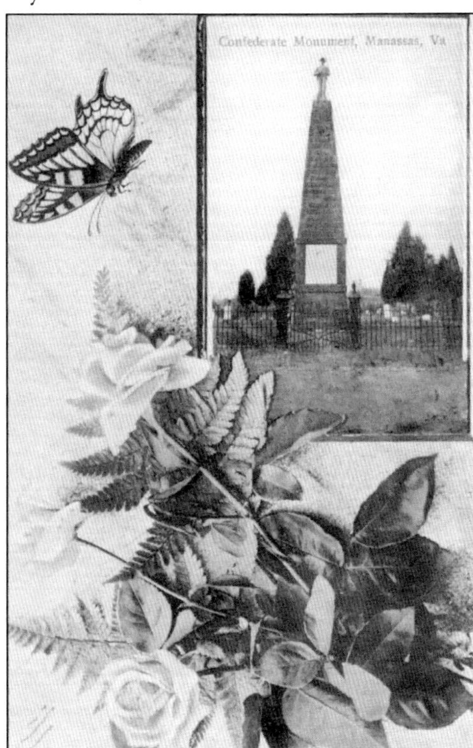

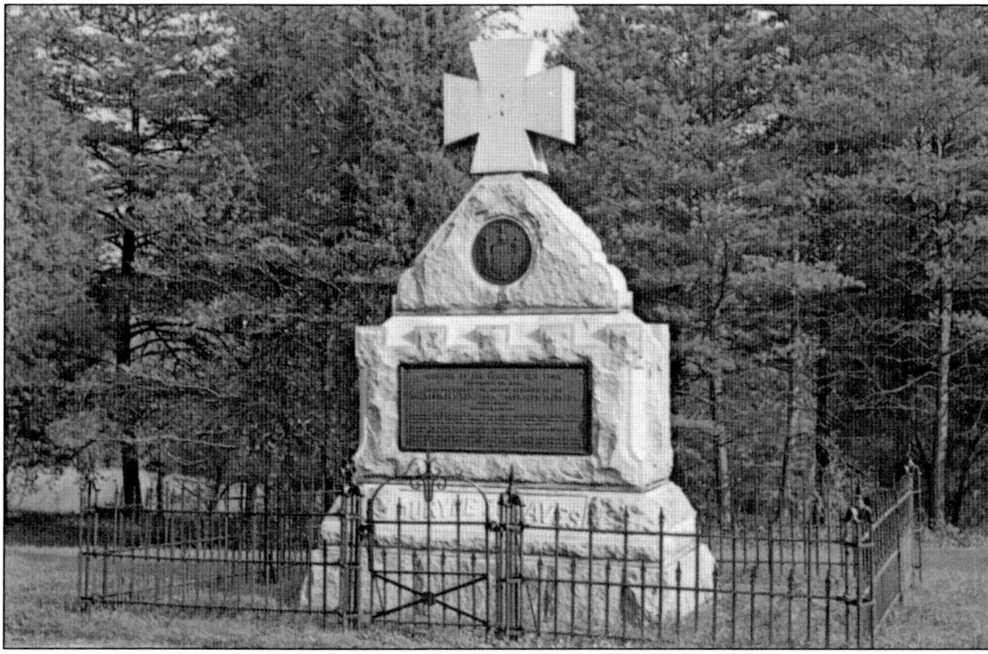

In 1905, the New York State Legislature approved $1,500 each to purchase land and erect three monuments to honor New York regiments that fought and fell on the Manassas battlefield, including this one honoring the Fifth Duryee Zouves, named for their organizer, wealthy Manhattan lumber merchant Abram Duryée. The many professional men who joined the volunteer regiment were known for their discipline, skill, bravery under fire, and colorful red breeches, inspired by the regalia of French colonial troops. The 5th New York encountered a surprise attack during the Battle of Second Manassas, as depicted below, and lost 124 men out of 462, despite a gallant defense. James Webb, a private in the 5th, won the Congressional Medal of Honor for selflessly warning an artillery battery during the battle.

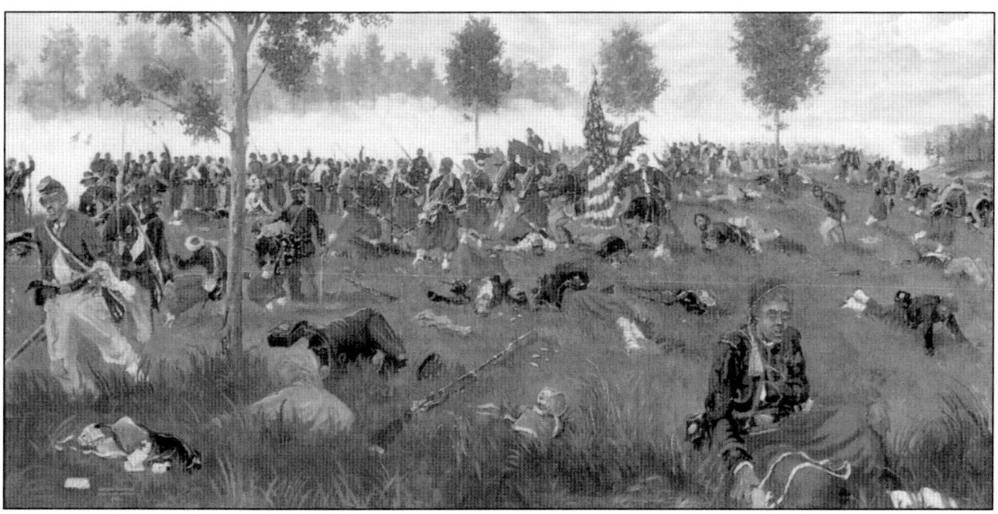

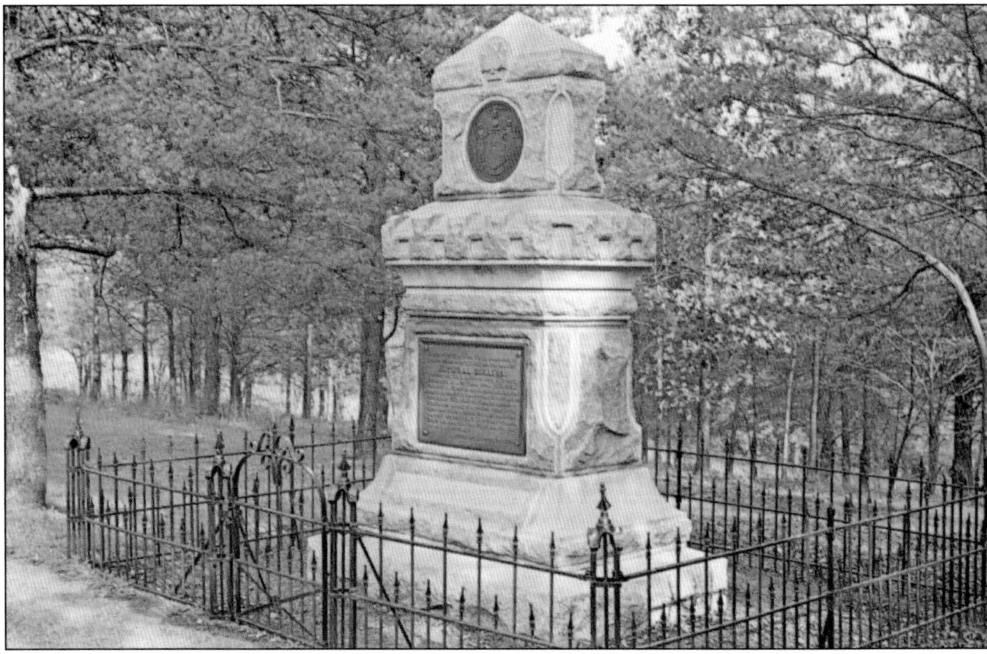

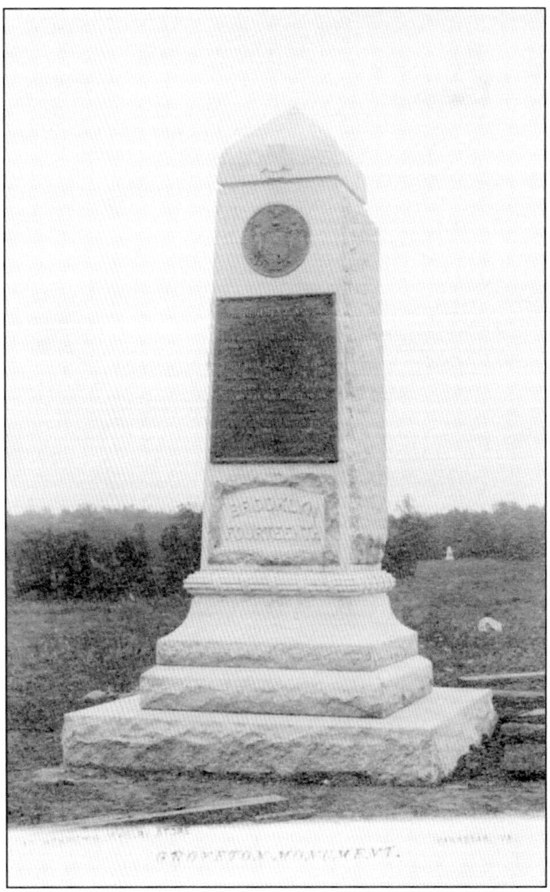

The New York City Board of Aldermen appropriated $500 toward the 1906 unveiling and dedication of this monument to the 10th New York Volunteers, which was one of three dedicated that rainy day in 1906. Known as the National Zouaves, the regiment lost nearly a third of its men during the Battle of Second Manassas and later participated in the Confederate surrender at Appomattox.

Also known as the "Brooklyn Chasseurs" (*chasseur* is a French term for "hunter") and the "Red Legged Devils" for their baggy bright red pants and brave fighting, the 14th New York fought in both the Battles of First and Second Manassas. Its monument stands in the Groveton area of the battlefield. As the regimental color bearer fell on this battlefield, he famously said, "Never mind me boys, save the colors."

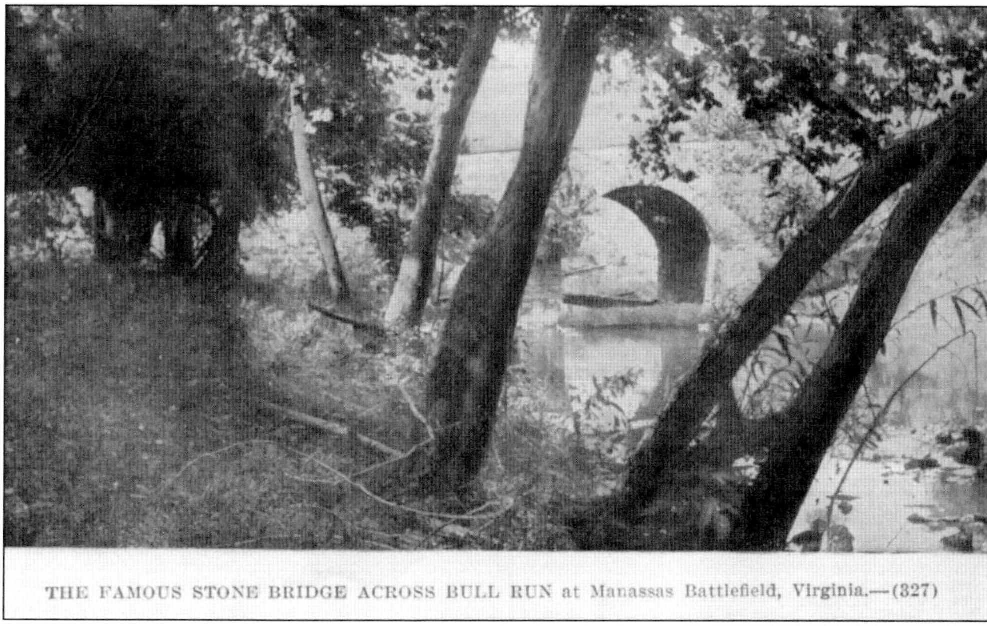

This early 1900s image shows the Stone Bridge as it must have looked when it was made famous in both battles of Manassas. Originally built in 1825, the two-arched bridge was constructed with native sandstone and carried traffic along the busy Warrenton Turnpike (now Route 29) until the Civil War.

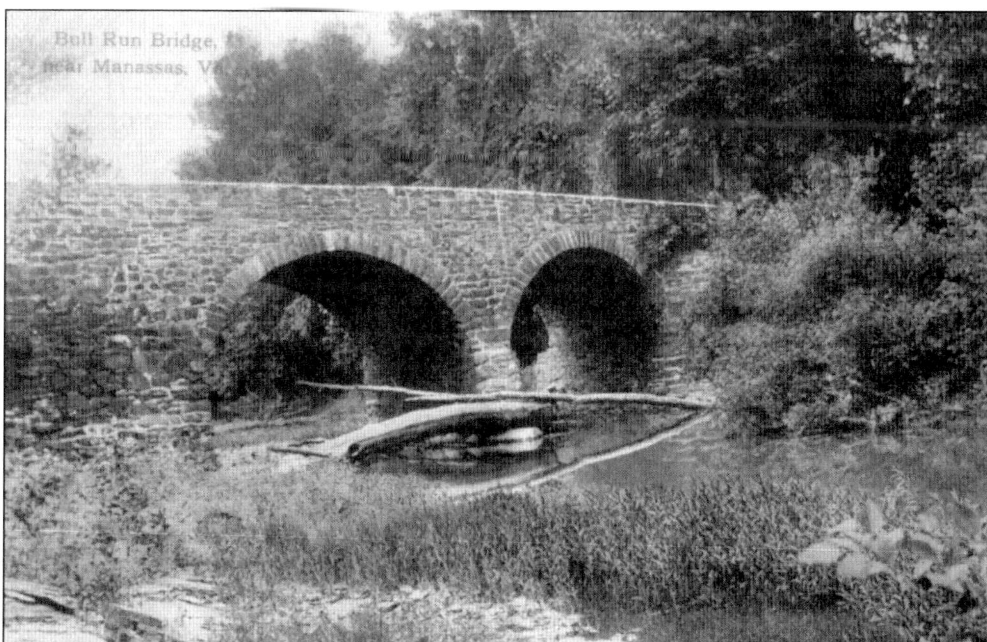

The bridge survived the Battle of First Manassas, despite the gunshots and artillery fire ringing the surrounding area. When Confederate forces withdrew from Manassas in March 1862, Gen. Joseph E. Johnston ordered the bridge destroyed to make it more difficult for Union troops to move across the Bull Run stream.

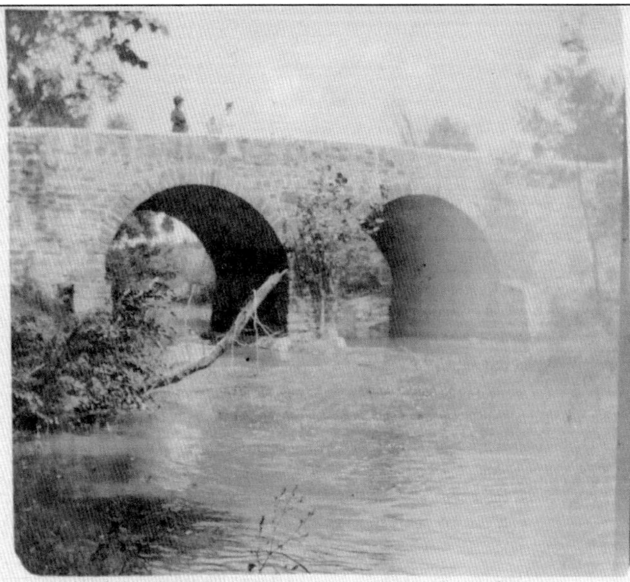

The Historic Stone bridge

The real-photo postcard at top shows strollers on the Stone Bridge, which had become both a historic and scenic destination in the early 1900s. Union army engineers built a temporary span on the original abutments after Confederates destroyed the bridge, and that bridge served Gen. John Pope's army at the Battle of Second Manassas, which took place August 28–30 in 1862. That battle ended much like the first battle—with a Confederate victory—and the temporary bridge was used by Union troops to retreat to Washington along the Warrenton Turnpike. When their forces had evacuated the battlefield, the Union army rear guard destroyed the bridge. In 1884, the bridge was completely rebuilt and remained open to traffic until 1926, when a new span for the realigned Warrenton Turnpike—now named the Lee Highway—was built downstream.

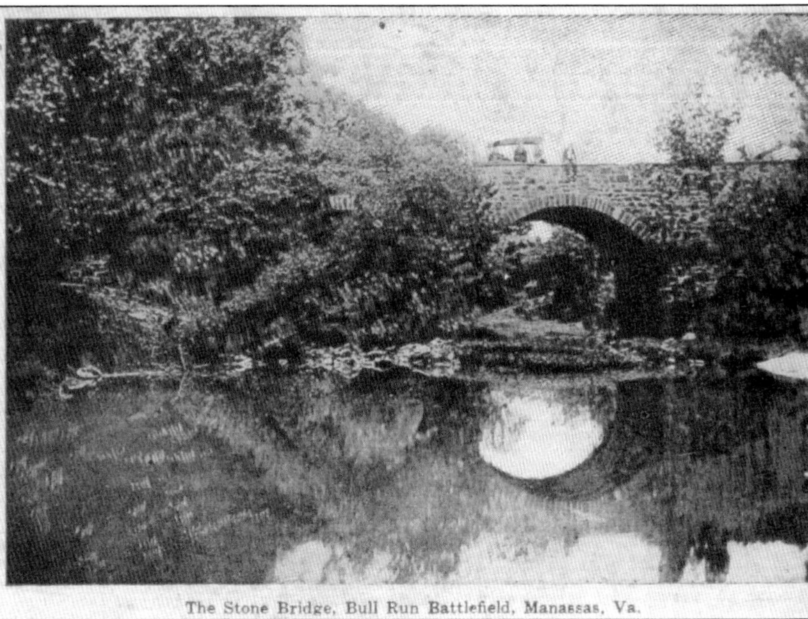

The Stone Bridge, Bull Run Battlefield, Manassas, Va.

"The Warrenton turnpike was already swarming with fugitives from the battle-field, going towards Centreville," *New York Tribune* correspondent Henry Villard later wrote of the retreat after the Battle of First Manassas. When he waited at the bridge for news, an officer he knew told him, "All is chaos in front. The battle is lost. Our troops are all giving way and falling back without orders. Get back to Centreville."

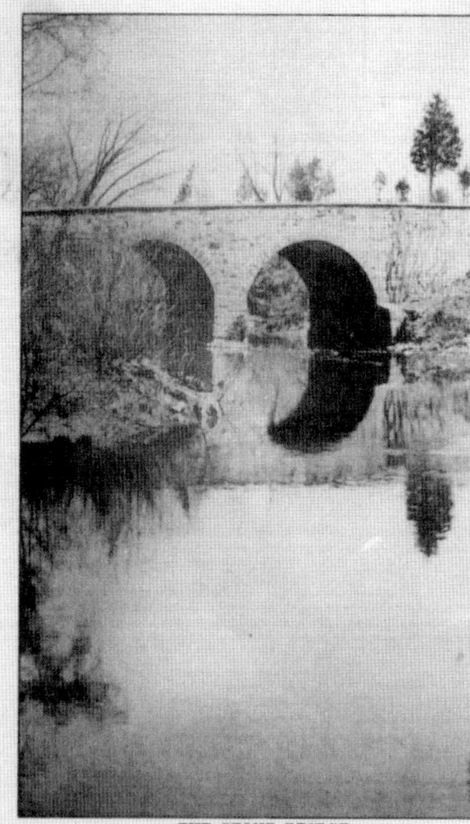

THE STONE BRIDGE,
BULL RUN BATTLEFIELDS, VIRGINIA

The Virginia Highway Commission gave the pyramid monument on the bridge to the United Daughters of the Confederacy Manassas Chapter in 1928. Prominent Manassas architect Albert Speiden accepted the monument on behalf of the UDC, noting its classical design and saying, "As we look at this pyramid and the hills beyond, we can recall many noble deeds of heroism." The National Park Service acquired the bridge in 1959.

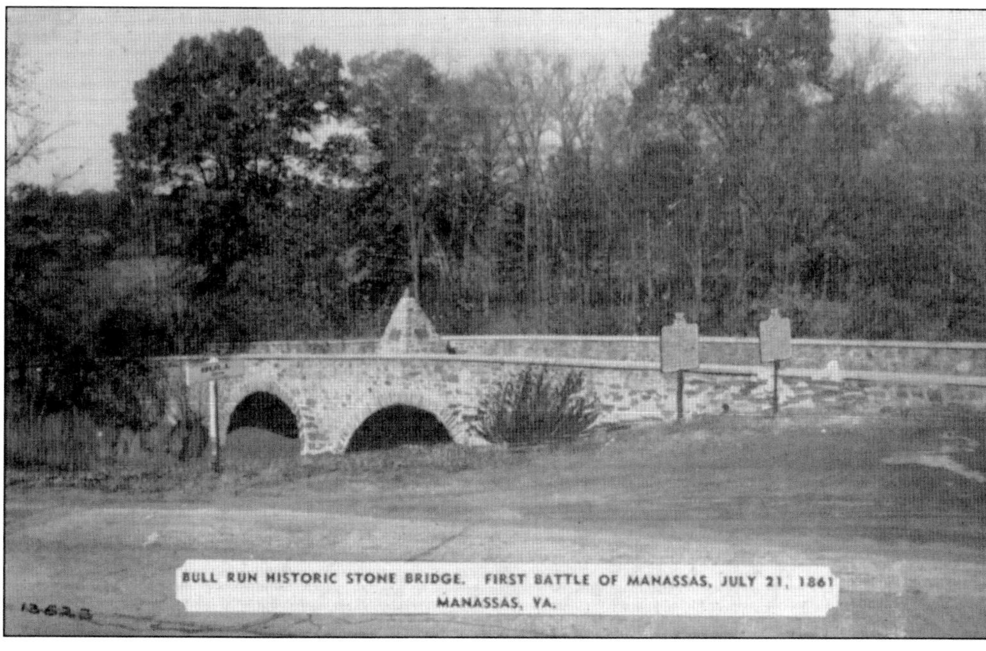

BULL RUN HISTORIC STONE BRIDGE. FIRST BATTLE OF MANASSAS, JULY 21, 1861
MANASSAS, VA.

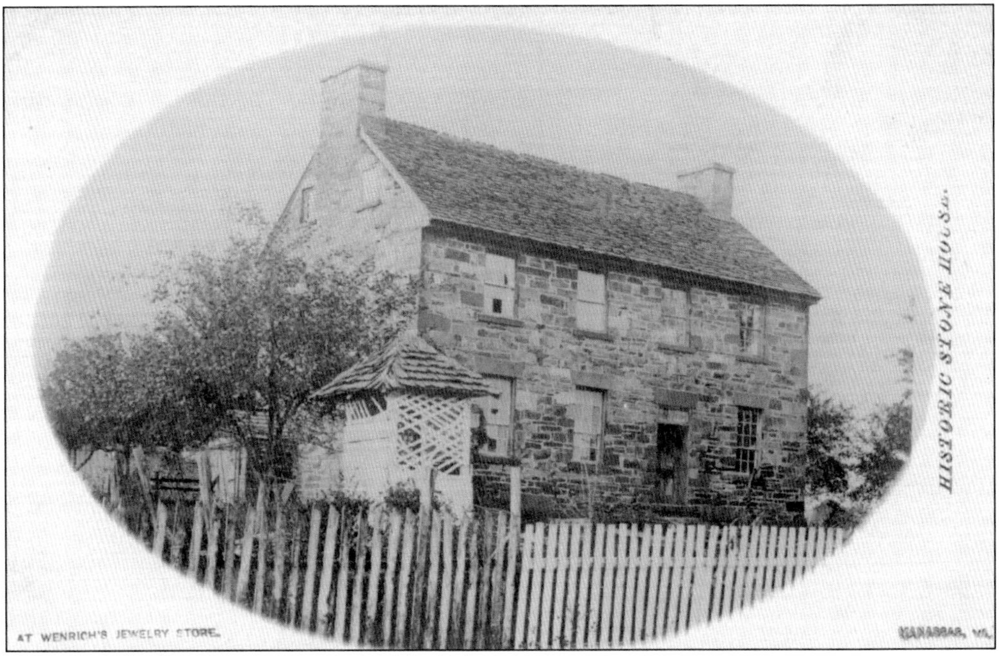

Built in 1848 of locally quarried sandstone, Thomas Clark operated the Stone House as a tavern or drover's rest along the Warrenton Turnpike (modern-day Route 29). Clark sold the house to farmers Henry and Jane Matthews in 1850. The Stone House stood sentry over peaceful farmland until 1861, when it sheltered wounded Union troops during the Battle of First Manassas, despite being under fire. Confederate troops soon retook the Stone House, capturing the wounded and 36 other Federal soldiers. During the Battle of Second Manassas, the defeated Union army retreated past the Stone House along the Warrenton Turnpike and left its wounded in the makeshift hospital. Once the battle ended, Confederates again gained control of the building and paroled captured Union soldiers there.

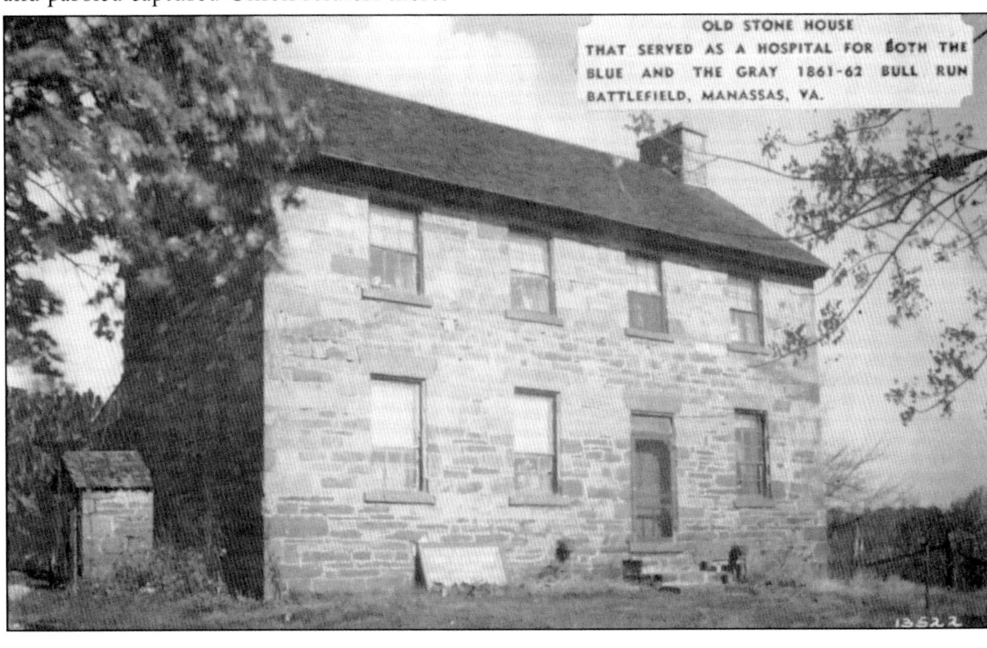

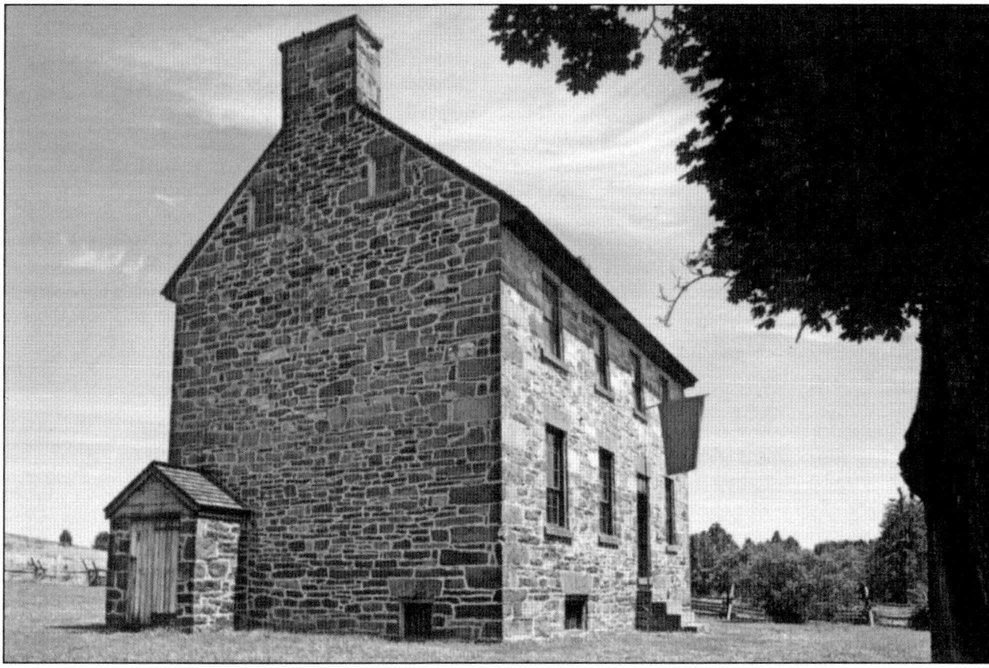

After the war, the Stone House was again a private home and briefly housed a hotel and a post office under two different owners. When *Washington Post* reporters visited the battlefield in advance of a veteran's reunion in 1915, they found that "in spite of the roughness of the road, however, between Fairfax, Centerville and Bull Run, the scenery and historic interest is more than enough to make the trip worth while." The reporters also mentioned battlefield landmarks: "The Old Stone house at the crossroads is in a splendid state of preservation, which is sure to bring back memories to any of the old soldiers who visit it." The National Park Service (NPS) acquired the Stone House in 1949 and restored it to its historic appearance in 1961.

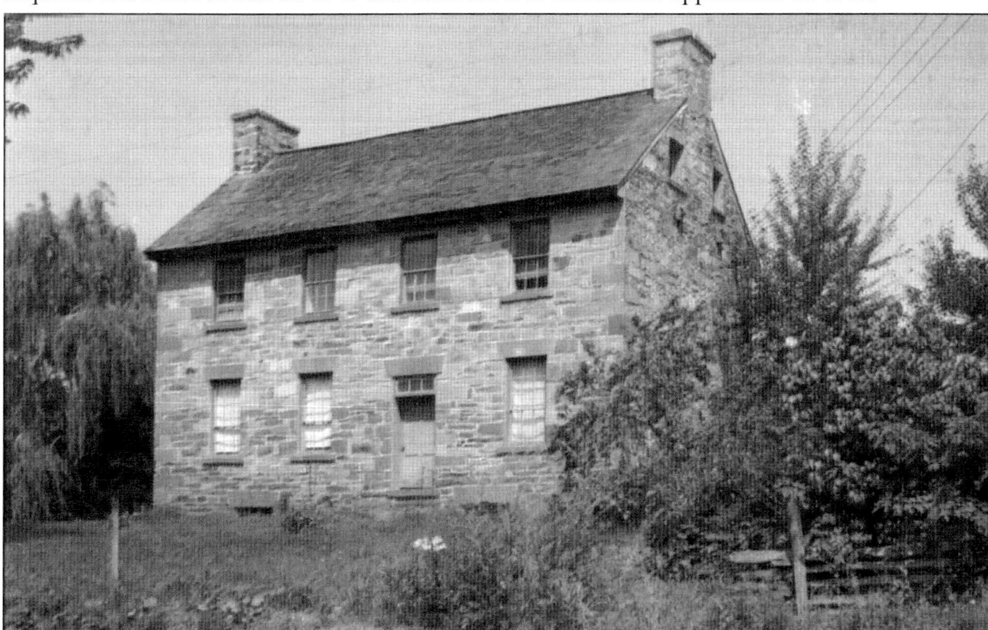

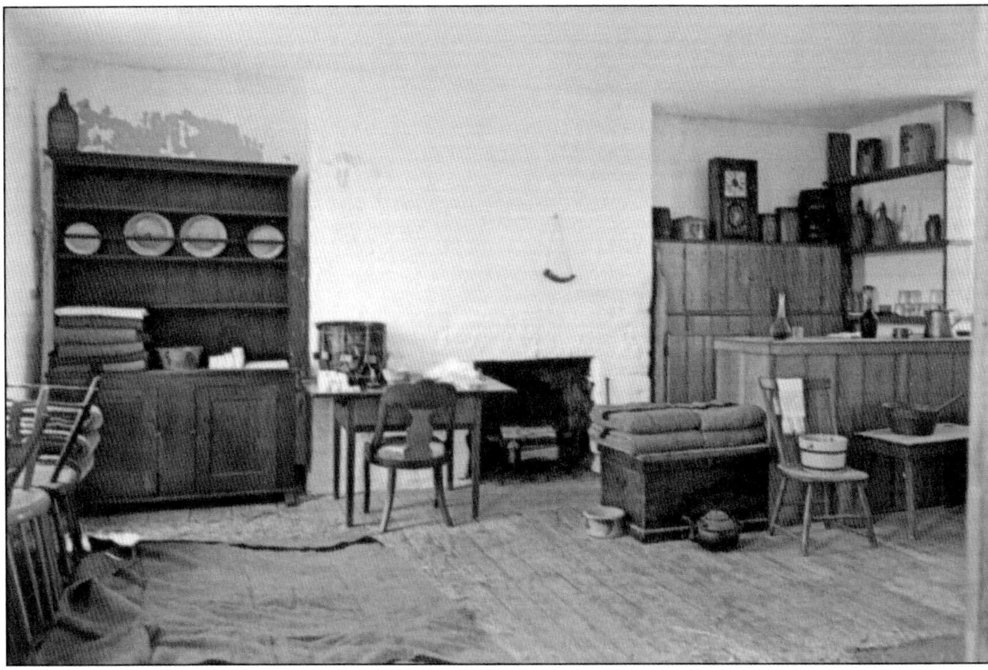

This image shows the Tavern Room inside the Stone House as it appeared in about 1970. The National Park Service has furnished this room to depict a Union field hospital where the wounded awaited treatment. The caption reads, "The furniture was stacked out of the way, straw spread to soak up the blood, and blankets put down for the men to lie on."

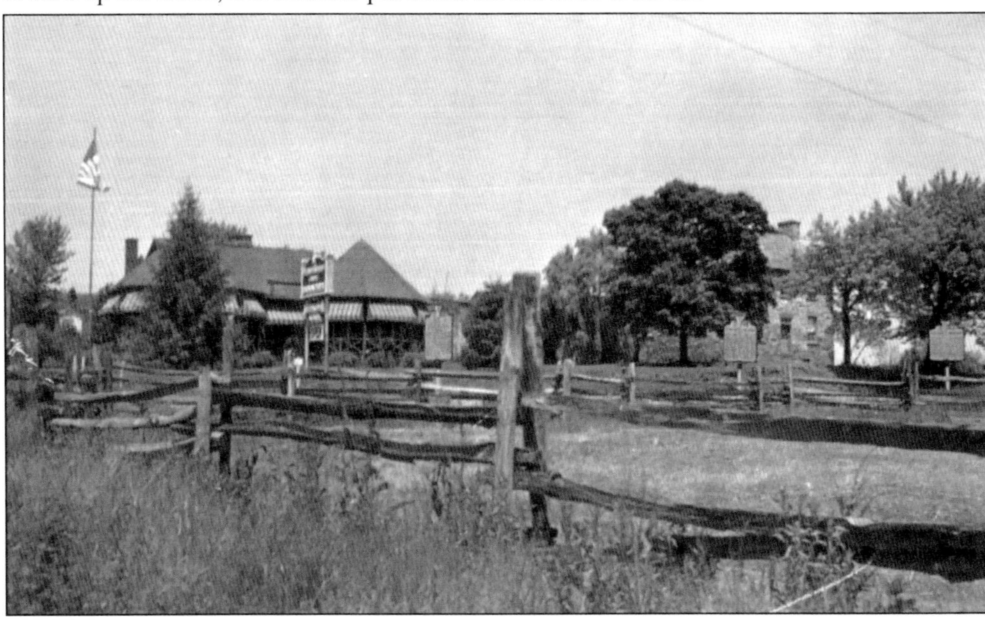

When the owners of the Stone House Inn, which adjoined the Stone House, decided to auction their business in 1957, the National Park Service raised $35,000 to buy the property. The inn included a restaurant, warehouse, and three cottages and was located on important historic ground. Once the NPS acquired the inn in 1958, it set about returning the area around the Stone House to its 1860s appearance.

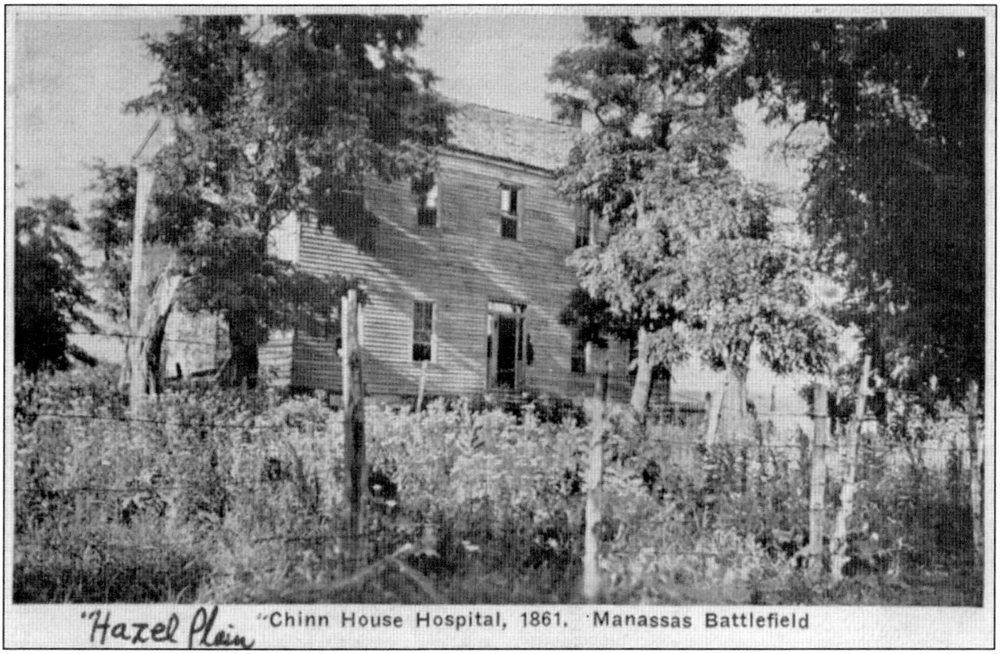

Shown here in an image from the 1870s, the house at Hazel Plain, also known as Chinn Ridge, was part of a successful 550-acre plantation near Sudley Road and Route 29 built in 1809 by Bernard Hooe. At the start of the Civil War, owner Benjamin Tasker Chinn, who also owned nearby Ben Lomond plantation, produced abundant quantities of corn, oats, and wine.

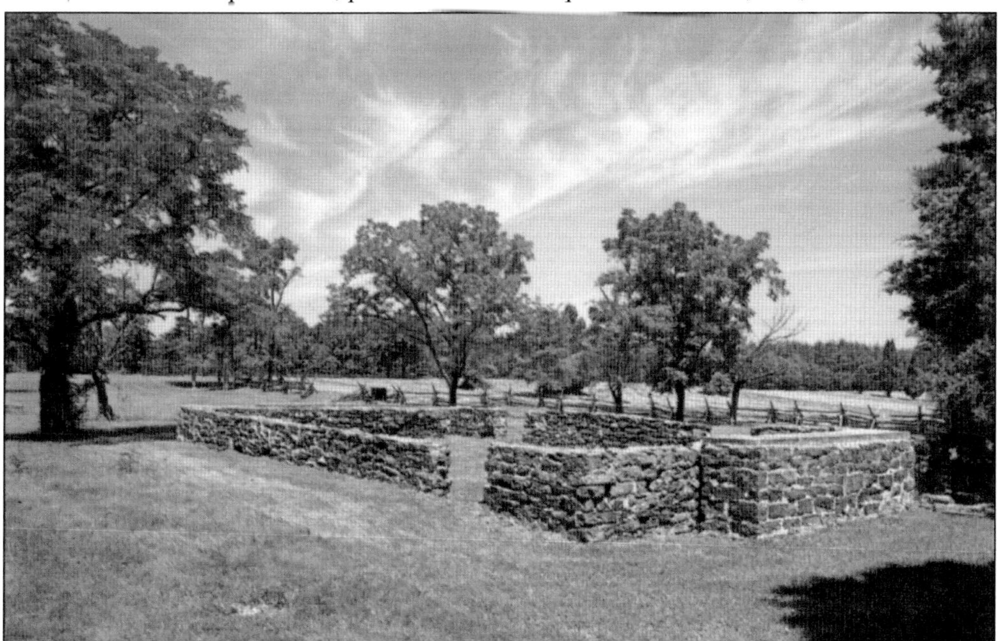

Because of its location on the battlefield, the Chinn House was used as a field hospital during both the Battles of First and Second Manassas. Although the house was an attraction for veterans and tourists after the war, it fell into disrepair and had to be demolished in 1950. All that remains of the house is this stone foundation, now part of Manassas National Battlefield Park.

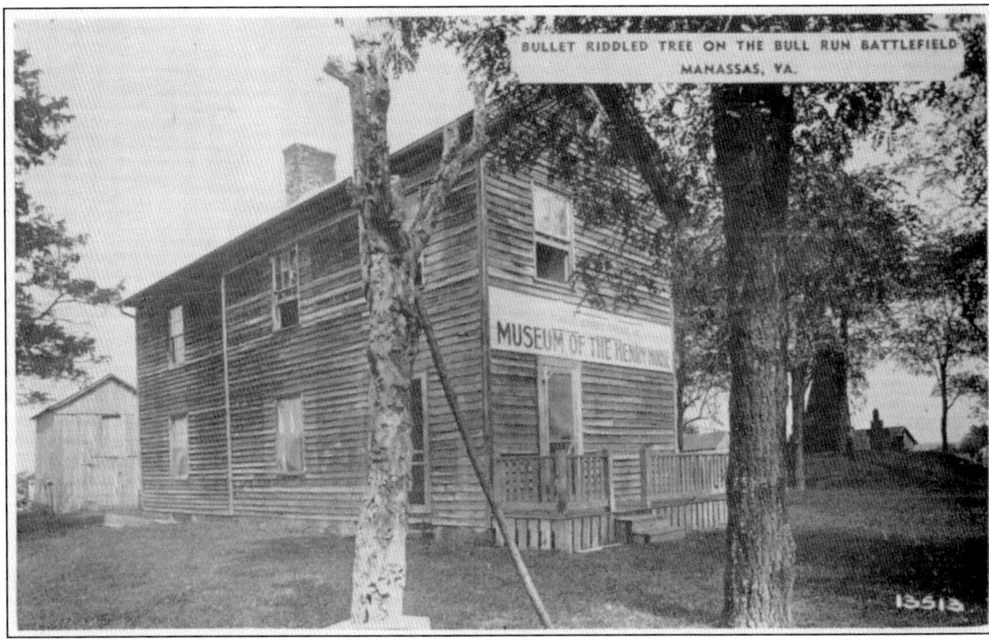

Henry family members first welcomed visitors to their home on Henry Hill, where they had established the first private museum with their own collection of artifacts. This image from the 1930s shows the house as a museum owned and maintained by the Sons of Confederate Veterans as part of the Manassas Battlefield Confederate Park, Inc.

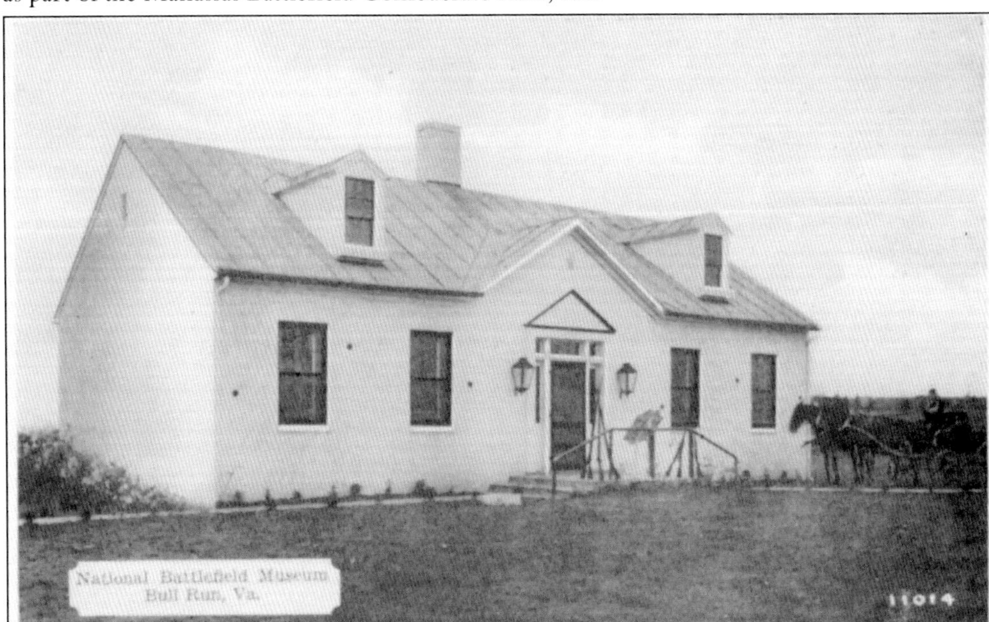

This private museum stood on the east side of the Stone Bridge in Fairfax County, no doubt capitalizing on its prime tourist location. It operated from the 1930s through the 1960s and was not affiliated with the Sons of Confederate Veterans, United Daughters of the Confederacy, the Roosevelt administration's Bull Run Recreational Demonstration Area, or the National Park Service.

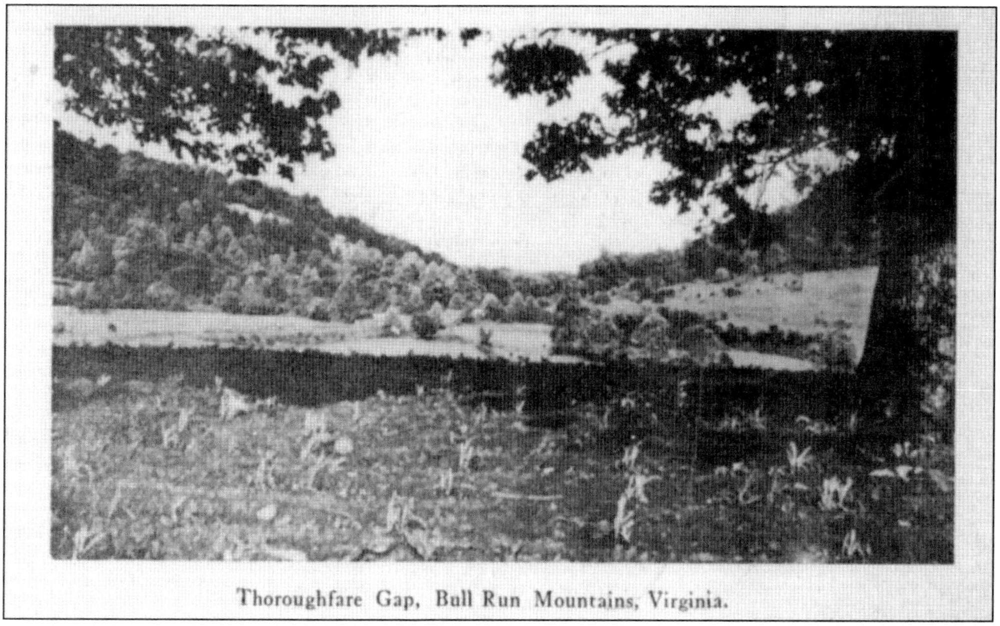

In 1946, this pristine view looks east through Thoroughfare Gap to the battlefield 12 miles away. Confederate general Joseph Johnston's troops traveled by train through here on their way to the Battle of First Manassas. Gen. Thomas "Stonewall" Jackson's troops passed through before raiding Manassas Junction, and General Robert E. Lee's forces gained control of the gap just before the Battle of Second Manassas.

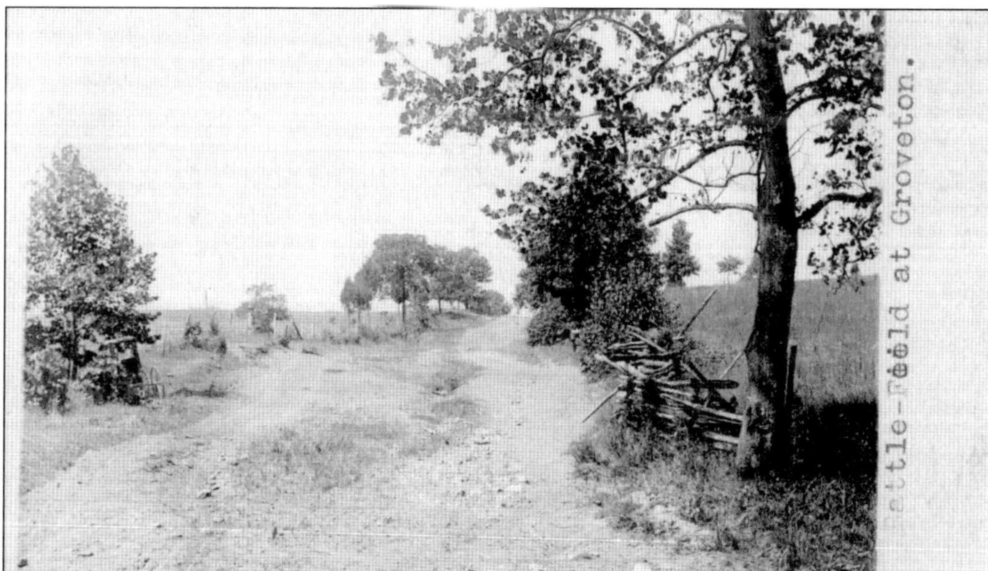

Confederate general Stonewall Jackson rested his troops north of the village of Groveton, waiting for reinforcements while eluding Union general John Pope's forces just before the Battle of Second Manassas. Jackson's men successfully attacked Pope's army from this area, confident that they could take cover along the unfinished Manassas Gap Railroad cut. Groveton remains unchanged in this early 1900s real-photo image.

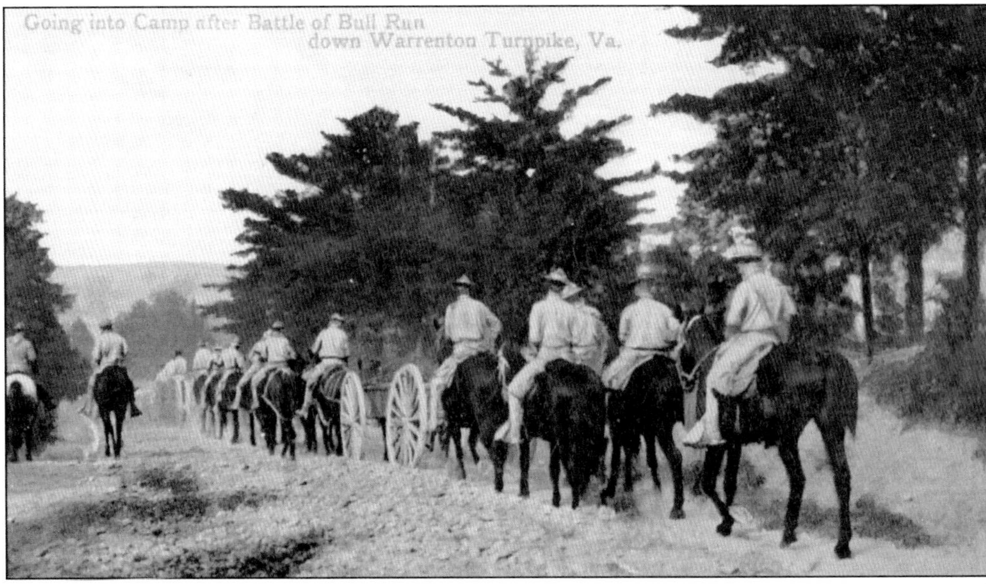

Twenty-six thousand soldiers again hoisted guns and debated strategy during the US Army's 1904 maneuvers on and around the battlefield. The large-scale practice and drills were designed to use lessons from the Battles of Manassas to teach a new generation of soldiers and to better their skills in organization, combat, intelligence, subsistence, and transportation.

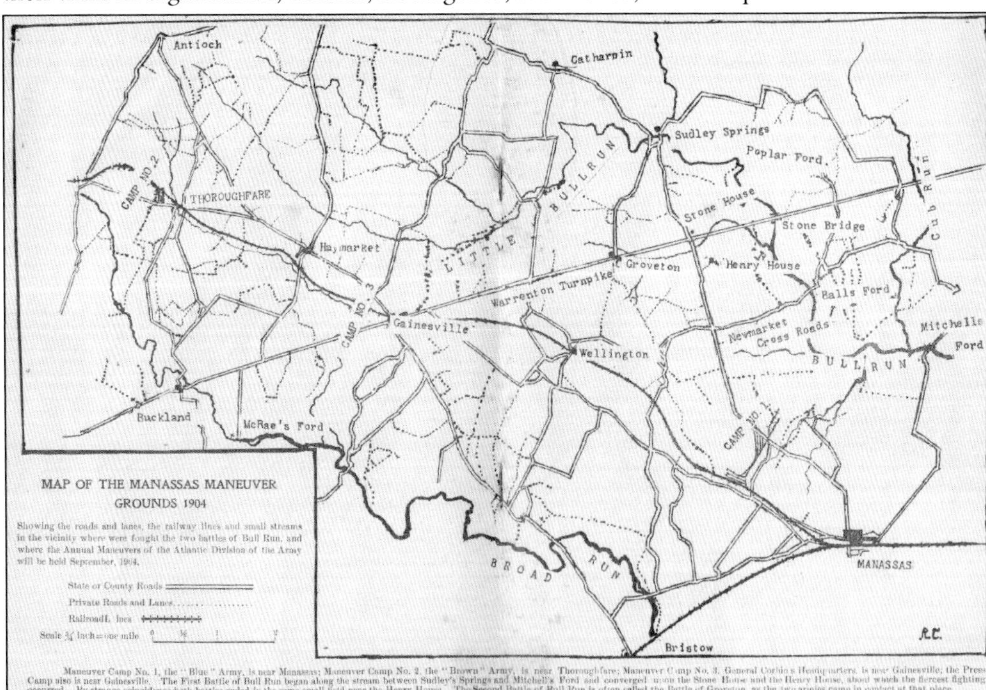

This souvenir map for spectators showed regular Army and Guard units spread out in camps from Manassas to Gainesville, and exercises that largely followed Civil War battle lines. An umpire officiated during the complex situational games and determined whether the Blue or Brown army was victorious in each exercise. Spectators toted picnics and watched the exercises, much as they did before the Battle of First Manassas.

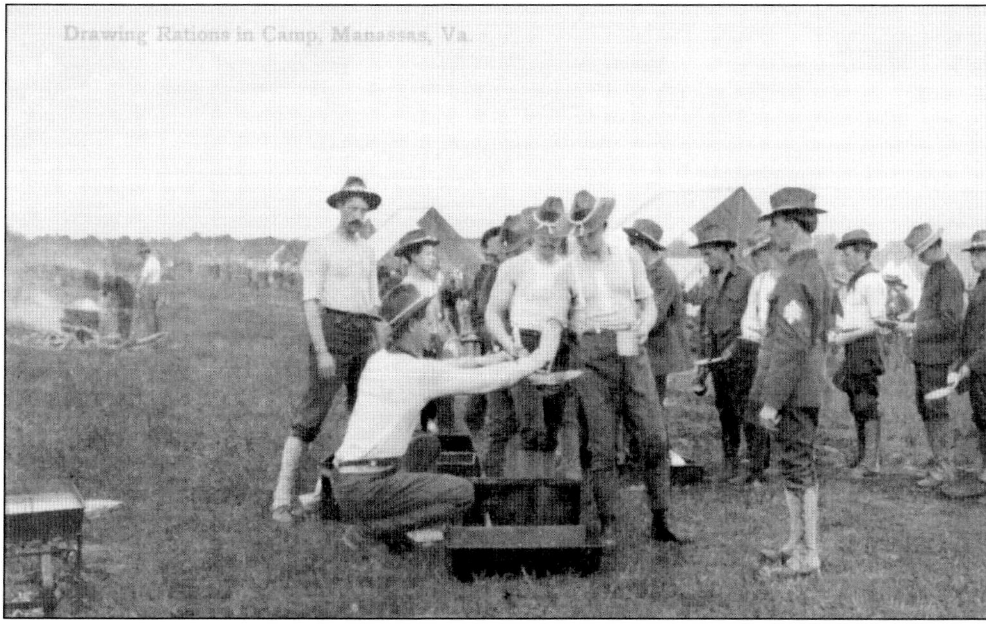

The 1904 maneuvers marked the first time in their careers that most infantry, artillery, cavalry, and others would live and train together, as shown above. Cavalry and artillery units from Fort Ethan Allen, near Burlington, Vermont, grew even closer as they marched to Manassas. The estimated 700-mile trek was expected to take three weeks and was described by the *Washington Post* as "the nature of an experiment." (Author's collection.)

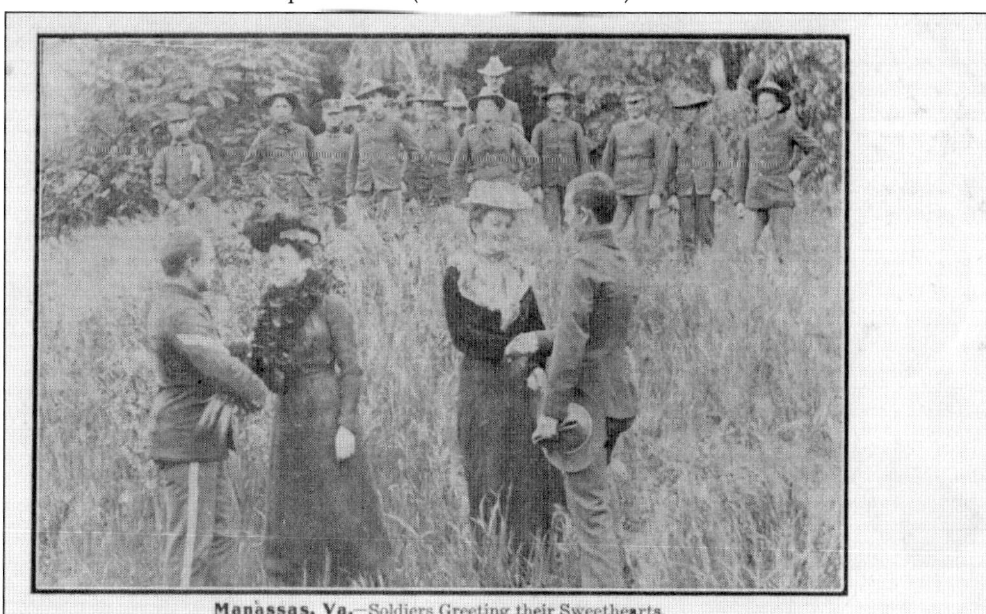

"What struck foreign observers as a complete novelty in the presence of ladies at manoeuvres, struck them also as a most agreeable novelty," the *Washington Post* reported. Locals were deeply partisan, cheering for the Brown army that approximated the movements of the Confederate army. Locals also enjoyed an economic boost from the 1904 exercises, selling all manner of food and drink at several times normal prices.

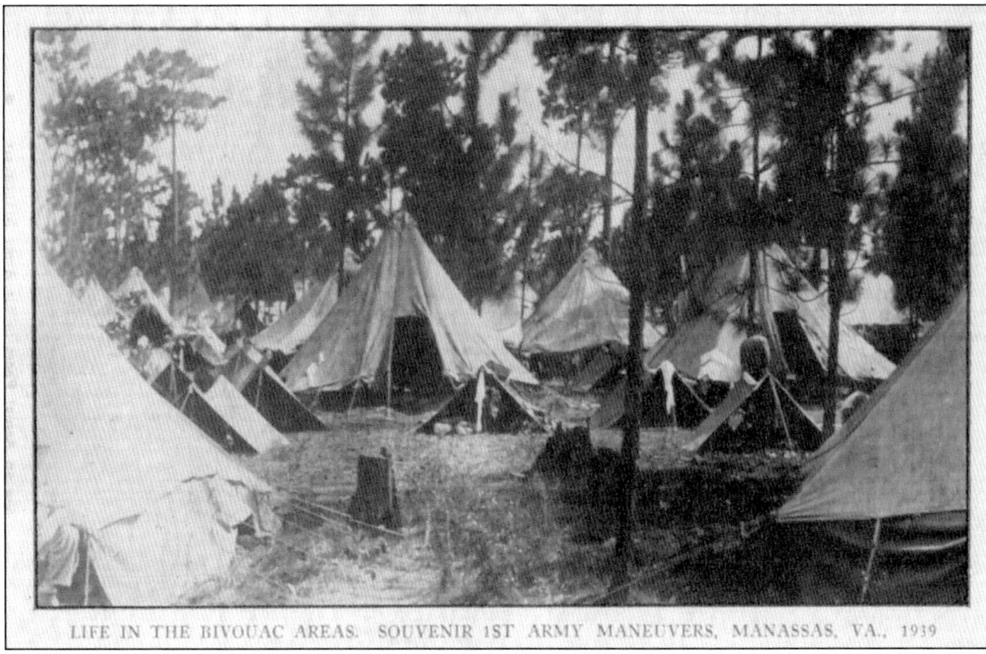

With clouds of war on the world's horizon, the Army returned again to the Manassas battlefield for the 1939 maneuvers. In 1861, Union troops took three days to advance from Fairfax to Manassas. In 1939, soldiers made the same march to Henry Hill in less than three hours, thanks to mechanized transports. This postcard's caption reads, "Not an actual photo of 1st Army Maneuvers."

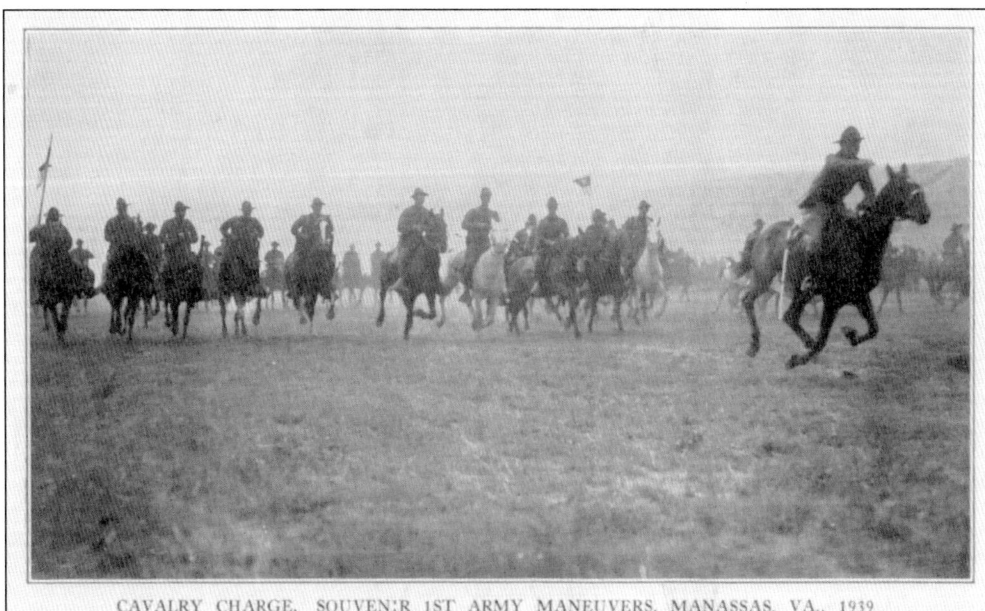

Manassas police chief W.T. Dutton told the *Washington Post* that during the 1939 maneuvers, the townspeople "expected a lot of trouble, but they've met some nice boys and are greatly surprised at the orderly conduct of the soldiers." Business was booming at area stores and restaurants, and the town worked to provide extra utilities, parking, and police patrols.

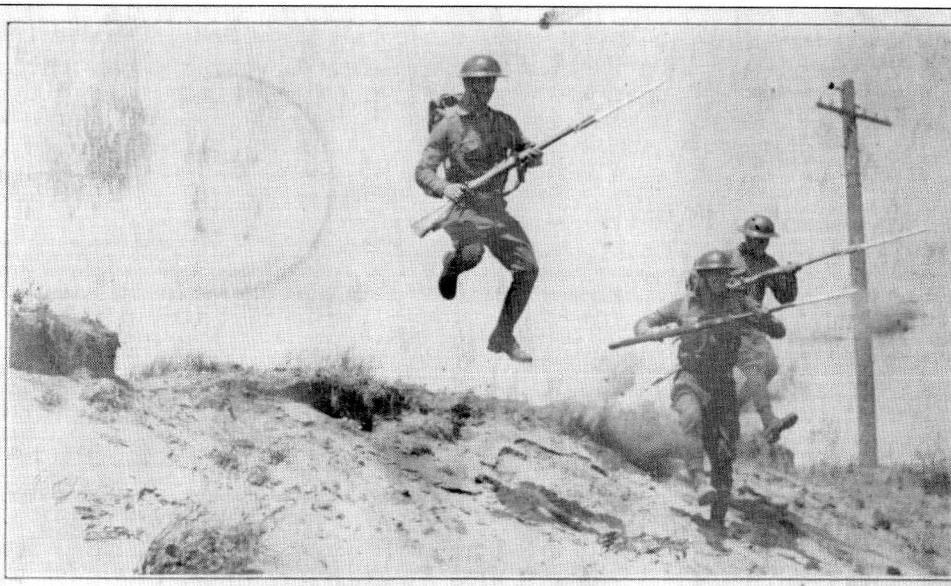

OVER THE TOP. SOUVENIR 1ST ARMY MANEUVERS, MANASSAS, VA., 1939

The 23,000 soldiers participating in the 1939 maneuvers set up camps across the area, including sites at the old Prince William Hotel near the railroad depot, on the Swavely School athletic fields, at the Stone House, and in Groveton. Soldiers arrived on hourly trains stopping at Manassas, Gainesville, and Haymarket. Notable Manassas families, including the McBrydes and the Marstellers, hosted parties for the officers, and merchants found the military influx good for business. Despite the use of planes and mechanized equipment unheard of in 1904, Col. George Allen admitted that the exercises revealed deficiencies in the Army. "These deficiencies were emphasized," Allen said. "But by being emphasized they were put in a better light for study and we believe the maneuvers accomplished a great deal of good."

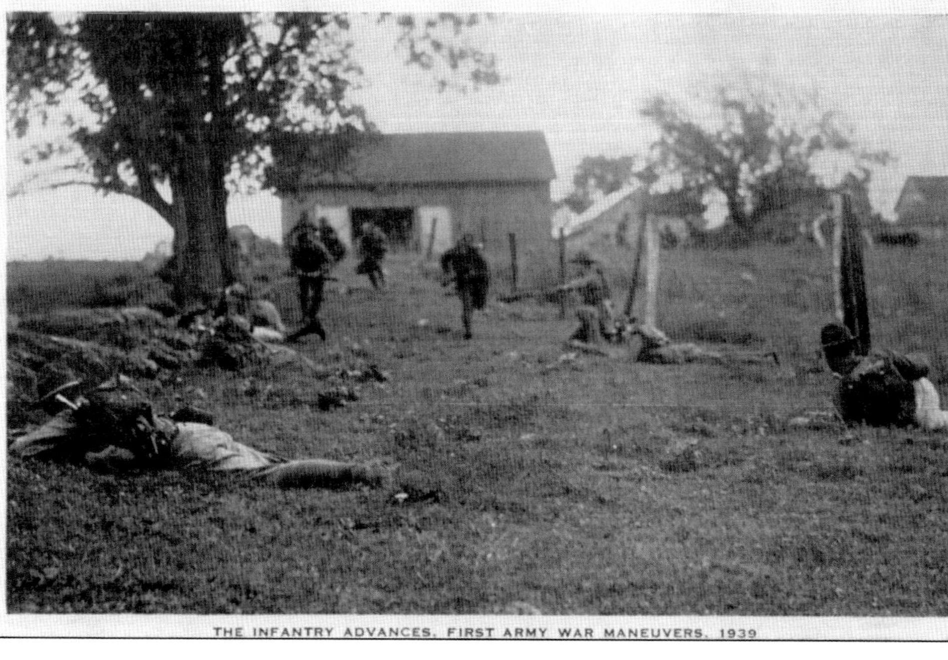

THE INFANTRY ADVANCES. FIRST ARMY WAR MANEUVERS, 1939

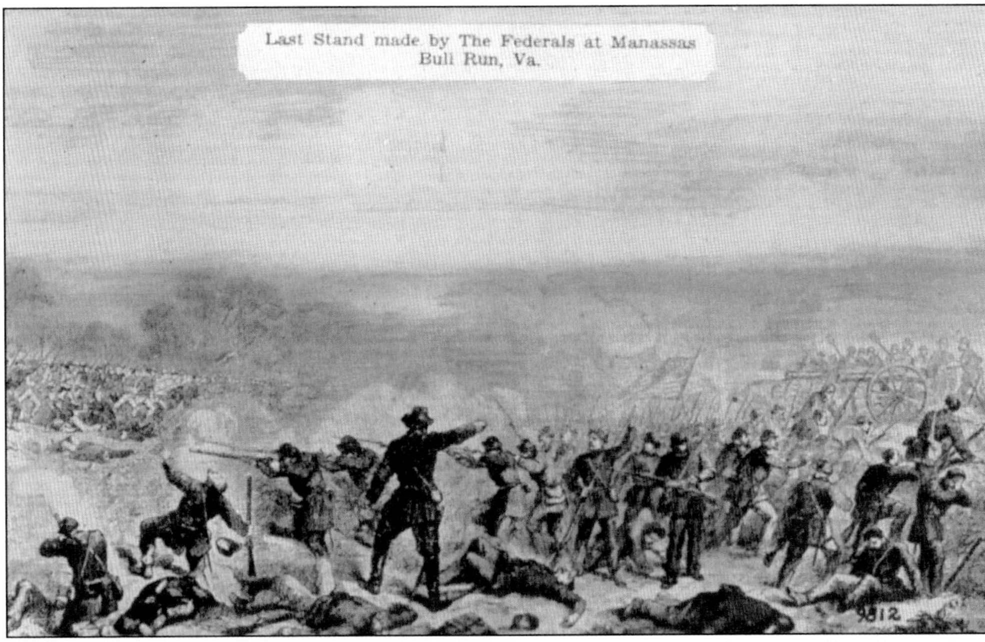

The monuments that Union soldiers erected to their fallen comrades at war's end remained on private land in the 1900s. George C. Round testified before a congressional subcommittee in 1902, urging the government to buy battlefield land on Henry Hill and Groveton, despite serving as the Henry family's legal counsel. Round never saw the establishment of a national park before his death in 1918.

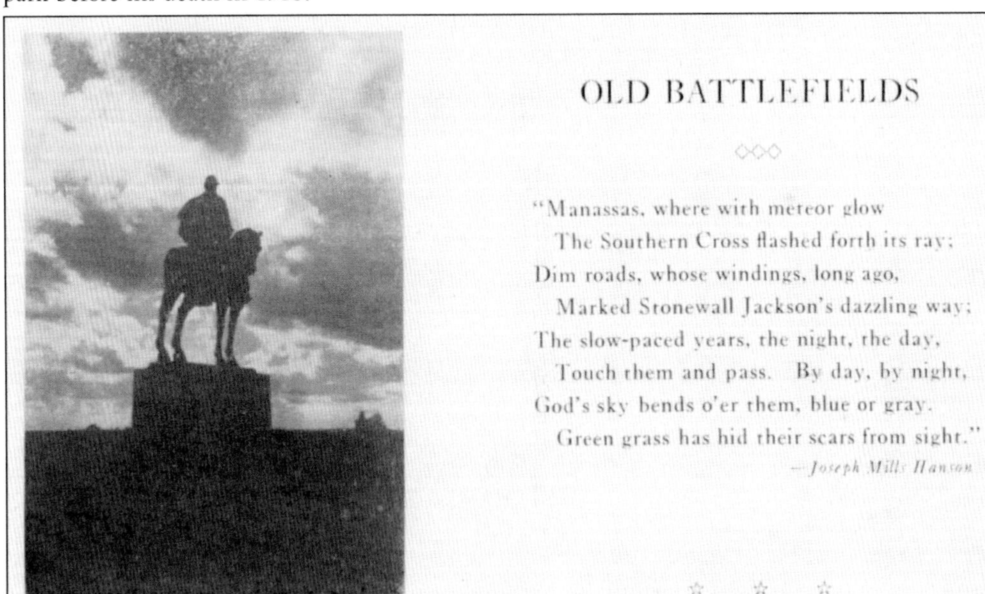

Postcards, poems, and popular culture paid tribute to Gen. Stonewall Jackson for years when the idea for a more permanent Stonewall Jackson memorial first emerged during the 75th anniversary of the Battle of First Manassas in 1936. By 1938, the Virginia General Assembly appropriated $25,000 for the erection of a statue depicting Stonewall Jackson's unassailable line on Henry Hill.

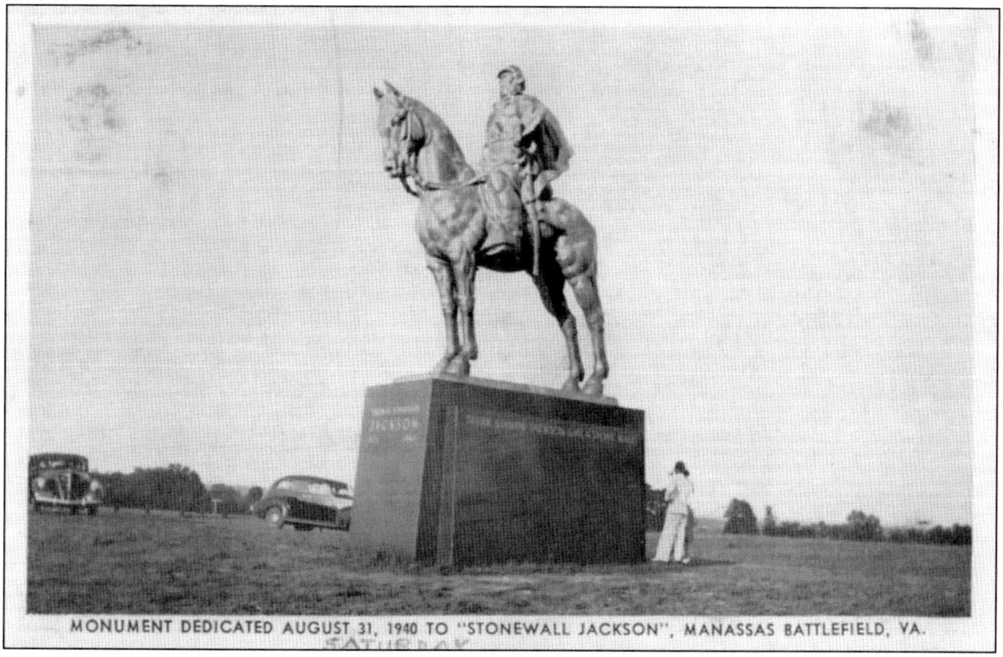

For those still struggling to create a national park, the Stonewall Jackson statue was far more than an imposing piece of granite. Creating the memorial would give Manassas a recognizable landmark that noted the heroic actions of a legendary Confederate general and a focal point for tourists. Although the Virginia Museum of Fine Arts had planned to review artistic submissions for the statue with the National Fine Arts Commission, state agencies finally chose Italian-born sculptor Joseph Pollia to craft the monument. Like most decisions associated with the preservation of the battlefield, Pollia faced criticism from veterans and Confederate organizations that disliked the way he portrayed Jackson and his horse. Pollia eventually addressed veterans' concerns and was praised in a local paper "for patience, for fortitude, and for gallantry" in the face of such disagreement.

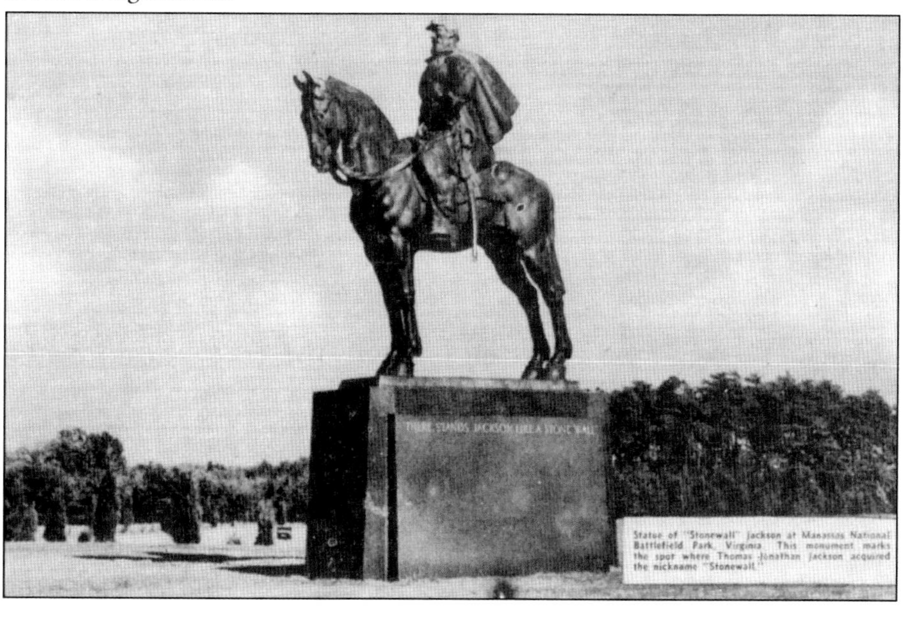

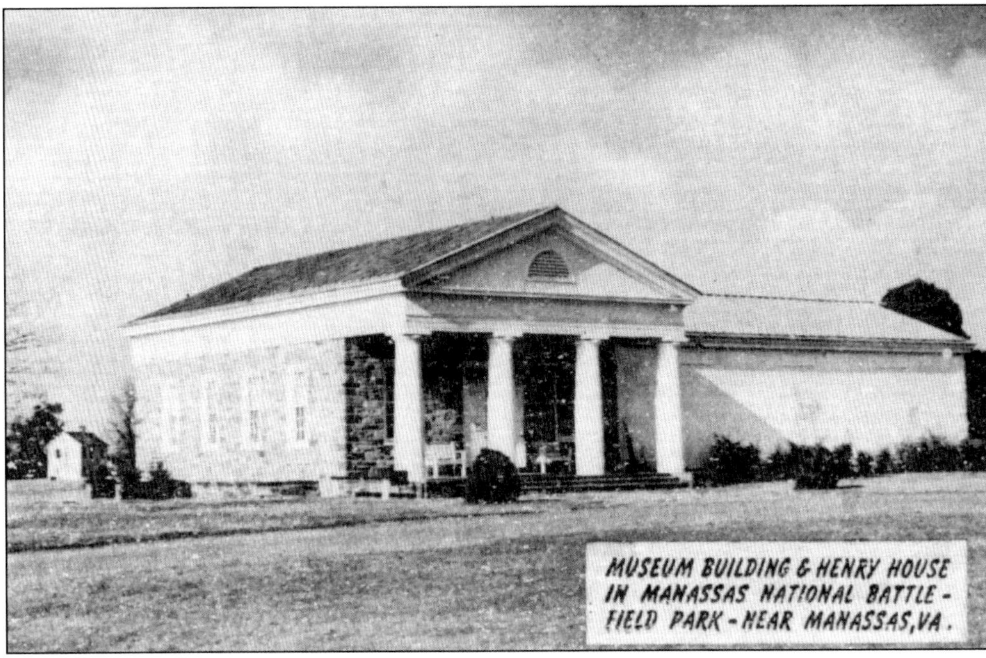

The long struggle to establish a Manassas National Battlefield Park came to fruition in 1940 when the federal government gained control of 1,600 acres and appropriated $56,000 to build a battlefield museum. The establishment of the park came after intense negotiations with private landowners and the Sons of Confederate Veterans, a group instrumental in creating the Confederate Park on Henry Hill. The 1938 deed of conveyance for the Henry Hill tract required the Park Service to place a plaque inside the museum lobby that recognized the significance of the Sons of Confederate Veterans' land gift to the federal government and suitable markers and memorials on the battlefield. The new two-story museum and administration building was constructed of native brownstone with a classically inspired portico and opened in 1942.

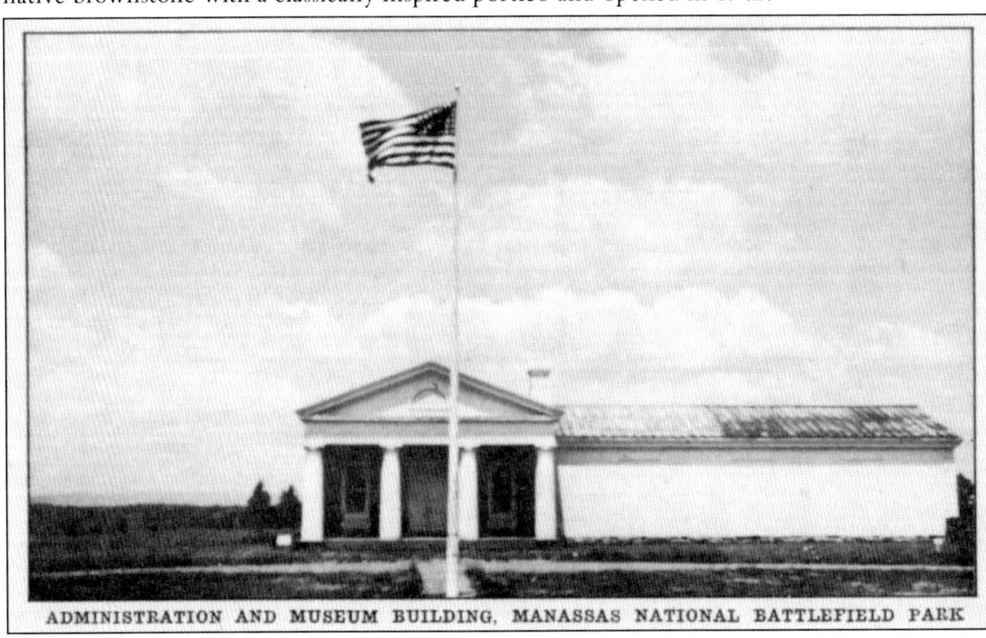

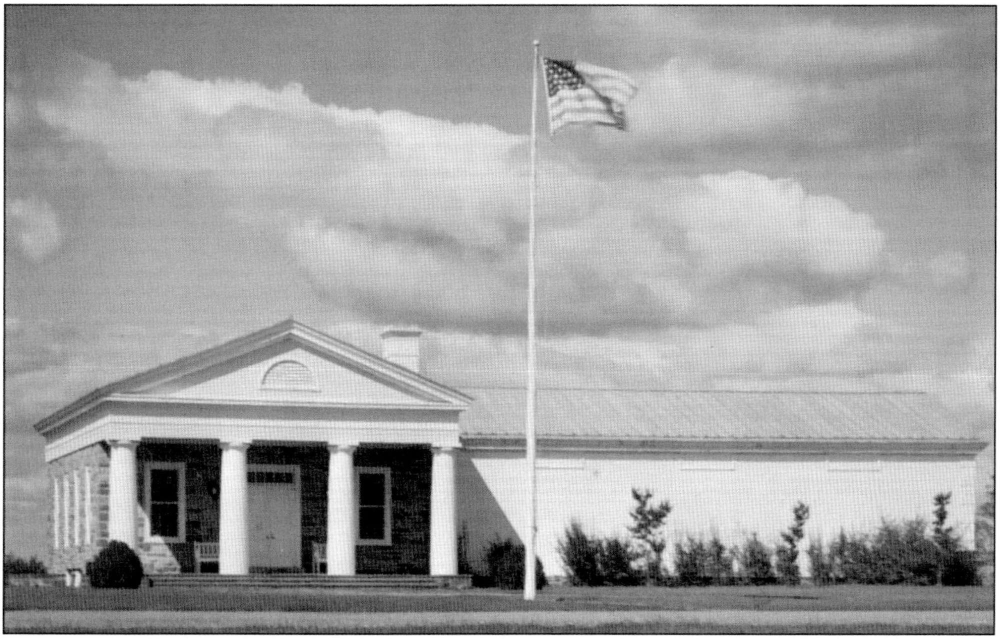

Soldiers again marched through the battlefield's hills and valleys during World War II, when officers from local military camps visited more frequently than tourists and local families. During the 1943 fiscal year, more than 10,000 military personnel—in comparison to an estimated 2,300 civilians—visited the park. The graduating classes from the nearby Marine Corps base at Quantico and the Army base at Fort Belvoir sent the largest numbers of soldiers, who studied tactical problems and held maneuvers. The Virginia Protective Force and the Virginia Reserve Militia conducted intensive infantry training at the park, and all military personnel enjoyed guided tours and Civil War lectures. The image below shows the Visitor Center's new auditorium wing.

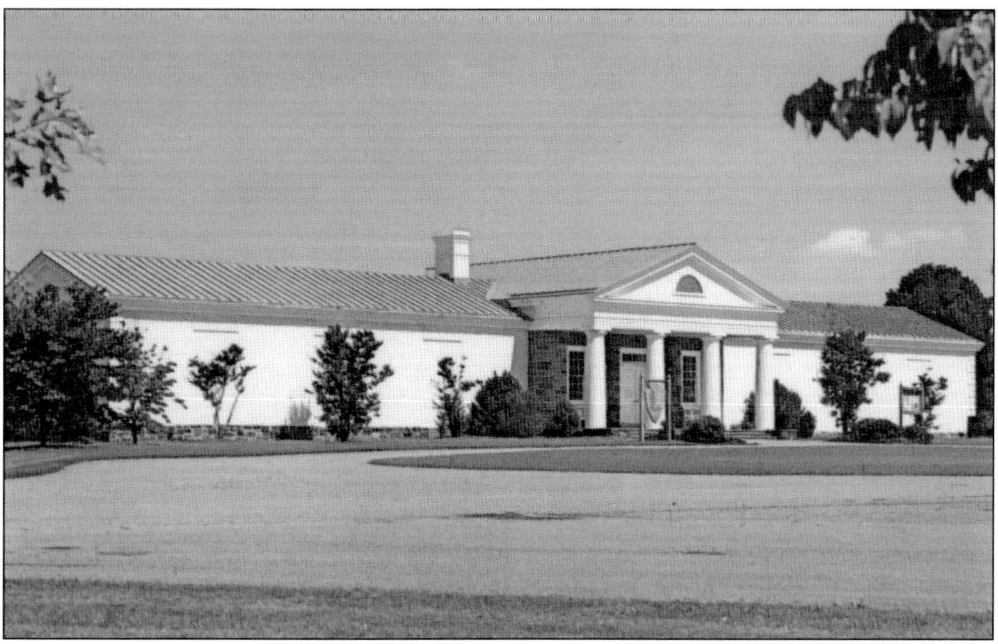

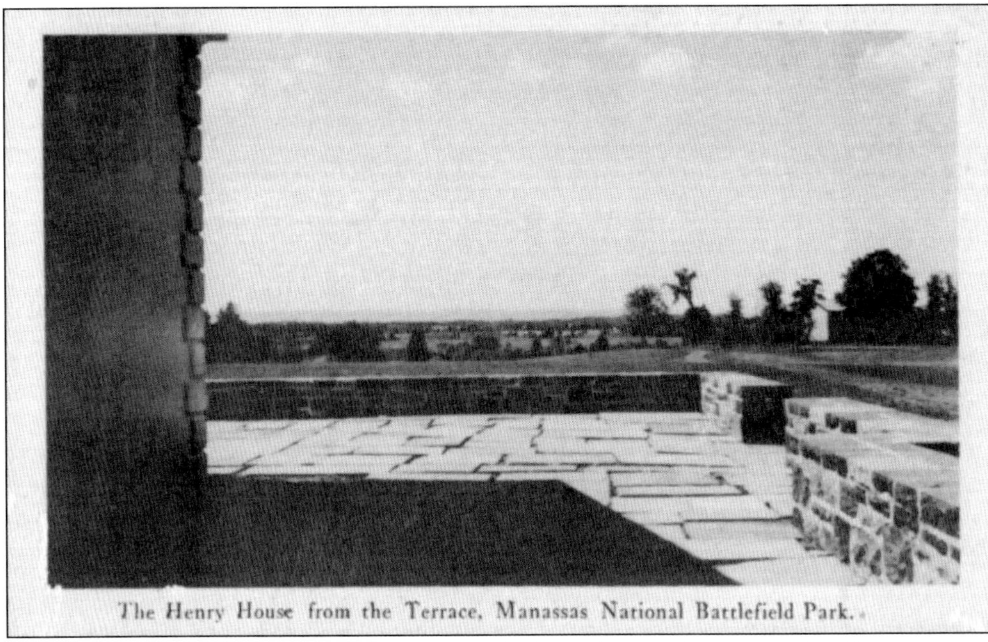

The park continued linking roads, installing trailside markers, and acquiring significant tracts of historic land throughout the 1950s and 1960s. Members of Congress who visited often supported efforts to fund land acquisition. The museum had a boost as well when an auditorium wing was added for park introductions and lectures. Park rangers still begin tours from this terrace.

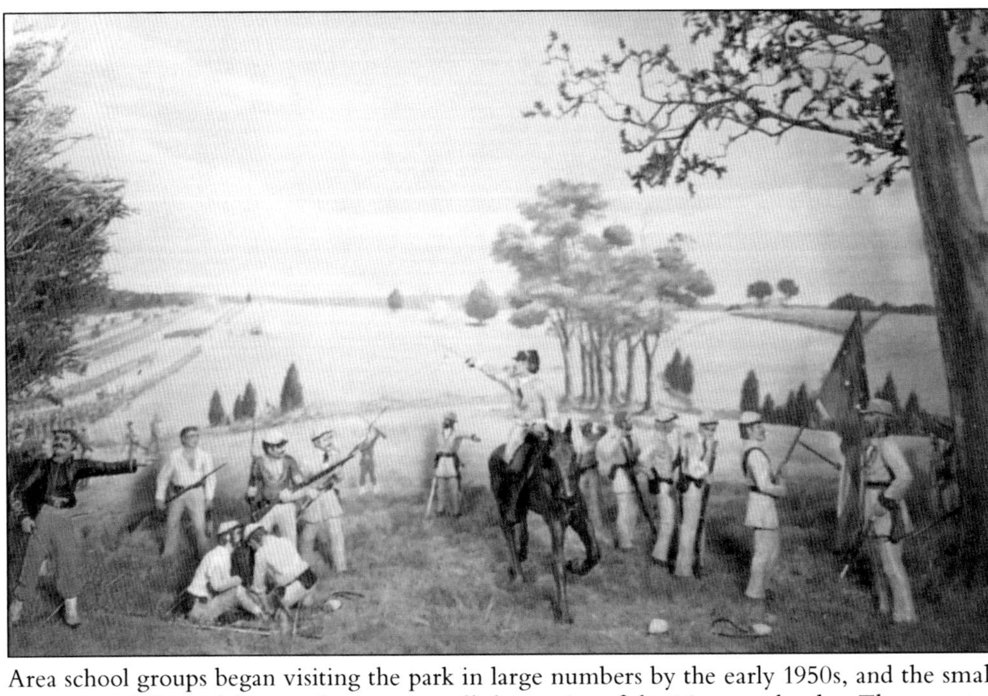

Area school groups began visiting the park in large numbers by the early 1950s, and the small museum staff looked for creative ways to tell the stories of the Manassas battles. They created electric maps with flashing lights signifying troop movements, taped narration, and this diorama depicting General Bee rallying Confederate troops.

George C. Round, the eager battlefield guide, quoted poet Joanquin Miller when he described Manassas as "the first in the alphabet of American battles," and the *Hartford Courant*, when it called Manassas "the most picturesque conflict of the war." Today, visitors can still view landmarks like this early 1900s battlefield image and the Stone Bridge, seen in this 1930s image, that are largely unchanged from the 1860s. The efforts to preserve these vistas did not end when Manassas became a national park. Proposals to hold battle reenactments, build a cemetery, build two different theme parks, build a shopping/office complex, and expand roads through and near the battlefield have met with resistance from a host of preservationists.

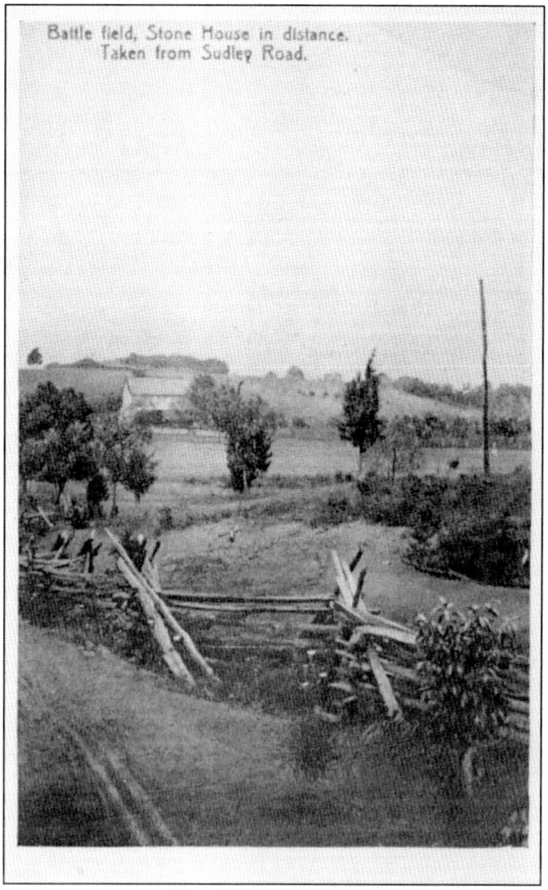

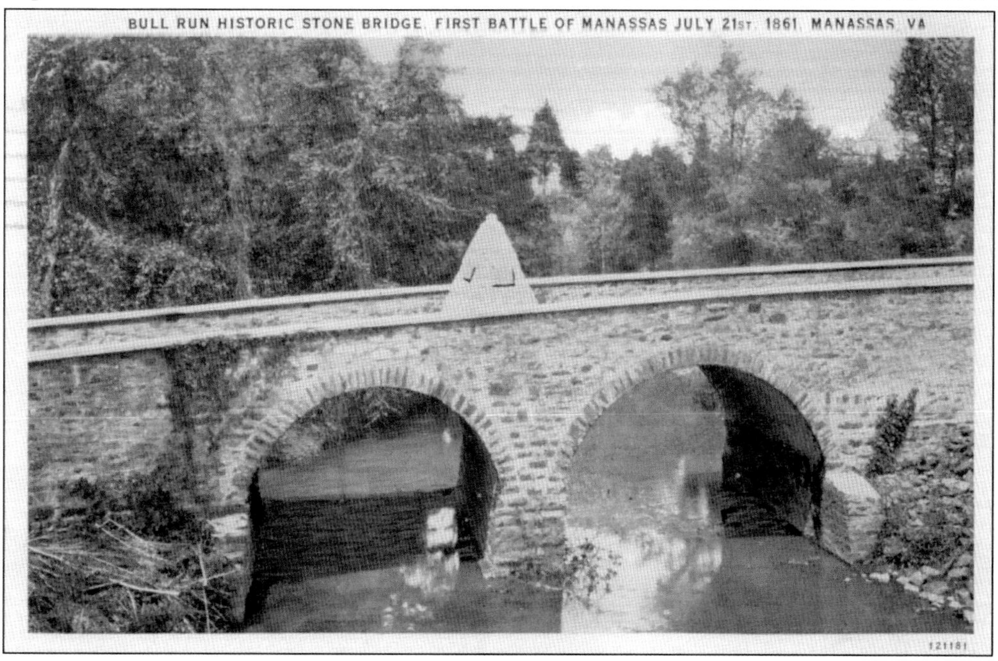

Bibliography

Good Housekeeping Club, Bethlehem. *Prince William, The Story of Its People and Places.* Richmond, VA: Work Projects Administration, 1941.

Koman, Rita G. *Manassas Mosaic: Creating a Community.* Virginia Beach: Donning Company Publishers, 2009.

Manassas Democrat, selected articles

Manassas Journal, selected articles

Manassas Museum Archives and Photograph Collection.

Mills, Charles A. *Echoes of Manassas.* Manassas, VA: Friends of the Manassas Museum, 1988.

Mulvaney, Kathleen. *Manassas A Place of Passages.* Charleston, SC: Arcadia Publishing, 1999.

100th Anniversary of the Manassas *National Jubilee of Peace July 1911–July 2011.* Manassas, VA: Manassas Museum.

Rabatin, June, ed. *Count the Ties to Manassas.* Manassas, VA: Manassas Museum, 1984.

Ratcliffe, R. Jackson, *This Was Manassas.* Manassas, VA: Good Printers, 1973.

Simmons, Catherine T. *Manassas, Virginia 1873-1973.* Manassas, VA: REF Typesetting and Publishing, 1986.

Townsend, Jan. *The Civil War in Prince William County.* Dumfries, VA: Prince William County Historical Commission, 2011.

Washington Post, selected articles

Wieder, Laurie C., ed. *Prince William: A Past to Preserve.* Dumfries, VA: Prince William County Historical Commission, 1998.

Zenzen, Joan M. *Battling for Manassas The Fifty Year Preservation Struggle at Manassas National Battlefield Park.* University Park: Pennsylvania State University Press, 1998.

About the Liberia Restoration Fund

Here in Virginia, it is hard to not stumble across a historic site. Worthy historic houses in need of leak-free roofs, draft-free windows, and crack-free walls vie for attention. Liberia, the 1825 Manassas plantation house, may be lesser known to the nation than nearby Mount Vernon or Monticello, but it has been at the center of some the nation's most tumultuous and newsworthy times.

Why is Liberia worth preserving? Historians will point out that Liberia had the rare opportunity to serve as headquarters for both Confederate and Union troops and to host both presidents Jefferson Davis and Abraham Lincoln. Architects will cite the home's sturdy brick walls that have never been altered. Schoolchildren will point to the faint scrawls of Civil War soldiers who were far from home and left their signatures on a Virginia plantation house wall.

Preserving Liberia is important for all of those reasons, and the Liberia Restoration Fund also supports preserving transformative, time-altering experiences all too rare in this digitized world: strolling up the long drive and catching a glimpse of the redbrick house while deer bound out of the woods, children gathering around a fire to learn what plantation slaves cooked, volunteers reading long-forgotten letters by candlelight, fathers and sons walking hand in hand through wooded paths cut by Eagle Scouts, and mothers and daughters perched on hay bales listening to the songs of hoopskirted ladies.

People can feel the past live around them at Liberia, but Liberia lives for the future too. Generations have yet to peek past its doors, to celebrate on its lawn, and to learn history not from a textbook, but from a living, breathing place.

Much has been done to stabilize the house and to restore its landscape, but much remains to be done. The author appreciates any donations to the Liberia Restoration Fund and thanks readers for supporting Liberia's preservation by purchasing this book.

Please see page 88 and visit www.manassasmuseum.org to learn more about Liberia and all the historic treasures of Manassas.